THE ARTISAN'S STAR

A NOVEL BY
GABRIELLA CONTESTABILE

Stelle Publications

This story is a work of fiction. Names, characters, places, and incidents are the products of the author's imagination or are used fictitiously.

Published by Stelle Publications

Cover design by Angie Jernejcic
Photographs of Ponte Vecchio, Lavender Fields, & Bicycles by Marisa McGrody www.marisaerin.com

Other photographs by Shutterstock

ISBN: 978-0-9960585-0-6

To Steve. For your unflinching integrity, and for believing in silver linings. Otherwise how would you have put up with me these 33 years?

And for beautiful Daniela. You are, and always will be, my *stellina.*

THE ARTISAN'S STAR

Il mondo dei profumi è un universo senza limiti: una fragranza può rievocare sensazioni, luoghi, persone, o ancora condurre in uno spazio di nuove dimensioni emozionali.

Perfumery is an unlimited world. In the creation of a scent it is possible to recall a feeling or a place, to move to an imaginary space or to invent new emotional dimensions.
—**Lorenzo Villoresi**

THE ARTISAN'S STAR

1

ELIO BARATI PUSHES OPEN THE BEDROOM SHUTTERS to an awakening Florence. The irises are everywhere now, on his dresser, in the windowsills, in the markets, in the fields, in his mother's garden. Soon the contests will start and his flowers will be among the contenders. In his sixty-plus years he's placed in the International Iris Competition three times—with the Ballerina bulbs unfurling throughout the room.

Its colors match the brushstroke of gauzy rose light spreading across the sky outside. Down below the Arno moves along its sludgy course as its bridges show signs of life; solitary figures walk or ride across to the click of a stiletto or the purr of a *motorino*.

Sofia stirs, the Chanel No. 5 leaping from the nape of her neck, from her pillowcase. The scent of the marina in Villefranche where he proposed, knee bent. The setting sun shimmered on the water, the pink and yellow stone houses glowed in the dusk.

"Elio, don't forget Romina comes home today," she murmurs.

"As if I would forget. We probably won't see her for another week."

He opens his closet door. Pressed jackets, shirts and trousers line up on cedar hangers over seven pairs of polished shoes, stuffed with shoetrees. He chooses the tan loafers, handmade just for him at Stefano Bremer. It takes four months to make the shoes. It takes Taddei, another friend, over four months to craft by hand the leather box that holds Elio's cuff links, each pair connected to a meaningful event in his life. He runs his hand over the gleaming surface. There is no mistaking the artisan's signature. He picks out a rose and lilac tie and a lavender-gray shirt, drapes the tie across the shirt to check the match.

Sofia is sitting up when he comes out. "She called from the airport. Told me she adored New York."

Across the white matelasse bedspread, he lays out a pair of anthracite gray trousers, the shirt and tie, a tan belt, a folded handkerchief that smells of lavender.

"Says she can't wait to go back."

"And how will she go back? Who will pay for it? Not me! She has to finish her portfolio! When you're applying to the *Accademia di Belle Arti* you should not be running off to work in some crazy gallery in New York!"

"She did some amazing watercolors before she left. Did you see the one of Porta San Frediano?"

"No! And I don't care. A real artist doesn't paint in watercolors! A real artist paints in oil."

"Her watercolors are brilliant, Elio. You can't deny that."

"Can you imagine Bellini painting in watercolor? Botticelli? Fra Angelico? Italians don't paint in watercolor. This is art for the English."

"I wouldn't mind a Turner over our mantle."

He stares at the empty wall that begs for a painting neither of them will agree on. Lovely Sofia stretches, gets out of bed. Her midnight blue silk nightgown slides around her slim but curvy figure. She plants a kiss on his cheek. "Our Romina's very international. She takes her inspiration from—"

"From crazy places! Here, I teach my daughter to enjoy the refinement and the traditions of our province. Forte dei Marmi, Castiglioncello, Volterra!"

"Places she's visited a thousand times and is bored with."

He ponders the unlikely possibility. "I would like to be so bored. Your daughter is as crazy as that gallery owner from Budapest who thinks a stroke of blue across a white canvas is art." He mimics painting a slash of color in the air. "I haven't a clue what she likes or wants!"

"True."

He shrugs, steps into his travertine-tiled bathroom to shave the old fashioned way, with a brush and razor.

"She said she learned a lot from working in that gallery," Sofia shouts from the bedroom.

"We don't have art galleries in Florence, I presume." He swirls the cream-filled brush furiously on his cheeks. "We taught the world about art. Better she focuses on her studies and comes to help in the perfumery from time to time."

"She has her own life now, Elio."

"Thanks to you. You're the one who told her it was all right to have her own apartment in an unsafe part of town." It's not really unsafe, but declaring it so helps his argument. He strokes the razor carefully along his cheek. "*Now* you see what's happened? We never see her. At least *I* rarely see her. She calls *you* from time to time. I'm not offended. You're her mother. But still, we used to go to jazz clubs, and we'd have a talk at Micheletto's. Of course we never agree on anything... Ouch!"

He's nicked himself.

Sofia stands in the doorway, rests her head against the wall. Her celadon eyes touch him like a balm.

"You know that's not true. She helps out enough at the shop. She has your sense of smell. When you and your daughter sell perfume, it's like a symphony."

"Yes, I play the strings. She plays the brass."

"But you play together beautifully. Conflict is good. Even da Vinci said, *When two people agree, one is unnecessary.*"

"You talk like a scientist." Another nick. "*Maledetto!*" He throws down the blade, splashes on Yardley English Lavender aftershave. Mistake. "Ay!"

Sofia goes into her enormous bathroom to shower. She didn't choose travertine. She wanted something fresh and Asian inspired: rose and gray granite. Squared off fixtures.

Elio checks himself in the mirror, straightens his tie. He steps out onto the terrace where Sofia's telescope still points up at the sky. If they'd never met, on that train to Genova, she would still be an astronomer now, or a famous astrophysicist, like her father. He caps the lens, goes back inside and locks the window shut.

Sofia likes her espresso dense and short, the way Elio makes it. So he's careful to press the grains in the *macchinetta* to lie smooth and loose. He waits for the sound of the espresso rising, and salvages it just in time, so there isn't a chance it will burn. He pours, tastes. Good.

As he quietly places the espresso on her nightstand, he smells the first spritz of her daytime perfume, Chanel Cristalle. He spins around and tiptoes towards the door.

"Elio!"

Too late.

"Don't forget Romina's birthday presents."

He sighs, walks to the antique dresser, picks up his gift for his daughter, along with Sofia's, a fat envelope with money inside. Sofia says it's hard to know what a young woman wants these days. Better to give her money and let her choose what she wants. She's been saving money to make yet another trip to the Angkor Wat temple in Cambodia

He shakes his head, grabs his suede jacket, runs out the front door, and takes hold of his bicycle. He can still jump on the seat as it's moving, and he can still take his hands off the handlebars as he rides down Via della Ninna.

He pedals across the Piazza della Signoria. Outside Rivoire, waiters roll out awnings and take chairs down from tables. He passes school children lining up in front of the Loggia dei Lanzi. He turns down Via dè Tornabuoni, where stylish patrons stand at bars to drink *caffè* and eat *cornetti* wrapped in paper napkins. A soot-covered vehicle with rotating brushes scrubs the pavement. He takes a detour along Via dei Calzaiuoli to ride fast around the Duomo, something he's loved doing since a child.

An American tourist stands in front of it but doesn't see its magnificence, doesn't know its history. If he did, he wouldn't be pushing buttons on his stupid handheld GPS. Elio screeches to a halt.

"Where do you want to go?" he asks.

The tourist's brow furrows. He can barely keep his eyes on Elio, so attracted he is to the backlit screen. "Um. Santa Croce."

"Then you don't need that. It's very close and very easy. Turn here to the right and go straight. It's impossible to get lost in Florence. The Duomo is in the center. Wherever you walk you will always go there. *Arrivederci!*"

He pedals away, turns down a street into the commercial sector. Merchants zigzag across narrow streets and pedestrian piazzas, from shop to café and back again. They leave their doors open so they can watch their shops while they talk about politics, soccer or the *porcini* they had with dinner. It's only eight o'clock and the first customers arrive at ten.

At Via della Vigna Nuova, Elio rings his bell, waves to Marina pounding a comforter inside her linen shop and admires willowy Lucilla as she wiggles out the front door of her flower shop, dragging a giant ficus tree

Minutes later he lifts the creaking gates in front of the oldest perfumery shop in Florence. Dust shimmers on his shoes and on the eight-point mosaic star at his feet. When he looks up, Marina's dark Moorish eyes lock on his. She blows him a kiss.

He quickly takes out his broom. The mosaic star must shine and invite. The star of tiny silver, graphite and terra tiles says, *This is more than a commercial shop.* This is a museum of perfumery, a celebration of Florentine artisanship. He sweeps boldly so dust leaps out of every crevice. A shimmer of powder covers his freshly polished shoes. He brushes it away with a swipe of his linen handkerchief.

Inside he dusts the Carrara marble counter. He stands crystal atomizers with trailing quilted pumps on mirrored trays, so they catch the light above. Sofia loves those sparkly, recessed lights because they look like tiny stars. Eh! He misses his Belle Époque chandelier with its honeyed amber light and naked angels swirling around.

She's right, though. A linear, more contemporary line gives the shop freshness, makes it easier to find things. He stands back, approves of the orderliness of it all. Fragrances line one side of the bright, rectangular room; cosmetics, the other. The perfume wall is, of course, his masterpiece. Each shelf displays an even row of cellophane-wrapped boxes, an atomizer of each scent and a beaker of scent strips. He's arranged the perfumes by fragrance family, not by brand. Branding is too commercial, he'd told Sofia. It belies the very nature of the perfumer's art. She agreed, even though he could tell she was not convinced.

He ignores the back of the store where Sofia's accessories boutique butts up against his perfumer's corner. She hangs the studded leather and jeweled belts on pewter hooks. She drapes scarves in silky folds over the glass counter. Leather agendas, wallets and key cases in the newest colors — teal, lavender, cinnamon—rest enshrined inside the glass alongside mother-of-pearl and tortoise shell evening bags. It doesn't sell, he will argue. And it takes away from our true mission. And what is that? she will ask. To educate the world about fragrance. To make the purchaser more aware of the perfumer's art: its nuance, its connection to our hearts and our minds. She will look at him with those brilliant and beautiful eyes of hers and declare their mission is otherwise. It's to sell things, she will say, so you can afford to continue to teach pretty women about perfumes. And she will smile and he will do as he does now. He will move a planter of pink irises from the counter to the shop window.

He raps on the glass to wave to Gabriele, the baker, as he pulls unsalted breads from ovens and slides them on racks to cool. Gabriele wipes flour-coated hands on his apron and waves back. Next door to Gabriele, Valentina, who reminds Elio of Audrey Hepburn, arranges English lavender soaps in the window of her new aromatherapy shop..

Elio turns on his favorite aria from *Turandot*, stands a glass vase filled with lilies beside his father's photograph, then finally a ceramic one with sunflowers by his mother's.

The aria reaches its crescendo, just at the point where the master stopped composing the opera. Puccini died before he could finish it, and when Toscanini conducted it for the first time at La Scala, he paused at just that point. This is where Elio stops too.

He closes the door behind him and goes across the street to Micheletto's bar.

Michele has Elio's *caffè latte* and *cornetto* ready. He would be a perfect son-in-law, so precise, so orderly. Elio studies his *caffè*. He folds his paper napkin into a sharp and perfect triangle and shaves away the milk foam that rises up ever so slightly over the side of his cup.

"*Ecco!* Now is perfect! Now I can drink!"

Handsome Michele pats Elio's hand, rolls his shirtsleeves over his sturdy forearms and continues to polish the counter. The lavender blue shirt suits him, compliments his eyes, his father's eyes. Elio misses old Luca to this day.

"Elio!"

He turns to see Enrico, owner of a new electronics store up the street, clink a spoon against his empty *spremuta* glass to let Michele know he is ready for another. The young man is far too gracious to tell him how rude he is.

"Have you given any thought to my proposal, Elio?" Enrico twists his emerald cufflinks so they lie straight against his snow-white cuffs.

"I don't need to give it any thought."

"Retirement is not so bad. Marcello's enjoying his."

"And I'm not ready for mine."

"Suit yourself."

Enrico downs his drink. Like a barbarian. The man has no sense of what his city fights so hard to preserve. Since he bought out Marco and Dajana, converting their art gallery into his new shop, he's become very rich and more irritating, especially when revving up the motor of the Lamborghini he doesn't know how to drive.

Enrico pulls out a silver card case and hands a card to Elio.

"When you come to your senses, let's talk. I invite you to join me for a drink at the Four Seasons."

"Out of my price range."

"It won't be if you sell."

"And what will you make of my jewel? A cell phone store? Another jeans franchise? *Per la Madonna!* Go to the devil!"

One of the regulars at the other end of the bar gives Elio a thumbs-up. Enrico stands, checks his reflection in the mirror and struts out.

Elio watches him go, then his eyes rest longingly on his shop window. A smile grows. His perfumery still dazzles, like an aging diva with its dark wood, white marble and twinkling overhead lights. His antique atomizers, some bartered for in foreign cities, others salvaged from flea market trash bins, sit on glass shelves that shimmer like a sheet of ice in the morning light.

Just then, Sofia rides up on her blue vespa, looking every bit the chic woman of Florence in her belted white jacket and snakeskin stilettos. He finishes the last few bites of his *cornetto* and reaches into his pocket. Michele gives him his habitual alarmed look. There's no point in offering to pay. The young man has never taken a single Euro from Elio. He rushes out as Sofia slips inside their shop, just missing getting hit by a *motorino* as he dashes across. *"Piano! Deficiente!"* he yells at the rider.

Standing inside the front window, Sofia ignores the outburst. She systematically opens blush and powder compacts so the new spring colors reflect in their small mirrors. She sets them on plexiglass stands, swivels up lipstick tubes, stands them alongside the blushes, matches nail enamels.

She also pays attention to the sun products: tubes and bottles filled with sunblocks and sun oils, the gamut from safe tanning to fast tanning. The gorgeous blonde model lolling on a beach in San Tropez, wearing nothing but an aquamarine belly ring, is sure to draw attention—as she should. Sofia's particularly fond of this fashion shot.

Elio's more focused on the fragrance part of his business. This season will be all about transparent florals. And there are the sassy new scents with a definite edginess. He rehearses the descriptions in his mind, edits as he goes along. Yes, the perfume companies send him a script, but he's an accomplished actor, not an amateur. He can improvise.

The door chimes. A tall German girl with purple hair and a nose ring steps boldly to the counter.

"Guten Morgen. Wie geht es Ihnen?" says Elio

"Grüß dich!" she replies with a grin. *"Geht mir gut.* Your German is wonderful."

He blushes, as much for her informal reply as for the compliment. She unfolds a clipping from Italian *Vogue.*

"Do you have this? It's the fragrance Sofia Coppola wore for her wedding"

"Hmmm." He stares at the distinctive bottle—then at the wedding photograph of the young filmmaker whose work he very much admires.

"At the Palazzo Margherita in Basilicata."

"Yes, I know. I read *Closer.*"

He sprays a scent strip. Any real perfumer knows that one must try a perfume first on paper, then on skin.

"You see," he says as he hands her the scent strip, "when you first smell this, you detect bergamot." He pauses, pinches his fingers together. "Bergamot is fresh. Then, in just five minutes, you will pick up the flowers, young and pretty flowers like you; violet, narcissus, peony, and a touch of aldehyde, more modern, no? And later, when you are with your boyfriend tonight it will become more sensual, with a hint of spicy musk."

Sofia frowns, but he shrugs it off. If he talks about perfume he talks about life, and life includes sex.

The door chimes again. Two British tourists enter. They blink in the dimness, frazzled from a morning flight and the tangle of traffic from Pisa airport. The man is dressed badly but the woman is not. She's in a swirling cotton skirt with a snug quilted jacket, the type of outfit his mother wore back in the Fifties. He notices these things. He watches as Romina's styles change with every year. But whatever she wears, she will always be his *stellina,* his little star, even with the double piercings in her ears and the long black hair that's always in her eyes.

"What *is* that lovely smell?"

The Englishwoman roots through his window display. She fawns over the irises in the window and leaves fingerprints on his bottles. She begins to annoy him with her *oohs* and *aahs.* He eyes Sofia and gestures that she should rub the smudged prints from the bottles, but she shakes her head, instead walking away to wrap up the transaction with the German girl.

He turns back in time to see the Englishwoman hold his most cherished atomizer up to the light.

"I just love this one, Peter. We can bring it to Allison as a souvenir."

Peter nods but opens the door and walks out to smoke a cigarette. Elio steps forward.

"That's not for sale, madam. It's a replica of an atomizer that once belonged to the czarina of Russia."

"Really? It's just so lovely. I understand your wanting to keep it."

She puts it down, turns and stares at a semicircle-shaped mahogany desk with rows of tiny perfume vials all around.

"That's a perfumer's organ, isn't it?"

"Oh yes." His eyes suddenly feel heavy. He jerks his hand to a chair and forces a smile. "If you'd like to sit down, I can mix some perfume oils so you have a bath oil made just for you."

The woman, now introducing herself as Sharon, is delighted. She likes essence of tea rose, lavender, hibiscus, but all the while she speaks, she keeps turning her head toward the purple irises in the window.

"Do you know that the iris is the symbol of Florence?" he asks. "It's what you smelled when you came in."

He opens a vial of iris absolute oil. Door chimes sound, but he leans forward so Sharon can inhale fully. Still, he catches a faint whiff of a scent he loves. It mingles with the powdery green and carrot scent of iris.

"Iris grows wild in Tuscany. The oil is from the orris root. Every Tuscan knows it. Our mothers would give us the orris root to chew on when our teeth hurt."

Sharon sniffs the vial again, nods.

From behind him someone says, "There are actually two species of irises used in perfumery, the iris *pallida* native to the Dalmatian coast and the iris *fiorentina* from Florence."

Romina laughs at her father's startled face.

"*Stellina*. I didn't expect you so early." Tears well up.

"Jet lag." Romina extends her hand to Sharon, who shakes it graciously. "Don't get up, Papa." She slides in next to Sharon.

"My father's an expert on the Florentine iris, which he believes to be the superior of the two."

Sharon dabs some of the iris oil on her wrist, brings her wrist to her nose.

"It's lovely, subtle, but surprising." She looks around. "There's something so Florence about this shop. More so than anywhere else we've been. Even that gorgeous star at the entrance makes me think of things made by hand."

"Ah!" Elio stands up.

Romina rolls her eyes.

"Do you know that during the Renaissance that star was a symbol for artisans who made perfumery and glass?"

Before Sharon can shake her head, he tells her this was his father's shop, has been in the family for centuries. How as a boy, he had a talent for identifying scents. Like Romina, he could name a woman's perfume as she came through the door; he could identify the notes inside after-shaves and eau de parfums, and he would play smelling games with his mother. She would blindfold him, pass tiny open vials under his nose and ask him to identify the notes. He would astonish her, and himself, with his accuracy. So he made himself a promise that when he turned seventeen he would go to Grasse to study perfumery. Once there he worked every day at a perfumer's organ, like this one, studying scents so he could one day create a great perfume.

"And did you eventually?" asks Sharon.

"Eventually what?"

"Create a perfume, like you wanted."

Elio shrugs. "No. My father died and I had to take over the shop and then *she* was born..."

"I'm not what stopped you, Papa."

"I know. I'm sorry. I didn't mean that, *stellina*."

"What my father means is that life got in the way," says Romina. " But he's also obsessed with Florence. He would never leave here. *I*, on the other hand, I prefer the Dalmatian iris."

Elio feels his face grow hot so he reaches for another vial. "I would mix this with the *iris fiorentina*. Cypress is also a scent of Florence. Let's look for another floral too."

If he keeps busy, he can ignore the feelings stirring up. And he doesn't want to look at today's sales figures. They're down twenty percent from last year.

Sharon studies the row of vials. "Do you have gardenia, by any chance?"

He starts, then nods. He fumbles as he opens the drawer, taking out a purple glass vial. He holds it a beat too long before offering to unstop it. Sharon seems to notice his hesitation because she explains herself. "I know it's an old scent. No one uses it anymore. But my mother wore it. I would hate it when I was young because it meant we were all going out to some grown-up's house and I'd have to sit at a table, bored, for hours. But it always reminds me of her."

He catches the regret in her voice, the sense of loss unresolved.

"My mother wore it too," he begins.

2

SHARON STARES AT THE EXOTIC YOUNG WOMAN in the photograph.

"Interesting. The flower." Even today, the sight of the robust sunflower, with its ungainly stem, in the hands of a young bride makes people pause.

Elio echoes her, forcing in a casual, enthusiastic note as he sets the vial down. "Yes, back then all the brides carried orange flowers. It was common practice. But my mother always distinguished between tradition and convention. Making fish on Christmas Eve was tradition. Lentils for New Year's, lamb for Easter. Irises in every room in our house for spring. Traditions she preserved. But convention, never! The orange flower was convention, so she had to refuse it. You know, her real name wasn't Elena. It was Eleni." He smiles, repeats the name to himself. "Eleni. Her Greek name. But until I was nine, I thought it was Elena. My father said it was the only concession she would make to a culture she abhorred. And!" He holds his finger in the air. "Do you know how I found out?" He slaps her knee without thinking, then realizes what he's done, but she smiles at him, so he talks on. "I found out when I was ten years old and tried to hide her passport so she couldn't go to Greece without me that summer. She used to take me all the time when I was small. But later she would go alone because she had a lover. So I saw her name, Eleni, and that's when she told me she would always be a stranger in a city that guards its heritage with the fervor of Savonarola." He laughs. Sharon does too.

"You see, Sharon, she was different from the other mothers here. She was foreign for one thing. And she didn't dress like they did. The style of the times was quite formal. You know how we Florentines think we are fashion leaders."

"Not a misnomer, I would say," agrees Sharon, nodding at Sophia.

"Yes, but we are thick-headed." Elio points to his head. Then he laughs. "You know that even the fascists, who tried so hard to dictate what women should wear, lost to us. They gave the edict that we were not to dress in the current fashion, which was then influenced by France or America. That we had to be more serious and, I suppose, conservative in our dress. No padded shoulders for women's suits, no imported fabrics. Well!" He shakes his head. "You can guess, my dear Sharon, that there was no way the Florentines would give in, not even to the fascists!"

Sharon nods, studies his face with curiosity.

"Now, there is the other side of course. The fashions of the Fifties were glorious, yes. Elegant. But, in Florence, we took it a bit too far. The ladies were stiff, in those stockings with the lines in back and those pocketbooks they would carry on their arms like this." Elio stands up, stiff, his elbows against his ribs. He eyes Sofia, who shakes her head as she continues to type numbers on the computer. She winks at him, though.

"My mother, on the other hand, she was *sexy*." He blushes a bit and sits down again. "Not in a cheap way, but in an *honest* way. She wore her hair loose. She wore sandals all the time, even in winter. And no stockings! The men would stare at her in the street when she rode her bicycle with me on the handlebars. She didn't care if her skirt blew up and they saw her legs. Why not? She had very nice legs."

A glance at Sofia, whose eyebrows are now raised, and he shrugs. Elena would never wear Sofia's shawls or lizard pumps. She would never walk the Vasarian corridor to do anything but mock the somber faces of the Medici titans. She detested formalities.

"But what she had was more than beauty. And she *was* beautiful. She had a spirit, she loved life, and that love was more important than everything, society, fashion, rules. And later, yes, it took over in ways... maybe, were not so good." He paused. "You know she rode a bicycle like I do, hands off the handlebars. That's how I learned to do it!"

Elio glances across the street. Sharon's husband is well ensconced with the Italian men at Michele's bar. They drink grappa to celebrate their team winning or losing. So Elio tells Sharon about Elena's love of gardenia, the flower and the perfume. But she rarely wore perfume of any kind, he explains. And when she did, well, it meant a change was coming.

3

HE'S GLAD WHEN SHARON LEAVES and the soccer match ends, so he can put away the vial and drink down a grappa himself. He keeps a small bottle in a cabinet for just these moments. But next to the cabinet is his mother's favorite watercolor of Greece, showing the brilliant bougainvillea against the white stone walls of his YaYa's house in Paros. And he remembers.

Why does he remember? Is it the colors brought out by the limpid, transparent light one finds only in Greece? Or is it the image, the bougainvillea, itself? The window's curve? The texture of stucco stippled on by a fine-tipped paintbrush? The smell of the paper, recalling the day Elena finished painting it? The day his YaYa's garden smelled of new blossoms pushing through the soil and creamy calla lilies rising up like white trumpets.

He sees Elena sometimes when he walks across the Florentine streets. He sees her in the stride of confident and sexually charged young women, with their bare brown legs and filmy see-through dresses. He tries not to look. He should not, but he sees in them that eroticism of his mother, the part of her she repressed for so long.

He breathes in their perfumes as they pass, hoping to find her inside them.

She's nowhere in any of those scents, however. Because if Elena was any perfume at all, she was the audacious gardenia, the scent no one knows or wears anymore, but the scent that will not die, not from memories, not from films, not from the archive of great and memorable fragrances. It remains, sculpted into his memory, as firm and unyielding as stone because it was the scent she wore the day he lost her forever.

The grappa goes down warm. He closes his eyes, feels his head go light, and without asking himself why he does this, he retrieves the vial, opens it, smells.

God, could she get angry, that Elena, Eleni, his mother! Like that morning she came in with flowers balanced on her hip as she swung through the perfumery door. Teasing, she passed the package under Elio's nose. The flowers from Sergio's shop were always tightly wrapped, but their spring vapors seeped through. He closed his eyes.

"Geranium, peony, iris."

"Brilliant." She kissed the top of his head, but that wasn't enough of a reward. Elio held out his hand. She slapped a hundred-lira coin in it and he ran across the street to Luca's café. Luca had white hair and happy blue eyes and always saved the gooiest hazelnut-chocolate *cornetto* for Elio. When Elio ran back into the shop, his mouth was covered in chocolate. Elena grabbed a towel to wipe it off.

"You know, Mamma, I smelled something else," he said between scrubs.

"I'm not surprised. Stay still a minute." She wiped off the last smudge. "And what would that be? "

"Mamma, I bet Maurizio wrapped the flowers for you."

"Yes, he was helping in the shop this morning. How did you know?"

"Because the paper smells like his hands. Here, smell." Elio shoved the crumpled paper under her nose. She sniffed, shook her head.

"If you say so. What do Maurizio's hands smell like?" As Elena asked, Gregorio entered, surprising them both. He tossed his son a cellophane wrapped box of Arpège. Elio grabbed for it and missed.

His cheeks burned. He picked the crushed box off the floor. "Like sweat, and rotten bananas."

"Doesn't say much for Maurizio's hands," said his father as he pulled new merchandise from a shipping crate. He tossed them to Elio, who scrambled to catch each one. "In the Guerlain section, Elio. The parfums first on the left, then eau de parfums, the eau de toilettes next to them, body lotions and dusting powders on the shelves below. Line them up right, okay."

That was something Elio knew how to do. He would line up each box, straight and even. He would twist the scent strips like curlicue ribbons.

"Gregorio, your son just said something amazing."

"He's always amazing. Let me guess. You brought in those flowers all wrapped up and he told you what was inside."

"Yes, in fact he—"

A loud thump outside made them start. Marina, whose mother, Rosaria, owned the linen shop down the street, had rammed her bicycle against the door. She laughed, waved her apologies and jumped back on her bike.

Gregorio tapped his forehead with his finger. "That girl is crazy."

"Elio was able to tell me that Maurizio had wrapped the flowers because the paper smelled like his hands."

"Don't you think it's time they buy her a new bicycle? The front wheel is twisted."

"Didn't you hear me, Gregorio?"

"Right. Elio, straighten that box just a tiny bit."

"Gregorio!"

"Come on, Elena, he's been exposed to this business his whole life. Yes, he's got a good sense of smell, but you exaggerate."

"Why can't you recognize that your son is gifted, that he just *might* have a special talent?"

Gregorio looked from her to the counter now strewn with after boxes.

"For God's-sakes, Elena, it's almost time to open and we have half a wall to finish."

"Good! Have fun finishing it!"

She threw a box across the counter, turned and walked back toward the stockroom. She roughly pushed aside the strands of beads at the entrance and disappeared into the darkness on the other side.

4

ELIO LOOKS OVER NOW AND SIGHS. They removed those beads years ago. Sophia had told him they needed a thick wooden door with a good lock. He bolts it shut now so he can go to lunch. He still closes his shop for two hours in the middle of the day, even though that's no longer common practice. Of course everyone around him stays open, including Marina. But it's yet another tradition he refuses to break.

The other is his midday walk through the streets of the Centro Storico, across Piazza della Repubblica, where Romina will undoubtedly meet up with her friends and tell them all about her "amazing" trip to New York. He does it to take in the familiar food smells that haven't changed over the decades. He does it because it eventually leads him to Vittorio's, where he'll sit at his reserved table by the window and receive a bowl of *pappa al pomodoro*, a dish of cannellini beans in sage, and a glass of wine. He does it to thumb his nose at a world that's changing far too fast. Certain things will never disappear, he tells himself as he lifts his face, eyes closed, to the afternoon sun. On buildings all around him are flowering window boxes with vines that sway in the wind. He listens to the shouts of children running home from school, even as some text on their cell phones.

He remembers doing the same when he was a boy. He would race his bicycle against his friend Tommaso and look up at open windows to hear forks and knives clink against plates, voices rising above the clatter as parents scolded children for not washing their hands before coming to the table and grandmothers stood at open portals to usher in the stragglers.

Elio realizes now that what he celebrates is the predictable, a quality he shunned as a young man and detested in his father. His mother once said that in life there were a few things one could always rely on. His father's daily routine was one of them. Gregorio was as precise and predictable as the eating habits of the Florentines.

And precise they were. In fact, if there was a topic on which the Florentines, and the Italians for that matter, were most persistently Germanic, it was that of mealtimes. At least in the old days. At six-thirty every morning, every bar swung its doors open and the smells of espresso and pastries wafted up and down the city streets. At twelve-thirty bewildered tourists, cash or travelers cheques in hand, were escorted to the front doors of shops and told to return at four. The merchants promptly locked the doors after they left. On cue, only seconds after the shops closed, the banks and other non-food businesses followed suit. Restaurants and bars began to fill for the midday *pranzo*. Homes filled too, with schoolchildren, parents and grandparents as they gathered around the table.

Back then children didn't leave home when they grew up. True, there was the period after the war when the farmers had lost their land and had to re-locate to the city where many started businesses. The golden era of the *mezzadria*, or sharecroppers, who'd cultivated the Tuscan landscape since the feudal age, ended mid-century with the commercialization of traditional agriculture.

Their children would work in their shops and the businesses would pass down through the generations, decade after decade. And then the vespa became popular, transporting young people out of Florence into other cities to find work. Once they left they never returned. The older merchants would gather in the cafés and complain about all they'd lost. They missed the land. They missed being farmers. The war had ruined everything, *blah, blah, blah,* little Elio thought while he sat at Luca's bar with his father, trying so very hard not to fall asleep.

Blah, blah, blah. How funny it all was then. Elio reflects on his childish impatience. Maybe that's what Romina thinks when he prattles on and on about Florence. Even though he doesn't see her do it, he's sure she rolls her eyes every time he tells her the story of how Michelangelo's *David* first appeared through the narrow columns of light into the Piazza della Signoria.

"You must be thinking of something very funny, Elio."

Vittorio pats his shoulder and places the bowl of *pappa al pomodoro*, then a knife and fork wrapped in a paper napkin, in front of him. His daughter Chiara brings a basket of bread and a half a carafe of wine. Elio breathes in the smells. The tomatoes and basil are from Vittorio's garden. The olive oil is from his own *cantina* and the bread in the *pappa* is stale, as it should be. The most honest meal in the world.

The local wine is not the best, but it's cheap, and so it's fine. As are the strong tan legs of a young woman who pedals by, cell phone to her ear, one hand guiding her bicycle through the street. She passes the *pietra serena* façade of the local bank. Young and new against old and enduring.

"*Bella!*"

He's barely noticed Vittorio standing over him. He watches the woman too, watches her long tawny hair swing across her slender back. If it weren't for his mother, Elio would gladly argue that Florentine women are the most beautiful in the world.

He feels the press of the hand of one of those women. He knows before he looks up because he smells Je Reviens from her skin. He looks up at Marina.

"You are always a Don Giovanni," she says, winking at him.

"Eh. All I can do is look now."

She pulls out a chair to sit down.

"That's a good thing. We should always stop to appreciate beauty."

"True." He feels his face grow warm. No matter how many years pass, she still makes his heart rush. Those dark, dark eyes slanting up, the strong cheekbones below.

"Vittorio." She signals that she wants a *pappa* too. Vittorio nods. *"Subito."*

Elio loves that she's there to lunch with him, but he wonders why. She never leaves her shop during the busy hour.

She must have seen the question in his eyes, or feels it.

She rearranges her long linen skirt. He can't resist glancing at her nipped waist, the drape of linen over thighs. She has always been a goddess to him, but now as she watches Vittorio fill her wine glass, eyes downcast, he knows, beyond any doubt that something is seriously wrong.

Vittorio leaves. Silence. Feeling bold because he will do anything for her, Elio reaches for her hand. Tears spill before she can even speak. "Marina."

She shakes her head, pulls her hand back.

"It's alright, Elio. You're my dearest friend. I will tell you first."

He has always relished this status in her life. He had it even while her husband was still alive. On many evenings, after locking up their respective shops, they would walk by the Arno together and remark at the colors of the sky at different times of day, during different seasons; at the hum of passersby and that the river still held a level of enchantment for them. They would talk about the delightful *baccala* with potatoes at Buca dell'Orafo, and the hip new wine bars they felt too old to walk into. Sometimes they talked about troubles and apprehensions, other times about dreams and hopes. They talked a lot about Romina's rebelliousness, Michele's intractable charm, and Sofia's intellect. The walk would usually end up at Caffè Gilli with a dish of Marco's handmade *cantuccini*, dipped one after the other into glasses of sweet *vin santo* until they were both drunk and giddy.

As she starts to talk Elio gulps down his wine. He can barely hear her. Inside the fog of her words she talks about the lump. It's in her right breast. She felt it many times but ignored it. There'd never been any cancer in her family, so why be concerned? Besides she's always been too pre-occupied with the remodel of her shop. And now that she has four grandchildren, well, time just slips away. In the fall she taught Franco to ride a bicycle and now he's racing all over the city. The youngest, Rosalia, is learning to walk and causes one catastrophe after another. The twins have so many food allergies she has to cook separate meals. She does it to help their mother, her youngest daughter, Clelia, whose law practice takes her to Rome for days at a time.

Elio hates that he does it and he knows she notices, but he looks away. Marina keeps talking. There will be treatments. There's an outstanding doctor at a clinic in Verona. She has it all planned, down to the smallest detail, but for the first time in her life...

"I'm frightened."

Frightened? Marina's never been frightened of anything. As a girl of sixteen, she defied the conventions of a sanctimonious city to sleep with her Australian lover, an athletic and strikingly seductive musician, twelve years her senior. The merchant wives with the trapezoid handbags would whisper about her when she walked down the street. She was the first woman in the commercial sector to take up the family business and make it a bigger success than her father had. Even though she was seven years older than Elio and quite a bit older than the younger proprietors, she embraced all the new technologies, all in the name of earning money for her children, grandchildren and great-grandchildren. "As long as there's money to be made, I want to be making it," she told Elio on her sixty-seventh birthday. And make it she did. She was the richest woman in the Centro Storico.

His mother said Marina was the person she trusted most. And he didn't need to ask why. If she promised to come by and read to him after school, she showed up. If he told Marina a secret, she kept it. If he got a nosebleed, she knew to apply something cold and tell him to hold his head back until the bleeding stopped. If a girl at school made fun of him, she knew what to say to make him feel better.

And, whenever they went to the *vendemmia,* she let him ride in her wobbly old Fiat Cinquecento so they could get to the vineyards long before his parents or anyone else. Marina taught him to squeeze the grape skins first as a test. The stickier your fingers, the more ready for picking. Then, of course, he'd stuff more in his mouth than he put in the basket. She'd been okay with that too.

The carafe of wine is empty. He doesn't remember drinking so many glasses. He doesn't remember seeing Vittorio clear away his unfinished *pappa*, or Marina write down the address of the hospital in Verona that she's looking into and place the paper in his hand. "Elio."

"I'm glad you're wearing my Je Reviens, Marina." He'd given her a vintage 1950s bottle of the fragrance created by Worth. "The new versions just get cheaper and cheaper. They don't have that smoky narcissus note, the note that makes me think of you all the time." His voice is breaking.

"You're not listening to me, Elio."

"It's that solitary sweet green scent too, the amyl salicylate. I learned to love chemical notes because of that note. Back then when I was a young man and I thought the only real fragrance oils came from nature, from the jasmine and the lavender fields of Provence, from the real animal-extracted musk. But that's *just* what the new Je Reviens is missing! What all the modern versions of the Fifties classics are missing!"

Heads turn because he's raising his voice.

"That marvelous nitro musk. So smoky and lush, so alive. Like, like...well, like you, Marina. Do you know why Worth called it Je Reviens? Because each of his perfumes was part of a love story. He wanted the story to say, *In the night, just before dawn, because I can't bear to say goodbye, I'm coming back to you.* So! The four fragrances! Dans la Nuit. Vers le Jour. Sans Adieu. And Je Reviens."

"I know what it means, Elio."

"That's why you wear it, Marina. You always come back. No matter what. When that bastard Eugenio broke your heart, you earned your reputation back. When Marco died, you grew this business. Your children would not have achieved so much without you." His face is so wet the tears slide over his lips as he keeps talking. He stops when she grabs his hand. She holds it there.

"Sometimes, Elio, there's a drumbeat that just does not stop. This may be mine. I'm okay with that."

"Okay! How can you be okay? Are you joking?" He yanks his hand away.

"I know you don't want to hear any of this, Elio, but I need your support now more than at any other time. It's no use to be angry with me."

"I'm not angry with you. Well, maybe I'm just angry about the situation."

The spicy topnotes of Je Reviens have wafted away. The narcissus is ever present.

"I know you'll come through this, Marina." He holds up a finger.

Vittorio puts down two shots of grappa. He rubs Marina's shoulder.

"I'm all right, Vittorio. Thank you."

"Can I get you something?" He raises an eyebrow. For a second Elio is jealous that Marina looks at him with such affection.

She squeezes the hand that still rests on her shoulder. "Maybe a *vin santo* after this." She laughs but can't control the tears that stream down her face. Vittorio hands her his handkerchief, which she rubs across her eyes, then crumples in her hand. "I'll wash and iron it for you. Better still, Vittorio, come to the shop and I'll give you a box of linen handkerchiefs from Ireland. The finest I've ever carried!"

"I still have seven boxes at home. My children give me one for every birthday, every Christmas and every feast of San Vittorio. They always make me think of you, Marina *bella!*"

He pats her shoulder again and runs to a customer who is waving his check in the air. Marina watches the strapping young man as he walks away.

"God bless him, Elio. He's as tuned in as his father was. Remember Gabriele, with that shiny bald head? Reminded me of Yul Brynner."

"How can I forget? I miss him still, Marina. He died too soon. Never got to enjoy retirement, his grandchildren. Nothing."

"True. Me, on the other hand. I've enjoyed everything!"

5

ELIO FEELS THE OLD DESIRE CHURN UP INSIDE HIM.

He'd returned from the perfumery school for his father's funeral. He was nineteen. She was twenty-six. And he saw her at the service with her new husband. For some reason, he couldn't stop staring at the profile of her strong lovely face behind the black lace veil, and her lips as red as a Florentine poppy. Maybe it was the grief. His father was gone. His mother had abandoned him long ago. He was an orphan and a young man with a now unsure future. Maybe that was why he desired her so much, so fast. As the Padre placed a bouquet of irises on Gregorio's coffin, Marina knelt down to kiss it. Elio, his young son, should have been shrouded in grief, should have been thinking about the father he'd just lost. But all he saw as she leaned over was the silver crucifix inside her cleavage.

That night, hours after her husband had gone to sleep, Elio knocked on her door. She led him into the back room to a pile of folded duvets where no one could hear them. As soon as he sat down she kissed him. He wondered why she took him in so willingly and why their lovemaking felt so right.

They were more friends than lovers. It was that real and that uncomplicated. Loving Marina was as natural as waking up or going to sleep, as organic as the Tuscan soil, as expected as a dazzling sunset over the Arno. When he left her shop early the next morning he felt not a shred of regret. He walked through empty streets to his father's perfumery and leaned his forehead against the iron gates, listening to the quiet pulsing of his heart.

"Do you remember the *Il Baccanale*, Marina?" he asks her now, aware his hand, which still holds hers, is sweating.

"Of course. The most exciting barrel roll ever. And I didn't forget the champion. He was gorgeous!"

Chiara appears at a nearby table, carrying a dish of salumi. Marina eyes the *mortadella*, *salame* and prosciutto in tight rolls on the plate around a mound of olives, and signals for Chiara to bring them a dish too.

"There was that walk up along Via dell'Opio Nel Corso to the Piazza Grande." Elio drops Marina's hand to make a squiggly motion with his. "I could never do it today."

"You wouldn't want to. Too crowded with tourists. It's not the same. I almost never go to Montepulciano."

"But the wine is still one of our finest." Elio snaps his fingers at Vittorio. "A *vino nobile* for a lady who is noble." He salutes Marina, then realizes with regret it's as if he's delivering a eulogy.

The wine arrives. They toast each other with their eyes and drink.

AT THE CENTER OF THE GRAY STONE Piazza Grande, so many years ago, performers in medieval dress unfurled red and white contrada flags. Contestants wearing their respective coats of arms lined up in pairs behind their barrels. A very young Marina threw a rose at Sergio, the irresistible Sicilian contestant with emerald eyes.

She held Elio's hand then, just as she does now at Vittorio's.

On the cold stone steps of the Palazzo Comunale in Montepulciano, the sunny August breeze rifled through their young hair. Contestants prepared to roll their barrels around the square, up into the narrow streets and down again along the road that spiraled around the outside of the medieval town and down to the autostrada.

The crowd thickened. The Sicilian and his partner pushed forward. Marina bit her lip. And it was just that gesture that made Elio whisper in her ear. Why don't we go away together. Marina? Leave Marco. You don't love him and he's far too old for you. You've always said you wanted to leave this part of Italy. Not enough passion, you say all the time. Rome, Naples, that's where you want to go, where the streets are aflame with laughter and song. We can even go to France.

Vittorio turns on the soccer match. Elio squeezes Marina's hand, looks at the age spots on his own lighten. Around him faces turn toward the television screen.

"Inter advances on Milan..."

A flurry of clapping, jeers behind them.

"Maledetti!" Vittorio presses his hands against his ears. "How is this possible!" he yells, hitting the bar with his hand.

Daria, the pharmacist, howls from her table, "Get over it, Vittorio! Milan hasn't won against Inter since Andreotti was Prime Minister!" In spite of the pit in his stomach, Elio laughs. His team is winning.

A plate of *salumi* and olives is placed in front of them. Chiara uncorks two bottles of sparkling water, slips the opener in her apron pocket. She sees their wine glasses are empty and gestures for her father to fill them.

Just as Inter rolls to victory, so did the Sicilian way back then. Everyone cheered. Marina whispered her answer beneath the roar, "I'm pregnant, Elio. It's too late for me to run away with you."

He hung his head as she told him she should have been bolder when she had the chance. "If we'd slept together before you left for Grasse we would have been forced to marry." Those were the rules back then. Funny times they were. "No. I have my life now, Elio, and you have yours. You are going to become a great perfumer."

"What if? What if?" he mumbles. Vittorio brings the *vin santo.*

"What are you saying, Elio?"

"Eh!" He shrugs. "It's this life we lead, Marina. Maybe if we, you and I, had run away then, that day in Montepulciano, it would have been better."

Chiara brings them a dish of *cantuccini*. Marina takes one.

"I would not be sick?" She dips the cookie in the sweet wine.

"It's possible." He defends the impulse he's ignored repeatedly through the years, to give up the shop, and go back to Grasse.

"And what would I have done in France?"

He opens his mouth to speak and she pops a *cantuccini* inside it. Irritated, he takes it out, puts it on his plate.

"Open a linen shop. Just like here. Instead of dupioni silk, you would sell *toile de jouy*, but we would have been together."

"We *are* together."

When the barrel roll ended, Marina looked down the hill at the Cathedral of San Basio, inside its basin of green and gold fields, as they drove away. Bells rang out from the *campanile*. He rolled down the windows to take in the smells of dry summer grass. At the bottom of the hill he turned on to the *autostrada* and looked back up, past the fields, at the graduated walls of Montepulciano, the home of *vino nobile*, this place where he cast out his last hope of ever marrying the woman he loved most in the world. He paused to stare at the apricot glow of its towers. At once a string of lights appeared like a diamond necklace around the darkening cypresses. The sky turned a smoky lavender and he wanted more than anything to keep driving north through Genova and Sanremo, over the border into Nice. Then he could continue to drive west to St. Tropez, or further still.

He should have done it then. He just should have done it.

6

ELIO SLIPS SLIM WHITE PAPER STRIPS into four vials whose colors rang from champagne to deep amber. He squints from the growing darkness outside. Suddenly the street lamps go on and spill a silvery sheen across the Carrara countertop. Just across the way the interior lights in Michele's bar dim. Votives flicker on tables. Monica, one of Michele's perky Romanian waitresses, turns on Brazilian music. Elio sambas about as he pulls out a saturated strip and hands it across his counter to Michele. Creamy amber notes waft around them. They suit the sensual dance he's mastered quite well. He ignores Michele's amused grin. He's not about to tell him where he learned the moves.

"The oriental notes are my favorite, they're carnal, they sink into your skin and become a part of you."

Michele sniffs, jerks his head back.

"Wow!"

"Yes. It's a wow. Strong at first, but once your skin drinks it in, it becomes softer, but more complicated."

"Well, interesting women are always complicated." Michele sniffs the strip a second time. "It does make me think of a liqueur."

"The best in anything is complicated. But just a bit. Too much and you get crazy. But what else is like a liqueur?"

Michele's distracted. He watches the door.

"Think hard, Michele. It defines us. And it smells different with every season."

Michele shrugs.

"Our earth! The Tuscan soil. When it's wet from rain, you smell it and you smell the bark of our trees. Together water, earth, wood, smell just like this. Like cognac. You don't remember, Michele, but on damp nights your father, bless his soul, would bring in large pans of hot coal to roll over your bed sheets so you wouldn't be cold. You could smell them smoldering against the linen sheets. So you just wanted to climb into bed, wrap the covers around you and—ah!" Elio wraps his arms around himself.

"A very old tradition, I know. But we were never cold then. We didn't have floor heat, or even hot water unless we heated it up the night before. But we just put things on. Scarves, hats, whatever—"

The *whatever* is a fuchsia shawl that catches his eyes. He knows it because he bought it for her last year and because it was a special shade of fuchsia, one he'd seen only once before, in a bougainvillea tree in Greece. He knows she wears it around her shoulders because her short leather jacket is not warm enough for a cool spring night. He knows her silky black hair will slide over it like lacquered ribbons. He knows that when she kisses his cheek he'll be the happiest he's been all day.

Romina taps on the window. Michele beams as she kisses him on both cheeks, swiveling her head just so, her cheek and her hair grazing his.

"So, Michele, it seems my father is giving you a fragrance lesson. *Salve.*"

She hugs and kisses her father too. Calyx. Grapefruit. He's always marveled how this scent, with its astringent modern edge, is still so approachable.

"You can't play this game without me, gentlemen. After all I *am* the champion."

She jumps up on the counter, crosses her long legs. How does she walk in those thigh-high boots with skyscraper heels? How does she keep her feet on the pedals of the *motorino* she zips around the city in? He's happy she's here, but he's not happy that she reaches into her jacket for a pack of Silk Cut. She slips a cigarette into her mouth, shakes the pack at Michele, who declines.

"You know I don't approve, *stellina*. A true *nose* never smokes." Elio pats his nose and shakes his head, but as she pulls an antique silver lighter from her pocket he takes it from her hand.

"*Per favore, stellina.* Let me do it."

She leans over to let him light the cigarette's tip, rests her hand on his. But the second she sees his unsteady hand, she stops, blows out the flame and pulls away. "It's okay, Papa. You're right. And it smells so nice in here, I wouldn't want to..."

She catches Michele looking at her. Unspoken words pass between them.

"Tell me what he's taught you, Michele."

"*Oof.* We're only just beginning. I'm a bit of an amateur, but willing to learn."

"Let's have a contest then. Papa, how about you blindfold us and make us guess the notes. What do you think, Michele?"

"Not me. You and your father play. This is a family affair."

"Well yes, since my mother taught me this game so many years ago." Elio waves his hand in the air to indicate all the years that have passed since the first time Elena tied a silk scarf around his head and had him sniff a strip doused in Shalimar.

"And the game hasn't changed a single bit since," Romina says, winking at the young man who probably wishes the wink would signify something more than good sportsmanship.

"Some things shouldn't change. Look at what they've done to the *David*."

"Come on, Papa. He's beautiful, all clean and so white."

"Too white! It's lost all its character! It doesn't look like Michelangelo's masterpiece. It looks like, like Disneyland! You know, Romina, I was just like you when I was young. I didn't understand anything either!"

"Oops, Michele! Here we go." Romina kicks back and folds her arms.

Elio ignores the gesture and tells them how he hated walking the endless corridors and galleries of the Uffizi when he was just a small boy while his father prattled on about the da Vinci drawings, the Giotto Madonnas, the light across the face of Botticelli's Venus. He would perk up, of course, when they left the Uffizi and went to the Accademia to see *David*.

"Do you know that it took four days and forty men to move this colossus from Michelangelo's studio to the Piazza della Signoria where they unveiled it for the first time? They had to break through archways to push the *David* through the streets into the piazza center, where crowds had gathered for days. Can you imagine how it must have felt to see such magnificence for the first time!" He clasps his hands.

"And that hunk no less magnificent today. He's still hot, even all cleaned up. Come on, Papa, blindfold me."

"All right, I don't sell many of these anyway." He ties one of Sophia's silk scarves in a secure knot around Romina's head.

"Now, *stellina*, a hard one for you because you're so smart. Michele on the other hand...he only knows coffee." He smiles at his young friend.

"That he does, admirably," says Romina behind her blindfold. "Makes the best *marocchino* in Florence, probably in all of Italy. With shaved chocolate, not powder."

Michele blushes.

"As it should be made. She's *your* daughter, Elio."

"Naturally."

Elio dips a strip into a pale rose liquid, passes it under her nose. An instant passes.

"Peony!"

"Brava!"

Now a warm, creamy scent.

"Sandalwood," she and Michele say in unison.

"Great first try, Michele." Elio tips the strip at him.

"You could try challenging me a bit, Papa."

"Okay, *stellina*. You asked for it."

He dips a third strip, sniffs, frowns, sniffs again.

The scent is faint. It's a green note but he can't name it. He dips the strip in a second time, saturating it. He holds it to his nose. Still weak.

"You're slowing down, Papa. I'm ready for the next one."

"Yes, yes. Here it is." Exasperated, he holds the strip out to her.

"Cypress!" she shouts. "Pretty damn obvious."

Not obvious to him. For the first time in over sixty years. He turns away, can't let them see his eyes. He spots one of his favorite perfume bottles on the counter.

"Wait, *stellina*. One more before you take off the scarf."

Elio lifts the crystal stopper from the pool of peach liquid. The overhead lights, like stars, send down sparkles of light that shimmy inside the crevices of the atomizer he holds in his hand. A whiff of voluptuous florals. He dabs the stopper inside her wrist and the crook of her arm. She brings her wrist to her nose first, then her arm.

"Is it the same smell, *stellina?*"

"It's the same and it's different. On my wrist it's sparkling, with a touch of something spicy. Inside the arm it's warmer, more sensual."

"Say a word. Something you can touch."

"Velvet."

"And music?"

"Jazz. Something sultry. Cool jazz. Miles Davis."

"A Touch of Blue?" hints Michele.

"Brilliant! That's just what it reminds me of."

Michele blushes again, probably relieved she can't see him.

"But, *stellina*, we're not finished! Can you name the notes?"

She buries her nose inside the crook of her arm. "Rose, orange flower, some muguet and a sexy, woody note. Like wet wood and wet earth when it rains. Sandalwood, off course." She rubs her thumb and forefinger together. "It's a bit smoky too." She cups her hands as if she's holding a goblet inside them.

"Yes, it's just that. That smell that comes up when you cup cognac in your hand."

He unties the blindfold.

"Now, *stellina,* the most important question. Why is the scent better inside your arm than on your wrist?" She feigns confusion. Then she looks at Michele, who looks away.

"Because it's closer to your heart."

"Brava!" shouts Elio. He clasps her face in his hands before kissing both her cheeks so hard he can feel her wince.

"Good! Now, Papa, it's your turn to play."

He shakes his head and begins to put the vials into a drawer.

"Not tonight, my *stellina.* I'm too tired."

7

HE WALKS WITH ROMINA AFTER THEY LOCK UP THE SHOP. The city streets are wet and slippery from an early evening rain that mists the air with a crystal-like shimmer of dust and stone, and she slips her arm into his as they step off the curb. Around them sift the smells of espresso and grappa and artichoke *crostini* and sweet aperitifs. There's the mellowing of Calyx from Romina's wrist just grazing his suede jacket. He thinks, I should not be wearing this jacket in the rain, but he shrugs.

As they approach Marina's shop, Romina lets go of his arm and raps on the window. Marina, folding a thick purple shawl, waves before turning back to her client, an unusually tall male customer in a Prince of Wales blazer. He holds a pair of brown leather gloves in his hand. Marina spreads the shawl over the counter, slips her hand under the fabric, lets the silk tassels spill over her arm.

She's telling the Englishman how the fabric was woven by hand in Prato. How warm it will be during the damp winter months in his country, in spite of its lightness. The man studies the fabric's color and suppleness, the leather handle of an umbrella hanging over his wrist. Remarkably he's not the least bit interested in flirting with Marina. He has one purpose and one purpose only, to buy the best shawl he can for the best price.

Romina raps again, presses her face hard against the glass, making Marina laugh and shake her head. She blows Romina a kiss, diverting attention again from her customer for no more than a second. The man frowns at first but smiles at Romina's apologetic shrug, and turns back to business. Marina reaches into the shelf behind her to pull out a second shawl in a gorgeous teal.

This is Marina, the quintessential businesswoman, at her finest. Buy two shawls and I'll give you an even bigger discount. Because, after all, Mr. Englishman you came all the way to Italy, and even if you come here often, these deals don't last. If you think one shawl will make your wife happy, two will make her ecstatic. And you can't afford to leave this here. Touch it. She crushes a handful of fabric in her hand, lets it go so it glides across the counter. He follows her lead and does the same. See how supple it is, how its colors undulate and glow under all forms of light. So she'll be beautiful in it, whether she's tossing it over her shoulder under the sun outside, or letting it drape over her bare arms as she dines with you by candlelight.

The embodiment of entrepreneurship, their Marina. On that evening years ago while they made love in her storage room, door chimes signaled the arrival of a customer. Marina, never one to lose business, wrapped herself in the duvet and ran out to greet her new client. The man, a Dane, could barely keep his eyes off her bare shoulders and the duvet folded around her. The burgundy satin against the caramel gold of her skin evoked a painting by Titian or Tintoretto, and that's what prompted him to pull out his pad of traveler's cheques to pay for four duvets and three Italian linen sheet sets.

"What are you laughing at now, Papa?"

He squeezes Romina's hand now resting on his forearm.

"Nothing. Nothing. Let me walk you all the way home."

"It's not necessary, but if you want to."

She raps on the window, waves goodbye to Marina. "Now there's a woman that will never grow old," she says.

"I know," he says, solemnly.

He wonders if he should tell her what he learned earlier today, but he decides against it. Instead he bows his head at Marina, who nods back, likely trusting he has kept her secret. Romina tries to pull him away. He realizes he's been standing there, frozen, staring at Marina who is now contentedly tapping numbers into her iPad.

"Come on, Papa. We'll take your favorite route, by the river."

"Yes. Yes, of course, *stellina.*"

They don't speak as they stroll by the tiny bars and *trattorie* buzzing with after-work clientele. They turn a corner into the Piazza della Signoria and walk quickly under the arches of the Uffizi. As they run across the street against the light, cars swerve around them but no one honks. Even the tempers of the ever-pragmatic Florentines mellow at dusk. The streetlights snap on just as they reach the stone railing along the Arno. Above them a gray sky begins to turn a faint lilac blue. Romina takes a deep breath and smiles. Elio smiles too as he takes in all the smells: the air-scrubbed freshness the rain leaves behind, the muddy stench of a river that moves far too slowly, and the intermittent whiff of spring flowers offering up their final burst of scent before closing petals for the night.

That's why he gives her the perfume, holds up the blue box with the name L'Heure Bleue scrolled across it.

She takes it. "Papa."

He says nothing. He's learned that there are times when a parent should remain silent, simply place a treasure in the palm of a child's hand, one she won't value at this point in time, but which will reveal its purpose when she most needs to hear the lesson only a parent's love can deliver.

She takes a dark blue bottle, shaped like a half moon, out of the box. A stopper of lavender-blue frosted glass flares out on the top. She lifts it out, holds it to her nose.

He can smell it from where he stands and it intensifies the fragrances around them, white petals closing around vapors that release too fast and spread too far.

Momentarily frightened, he takes up her arm.

Again she tells him it's too late and he doesn't need to accompany her all the way, but he relishes the walk and he's not entirely comfortable with her living in Oltrarno. Oltrarno means *the other side of the Arno*, which is probably why Romina chooses to live there. They all say it's fine, a bit bohemian and the real Florence. Still, the galleries and art restorers' shops shutter and close early, the now dark streets are often deserted. A beautiful young woman should not be making her way alone.

She laughs at his concern and leads him into one of Oltrarno's smallest and oldest *piazzettas*.

"A hidden treasure," she says.

"It's desolate and dark."

"That's why I come here, " she says dryly.

A few *motorini* zip by. Streetlamps light up the damp cobbled streets.

"I need to tell you something, Papa." Pulling herself up on the edge of a street fountain, she pushes up the sleeves of her sweater.

"*Va bene.* Something wrong?" He can't imagine that anything would be. She's seemed so content since she's come home.

"No. Just the opposite." An electrifying smile crosses her face. "Do you remember Claudio, Francesca's son?"

"Claudio? Oh! Yes. I'm afraid so. Haven't seen that vagabond in years."

"Well! I met that vagabond in New York."

"New York?"

She laughs at his startled look. "It was quite by chance. At the film festival in Tribeca. We were there alone, without dates I mean, there were lots of people, and I ran into him in the lobby. It was an Italian film by Michelangelo Frammartino. You know, *Alberi*?"

"Yes, of course. He's quite the talent. Like Tornatore or the Taviani brothers. It's about time we made a name for ourselves in film again, *stellina*. We've been silent for far too long. After *Cinema Paradiso* and that miraculous *Il Postino*, we've done nothing memorable. Maybe *La Grande Bellezza*. Who knows? The French meanwhile—"

"He's quite good-looking."

"No! He needs a haircut. I saw him in *Italia Oggi*. Next to that new director from France he looks like a derelict."

"I wasn't talking about Frammartino, Papa."

"No? Who then?"

He's distracted by a svelte young woman at the edge of the fountain whose thick red curls toss about like the hair of Medusa

"I was talking about Claudio."

"Him? You are joking?"

"No." She shakes her head and reaches down to brush a speck of dust off her boot. Silky hair spills over her shoulders, and for a second, he wants to pull it.

Instead he turns away and walks toward the grand metal-studded Porta San Frediano.

"Can you imagine, *stellina,* the noise of these doors creaking open when the guards pushed them out every morning?"

"How many centuries ago?"

The frustration in her voice doesn't distract him. "And the horses would come in, pulling carts piled high with fruit and fabric and vegetables. What that must have been like, *stellina!* Those horses kicking up dust as they rode by."

She takes a deep breath as if bracing herself. "I find the history of this *porta* fascinating, Papa."

"You do?"

"Yes. It's a story about us as Florentines."

Where is she going with this?

"It's about our adaptability. You told me the Porta was built as part of the third medieval wall. Every time our city had to expand out of its walls to create more *borghi,* it needed another enclosure to protect it from rival armies. We had to expand and change along with the times. We're quite good at it."

She raises an eyebrow. Avoiding the look, Elio lifts up one of the thick metal rings where the Florentines of the Trecento would tie their horses and lets go. It clangs with such force, Romina jumps, as do two men strolling up ahead. Elio shrugs an insincere apology and Romina rolls her eyes.

"I'm sorry. My father likes to play."

The strollers nod and keep walking.

"*Especially* when he wants to change the subject."

"Me? Change the subject? Never!"

"You know—" She takes a deep breath. "I really loved being in New York, Papa."

"Yes, yes, your mother told me. *You* told me."

"But I haven't told you everything."

"We should one day stop again at the Brancacci chapel."

"To look at the Lippi frescoes."

"Yes, that's just what I was going to say."

"I felt very connected in New York." She digs her hands into her pockets. "I felt like I belonged there, more than here."

Elio's eyes shift right. Where is there another landmark?

"And I really like Claudio, Papa."

He takes a minute to let this sink it. "What does that mean?"

"Exactly what you think, or fear, it means. We hit it off, spent lots of time together. We're a couple to put it bluntly."

"I think I need a grappa instead of a hot chocolate."

"Perhaps two. My treat."

She slides her arm through his and kisses the top of his head. He laments the loss of a simpler time, when she was still a child and he could order her not to keep company with someone he didn't like. She never listened even then, of course, but now he has even less of a say. The arm that wraps so warmly around his, in spite of their differences, has wrapped around the shoulders of many young men, some older men too. He lost track many years ago, but he's never been one to lecture her about what he perceives to be a rather cavalier attitude toward relationships and sex. It's a new generation and he's well aware his was another time. He also knows he won't be happy whatever her choices. Were she to enter into a full-fledged relationship, engagement ring and all, he would feel he was losing her. If she continued her free-spirited, a boyfriend in every port lifestyle, he would continue to feel threatened by every new suitor and scandalized by every new affair. It's good she's living on her own and travels so much. He can pretend none of this goes on.

He halts in front of the church of Santa Maria del Carmine.

"Ah, the Brancacci Chapel, *stellina!*" He clasps his hands. "Some of the finest Renaissance frescoes in Florence! And so few tourists know it!"

"Good. Keeps them away."

"I agree with you, *stellina*. This is more *fiorentino* than our neighborhood, no?"

"I like it that way, Papa. Although I hated it when I was little and you would take me from fresco to fresco and go on and on—"

"Filippo Lippi was the master of all Renaissance frescoes!"

"Imagine that! And who was it that told me Masaccio was the James Dean of Renaissance Art?"

He ignores her sarcasm. "I told you for a reason. It was Masaccio who established new traditions in Florentine art with *chiaroscuro*, perspective, his brilliant unified lighting. His figures were so naturally rendered, he became one of the founders of the Renaissance style everyone talks about all around the world." He flails his arms about as he pontificates.

"What a surprise!"

He has to laugh with her, so effusive are his outbursts evoked by the appearance of a church façade on a foggy night.

"Speaking about establishing new traditions, Claudio's done that in New York."

"Hmmp. I've heard. Owns two restaurants, or three. I forget."

"Two, both very successful, and in the trendiest parts of the city. He has a knack for business, Papa, and a good eye. Each place is so cool. Some of the décor is modern, some antique. He has a way of putting unlikely things together, and making them magical."

"I'll bet the food isn't magical. Or edible, from what I hear about America."

"Oh, but you're wrong. The food is equally inspired." She adjusts the fuchsia shawl around her shoulders and straightens her back. She wears the shawl as elegantly as her mother does, but he would never tell her that.

"It can't be better than our food here. "

"In some ways it is."

"I don't believe it!"

"Believe it, or come with me next time."

"Next time where?"

"Where else? To New York."

"Are you crazy! And you're not going back either! All those miles and all that money to eat bastardized Italian food."

"It's not bastardized. It's fusion cuisine, Italian with Asian influences. Flavors you never would have thought to put together just burst on your tongue. And around you as you dine are artifacts from all over the world." She closes her eyes, twirls around. Her perfume twirls with her, mixing with the air and her energy and becoming something he can't recognize.

The sensation he felt earlier when he held the cypress strip comes over him again, but he can't dispute that there is something electrifying about her in this instant. He turns away to a blink back a tear and looks back in time to see her furiously punch keys on her cell phone.

The *cioccolateria* Hemingway smells of cedar, burning wood, liqueurs. Soothing chatter from the tables and the bar fills the room. The hostess, Giovanna, wears a form-fitting red dress that does her dancer's body justice. She leans over, just enough to show cleavage, as she lights long tapered candles. The second hostess, Emma, sets folded napkins beside square white porcelain plates. Giovanna smiles at Elio and blows out the match. He feels the weight of the day lift all so slightly off his shoulders.

Maybe he's seeking comfort because of Marina's shocking revelation, or he's happy Romina's finally home. More than likely he wants to pretend their earlier conversation never happened. Or perhaps he just needs to settle down in a wicker chair at a round wooden table and stare up at the black-and-white prints of "Papa Hemingway" on the wall to remember how his reading of *A Moveable Feast* made the six-year-old Romina want to study in Paris one day and live around the world and drink in cafés, not to write but to sketch, and she would drink scotch too like the writer did and ride a tiger in India when she was old enough to go alone. He can blame that one splendid novel for her wanderlust.

But now Giovanna is sitting beside him, her scent hinting at something, while Emma brings two cups of the spry red-pepper-tinged hot chocolate to their table. The numerous gold bangles on her wrist jingle as she rambles on and on about the spice market in Istanbul.

"Can you imagine, Romina, Elio, risotto Milanese with Turkish saffron! I left the Bazaar with baskets of bracelets—all kinds, red, purple, yellow, gold, all for a bargain." She winks at Romina, another fantastic bargainer, as good as anyone except the venerable Marina, against whom no one, hands down, could compete.

Elio rubs the cloth napkin by his plate and bites his lip.

8

"I KNOW JUST WHAT YOU'RE SAYING, Giovanna," Romina chimes in and now she's lost to Elio as she waxes on about the hot air balloon ride she took over Cappadoccia at sunrise. "There were about fifty balloons up in the air then, over that creamy tundra landscape that looks like the moon." She goes on to talk about the whirling dervishes in a cave theater, the tiny cups of tea served in the souks. "The food would make me go back there any day!"

"The food in Turkey is not as good as what you eat here at Giovanna's," says Elio, wondering why the chocolate doesn't smell as lush as he remembers it.

"But Giovanna's gets better with every visit to Istanbul!" says Giovanna, patting her chest.

And it's in the middle of her description of on a new red pepper Hemingway would now add to its world famous hot chocolate that Romina runs to the door. Elio recognizes Claudio, of course. He recognizes him as the adult incarnation of the adolescent who, at seventeen, was apprehended not once, but twice for smoking marijuana outside the Baptistry, right in front of Ghiberti's doors of Paradise. The teenager Claudio might have considered himself in Elysium that night, that's how high he was, how oblivious to the *carabiniere* dragging him into his squad car just around the corner from the most revered piazza in Florence.

Elio had tolerated this *delinquente* for years because his mother, Francesca, is so incredibly charismatic. He can forgive her Argentinian upbringing and preference for new world wines to the venerable Brunellos and Montepulcianos. Her irreverence is irresistible.

Romina throws her arms around Claudio and kisses him on the mouth. He strokes her cheek. He's far too thin and his eyes, not hazel but yellow, like a tiger. The dark hair is too long, if stylishly cut; his teeth, perfect like a Californian. And Elio wonders why everyone in Hemingway seems to know something he just heard about less than an hour ago.

"I left the minute I got your text," he tells Romina, holding up the infernal smart phone. Elio scowls.

He extends his hand because the vagabond extends his. It's warm and firm. Not defiant, as he had hoped. The shirt cuffs are frayed as is the style with young people today, but the quality is unmistakably good.

"I'm pleased to meet you, Mr. Barati, and pleased you have such good taste in cafés." He nods at a beaming Giovanna. "Your daughter told me I would find both of you here on most evenings."

"And on this evening in particular," Elio casts a reproachful glance at his daughter.

One of Giovanna's waiters places a cup of hot chocolate in front of Claudio, who nods graciously.

"Giovanna and Emma only use chocolate *di prima qualita*. The best. Probably just a sweet beverage to you." Elio holds up his cup.

"Not at all, Mr. Barati. My mother educated me on the history of chocolate when I was five years old, not in Buenos Aires, but here at Marzocco's. Remember it was the Mayas and the Aztecs who roasted and ground the beans to make *cacahautl*, the chocolate drink Cortez drank thirty cups of a day." Claudio rubs Romina's shoulder as he speaks. Elio doesn't like that she seems to enjoy it.

"Even I couldn't drink thirty cups of chocolate," says Giovanna.

"I could!" giggles Romina.

"Cortez thought the chocolate too bitter, " says Elio as he looks Claudio straight in the eye. "He took the beans back to Spain and it was the Spanish monks who first made cocoa into chocolate. Of course this is all academic because the best chocolate is made here in Florence, here in Hemingway, Marzocco's, and of course at Amadei, and at Cioccolato Molto Bene."

Giovanna clasps her hands and blows him a kiss. "You are our best diplomat, Elio! But don't forget Vestri and Caffè Giacosa."

"But, Mr. Barati, fine chocolates have been made by the Dutch, the Belgians, definitely the Swiss and today, even the Japanese—"

Romina shakes her head at Claudio and he stops.

"Papa, Claudio lives in Greenwich Village. He has the most perfect apartment, on top of an all-glass tower overlooking the Hudson. We don't get the sunrises, but the sunsets, Papa, you would die! So lovely."

We don't get sunrises!

"I hear your restaurants are quite successful, Claudio. From what your mother tells me, you've made millions."

"You flatter me, Mr. Barati. Not yet millions, but close."

"You would need millions to live in New York," chimes in Giovanna.

"Oh, but it's so worth it," gushes Romina.

Elio looks down at the floor.

It was impossible for her to become more beautiful than at this moment as she talks about the streets of the Lower East Side, the pungent smells of falafel from Pakistani street vendors, the grit of the subway stairs as she runs toward the screeching train where she crowds into the rattling car among faces of every ethnic origin, bad coffee sloshing inside a paper cup in her hand.

"I feel like I'm part of a community in New York, as odd as that seems because the city is so large. You're part of things but you're anonymous at the same time," she says, folding her arms on the table and staring at one of the Papa portraits on the wall.

Emma, waved over by Giovanna, pulls out a chair and sits down, but not without a tray of grappa glasses for everyone.

"You are the spirit of our café, Romina, just as your father was at one time. Now you carry the tradition."

She must have seen the confusion in his face because she adds, "It is the tradition of the Papa on the wall. He was an *artista* and an *errabonda*, a vagabond, because he was a traveler. And when you travel, no one knows you so you don't have to behave yourself. *Salute!*" She passes the grappa. Elio downs his before the others pick up their glasses.

Romina's talking to Giovanna now, about the second time she ran into Claudio. How odd that they were always finding each other in such a large city. But they both frequented the Chelsea galleries, Romina to study the work and Claudio to look for abstracts to balance the all-white leather sofa he had imported from Italy. He has exceptional taste. *Papa, you might not like it. Modern, edgy stuff.*

So it's fitting Claudio should like Rothkos and Morandis on his walls. "All those triangles and squares," Elio comments. But there are windows all around the apartment and the triangles change with the light, not just their colors but also their depth and perspective. "You need to participate in contemporary art," she says, and keeps talking in a language that makes no sense to him.

He doesn't like Rothko. Or Pollock. He only tolerates Morandi because he's Italian and the serenity in his forms is soothing, although he'd never admit it to anyone, much less to Romina. It has less to do with his more traditional artistic inclinations than it does with his sense of inadequacy, especially now as Claudio, who seems quite the critic, is going on about abstraction in art.

"It's the same journey because whether a painter works from landscape, still life, figure, memory or imagination, she is basically working from life, from the world around her and her relation to it. She feels it viscerally. She expresses it in whatever form and in whatever medium she's drawn to. The world, in effect, is the stimulus from which all creative impulse is derived and what the artist creates is his perception of it, how it makes him feel, how he lives inside it."

"Ah!" says Giovanna. "Just like Papa Hemingway."

"You're quite the art connoisseur for a businessman," says Elio.

"You remember I was an art student as a young man. Not at the Accademia, of course. I don't have your daughter's dazzling talent. I was more of an art historian. Even then I knew my limits. And my professors were quick to remind me of them." He laughs, then gets serious.

"Fact is, we all know that between the ability to appreciate great art and the ability to create it is a giant chasm. I know what's good, I know what's brilliant, which is why I cite Romina. I believe she has a career ahead of her as an artist, but I know I could never do the same. My art is my business. Just like you, Mr. Barati."

"But Papa once created a perfume."

"Well, *stellina*, if one can call perfumery art in the same way as sculpture, as painting—"

"Why not, Mr. Barati! It's an act of creation. It comes from your heart. It's your perception of the world."

And now he wants to know about Elio's perfume. Does he have a name for it? How did he see it taking shape over time? More specifically, how did Elio first become inspired to create a perfume at all?

Elio nods. How should he start? How does he explain the incipient idea that first came in the middle of the night after his mother placed a cup of tea with honey on his nightstand? Or the tears that filled his eyes every time he smelled gardenia on the clothes she took off, folded and placed inside her armoire after a night out. Or the more hopeful scent of iris floating in the winds outside the family house in Castellina, where they went every weekend when he was a small boy.

That small stone house with its crenellated roof was the one place where he could pretend. It was where his mother gardened, his father refurbished antiques, and where his parents actually laughed together from time to time. Elio the boy played warrior all along the hill overlooking the valleys. He would lift his arms and swerve around the tomato plants, pretending to be an American warplane shooting down torpedoes. He loved the house. He loved that its apricot walls were as thick as a fortress and felt cold when you touched them, even in summer, that the dark green shutters squeaked as you pushed them out, that there was a huge veranda with a swinging seat, that the flowers in the garden rose up in patterns of fragrant color: lavender, yellow, rose, white. That the house stood alone, high on a hill, protected from invaders should there ever be another war, and in full view of the sunflowers surrounding it.

There were legends that tied him to the green and gold countryside around Florence, especially the war stories told by Luca, Michele's father, after a Sunday dinner in Castellina. While Gregorio poured out yet another cup of espresso from the Neopolitan *macchinetta* that had been in the family for what felt like centuries, Luca recounted how one day a local farmer had found a dead German soldier in the fields. That farmer had an overworked sense of humor. So he propped the soldier up against a pile of wheat with a cigarette in his mouth, and the sight of him scared all the local farmers. Elio laughed alongside his father, and wondered if Luca was just that farmer.

Luca plunged in about the day the German soldiers marched out of the city after the war. Snipers shot at them from windows. Everyone had to run for cover and even today there are shell marks on the outside walls of buildings not far from their shop. Elio asked Luca to describe the smell of gun smoke. The only guns Elio had ever seen were those carried by the guards outside the Palazzo Vecchio. His father didn't hunt and his mother wouldn't let him have a water gun to play with. But, when Luca told stories, Elio forgot about all the things his parents wouldn't let him have. Luca made the dull gray city of Florence come alive.

This is what the adult Elio remembers as he tells Claudio that to his father, Gregorio, the Florentines were the most resilient and resourceful people in Italy.

"You know what he would say to me, Claudio?" He clasps the young man's hand without thinking; he's on a roll.

"That we Florentines are the descendants of the great artists, artisans and thinkers of the Renaissance. Yes, but all those people are dead I would say, and he would laugh."

Elio laughs hard now and the others with him. "He would laugh but he would still drag me to the Uffizi and prattle on and on about the Giotto Madonnas, the Botticelli light, the drawings of da Vinci, blah, blah blah."

"But you liked going to see the *David*, Papa."

"Ah, Romina, yes! But that is another question. The *Gigante* was—is—magnificent. Do you know, Claudio, that it took four days and forty men to move that colossus from Michelangelo's studio to the Piazza della Signoria? They had to break tops of archways to push *David* through the streets!"

"Impressive," says Claudio.

Giovanna nods. "It's true. My mother told me the story."

Elio pauses. Giovanna's placed an Amaretto with a twist of lemon beside him. Citrus, the scent of possibility, an appropriate introduction to the velvety bitter drink he now lifts from the table.

9

HE HELD A GIANT LEMON IN HIS HAND. He was only eight years old, and beside him, Elena, surrounded by the blue ozonic scent of the Aegean, told him to smell, to squeeze it hard. "It's a Calabrian orange that's a bit tart like a lemon, but not as sour." She sliced off a piece with her penknife and handed it to him.

It wasn't as sour as he supposed, but he still didn't like it much. He just wanted to know why it was called bergamot instead of orange or lemon, which is what it really was. And the word itself was odd. It sounded French and here they were by the sea in Greece, on his mother's island, Paros, and she was telling him how bergamot grew on small trees that blossomed only in winter in Reggio Calabria, a place he had never visited, even though his mother seemed to know it well enough to describe the smells of fruit the farmers would twist off the trees and hurl into baskets on the ground.

"Bergamot makes the scent jump out at you, not in an aggressive way, but like fireworks or a splatter of shooting stars. It wakes you up."

Elio smelled the cut bergamot again. It wasn't so bad. It had a lift that fit with the burning sun, the salty briny whiff of the sea and the piles of fresh fish, eyes glistening wide. He sniffed again and he liked that the scent poured into one's nostrils like the pop of a ship's sail before it plunged out into the sea.

"We have bergamot in our perfumes," she'd said, sitting up higher on the rock. She hiked up her skirt so her bare legs and feet could find a cool place on the wet moss-covered rock and she picked up the tray of oysters she'd set aside.

"Mmm. You have to try one, Topolino."

She sucked each one down. Elio saw the fisherman Costa watching her.

"Why do ladies want to smell like lemons?"

She took the cut lemon piece from his hand, sucked in the juice. He wondered why she didn't pucker up her face.

"Lemon is clean. It opens everything up. Now my mouth is fresh, I will have another oyster." She stopped, tickled his stomach until he laughed.

"But first you must try one." She handed him a cold oyster shell. It looked rotten. But the glistening flesh went down easy. He liked the salty gelatinous taste and that he liked what she liked.

"Bergamot is in many great fragrances because it opens up the scent, like the first page in a good book. It makes you want more. Take Shalimar."

She held out her wrist, and he could smell Shalimar but with all sorts of interference: oyster ink and hand cream, the lemon juice along the back of her hand.

When Elio looked up, Costa was still watching. At the time Elio had yet to learn the man's name but he would soon, and he'd also learn to hate it.

"Shalimar has bergamot in the top note. The perfumer had to put it there because the rest of the composition was too strong."

He frowned.

"Some people thought it was too serious and even a bit naughty."

"Naughty? How?"

And she started to tell him, but all the while she was locking eyes with the robust, dark-eyed fisherman now hard at work. He tapped the flesh of each fish, checked the eye, then threw the fish into one of two bins. All the while the sea rolled in behind him, all dark blue and shimmery under the sun.

I wish Florence could be like this, the boy Elio thought at the time. He liked the that his linen shirt felt so light along his back and that he could run free in his bare feet. He liked that he could eat with his hands here, that his mother drank something called ouzo that smelled like anise but fresher. And even though she sipped it across the table from the fisherman, it was no less pleasing to Elio because the fisherman didn't ignore him completely. He bought him a lemon ice and took him into the fishing boat later so they could watch the sunset from inside the sea, not just from the shore, and so he could learn a few Greek words to share with his YaYa later that evening.

Costa asked Elio if there was a fish market in Florence, and Elio nodded enthusiastically. They would go every Friday morning, and the fish there were equally fresh and dewy-eyed, but their smells were masked by the smells of the city, by the soot and the scrubbing street brushes and the perfumes of ladies, and by the roasting meats and pastas.

He talked on and on and the man Costa listened, and he tried to ignore how Costa looked at his mother and how she seemed to change in his presence.

"ARE YOU ALRIGHT, MR. BARATI?"

Elio starts.

"I think maybe it was my mother's garden that inspired me to become a perfumer. I would smell things at different times of the day. In the morning. In the afternoon. At early night. And I noticed some scents made me happy. Some made me sad. Gardenia always made me sad. She never grew the flower. She wore the perfume. "

Someone clasps his hand on the table, the wrists smelling of Calyx.

Around them the locals of Florence gather. Elio stares transfixed at the bartender who carefully measures out Strega, a liqueur from Benevento using Florentine iris. Young people, women in billowy tunics and silver sandals, men in supple linen shirts, trousers cuffed, crowd around the bar, holding Negronis or grappa, or hot chocolate, or tiny crostini of olive paste or chicken livers. Voices interlock. Conversations take hold.

Except at his table where everyone seems to have gone silent. He tries to stand but can't.

He tries again and wobbles from the wine and the grappa. Claudio and Romina each grab an elbow. He tries to focus on Papa Hemingway's photo on the wall, a mass of white, black and silver. The mustache melts into a blob across the writer's face. He steadies himself.

"You don't all have to leave. I'm an old man, I... The night is young. Go out dancing. I will find my way home." He starts to sway so Romina eases him back into his chair. He rests his throbbing forehead in his hands. She sits across from him.

"Papa?"

"Yes, *cara.*"

"Are you and Mamma going to Castellina this weekend?"

He perks up. "Yes! I have to see how my irises are faring." He holds up one finger, grabs Claudio's hand and squeezes it. "Claudio, you will not believe how well they grew this year. The Florentina and the Ciel de Mer. Magnificent!" He kisses his fingers in the air.

"I'm sure Claudio would love to come and see your irises, Papa."

"What?"

Romina looks from Claudio to her father. "Can I bring Claudio to Castellina when you're there this weekend? Just for one night."

"*Oof!* Of course! Come for the whole weekend. I have a *maialino* to roast and the chestnut cake. Ah. The chestnut cake."

Romina frowns at Claudio, surprised her father is so enthusiastic and probably not so excited about chestnut cake, but who cares? A little Tuscan tradition would be good for them both, even if it does involve savoring the rather boring delicacy of piglet. But his crocuses are brilliant and bountiful, as are his lilacs and his cherished irises, the most resplendent in all the province. And he'll take both Romina and Claudio for a long walk, past the stone house, down the hill into the flowering fields where the land smells of life itself and where one's memories take hold and rise up, like the towering cypresses that stand guard from season to season. These young people do not know what they hold in their hands, he thinks, before he passes out.

10

HIS FATHER NUDGED HIM AWAKE as the train from Genova screeched into the Nice station. Elena yanked their suitcases down from the racks. Travelers pushed past. Gregorio pulled down the window.

Opening his eyes to swirls of smoke from the clanging locomotive up front, Elio scrambled up on the seat and stuck his head out the window. French baggage handlers in neat jackets and caps shouted across the rails. Squared-off manicured hedges, spotted here and there with pink flowers, rimmed the length of the station. Above them the sky was the bluest he'd ever seen. Tall flags unfurled in waves of blue, white and red instead of green, white and red. From the window opposite, a child reached out to buy a package of vanilla biscuits from a shouting vendor with a cart. The smell made him hungry. A bright sun burned across his forehead.

Otherwise, France was hardly the marvel his mother had described. True, the palms lining the traffic-plagued Promenade des Anglais were as tall as giants, and the white stone beaches stretched on for miles. Beyond them a shimmering blue green sea burst into salty white foam over the few brave bathers. Grand hotels in pastel colors, arrayed along one side of the boulevard, made Elio think of dusty gilded rooms haunted by French women in flouncy dresses and powdered wigs.

While his mother drove the rented Citroën convertible through the city and onto the *autostrada*, arms flailing and lips swearing at anyone who cut her off, his father tapped numbers onto his adding machine and Elio did his best to stay awake. This was going to be one boring holiday.

Or so he thought until they swerved off the *autostrada* and turned up into hills of Grasse. It was the honeyed mimosa that forced his posture upright to view the old gray town sinking into the marshy hills. Around him drifted vapors of jonquil, lilac, lavender, and jasmine—that lustrous and intoxicating oil from which every great scent was made. Or so his mother has told him. Only it smelled so much better at night, like under the jasmine tree in Positano that summer before. Its branches spread out over the hotel entrance, so when Elio and his parents stepped out for dinner, it was the first thing they smelled. His mother pulled down a cluster, and Elio couldn't decide what smelled prettier, the perfume on her wrists, or the flower with which she stroked his cheek.

All the smells were sweeter and rounder in France, harder to define. He knew the earthy green smells of his home province: cypress, sage, chestnut. In Italy, even the florals had a sturdy, constructed air. From the nut-like espresso streaming like chocolate syrup from Luca's machine, to *cornetti* filled with *crème anglaise*, to the tomato and basil simmering inside *pappa al pomodoro* and the flowers growing in color families throughout his mother's garden—these smells colored his life, made him smile and made him cry, made him want to do some things and not do others, made him sense what was about to happen, even when others around him seemed unaware. Those smells, whenever they woke him up to a realization, came together in a harmony he wished existed between his two parents, who now argued. And they continued to argue all the way up along the rain-soaked road and deep into an uninviting hill town that would enclose and enchant Elio for decades of his future life.

AT FIRST GLANCE, Gregorio was even less interested in the perfume school than his son. He excused himself, sat down at a café across the street, and proceeded, with nicotine stained fingers, to unfurl even more white paper from his adding machine, eyes squinting above the cigarette that seemed glued to his lower lip.

Elio, for his part, thought the school building entirely too big and austere in spite of its daffodil-colored stone and blocks of red geraniums rimming iron terraces in an all too even symmetry. But as he walked through the wrought iron gates into the patchwork gardens, the lush shrubbery and the tall slender trees could have been the school's ambassadors. Come in, you will like what's inside. Push through those massive wood doors, step into the round marble vestibule and stare up at the stained glass skylight. See how the sun pushes through those tiny mosaic-like squares of colored glass, spilling sparkles of blue, rose and gold down onto the walls, the paintings, your beautiful mother's face. Yes, the marble is from the quarries of Carrara. And it gleams so bright the artwork jumps out at you. Take the time to look at pictures upon pictures of perfume bottles in every shape imaginable, each smooth or faceted creation larger than life, each shape reminiscent of a distinct period in history. Your father is missing something important, even though he claims to be an art historian as he drags you to the Uffizi and the Bargello. But let him stay where he sits. This morning is for you and your mother.

Let her guide you. Go on. She's already way ahead. Yes, she's turned to glimpse back at the garden and the Belle Époque gates at the end of the long gravel path that leads from the school grounds to the street outside. But it won't be for long. She's already turned back and stares ahead at the museum rooms with a focus you've not seen before. Your mother has a mission, one that will reveal itself to you. The sketch she's staring at is a significant one, even though it may not appear so.

"Look, Elio! Jicky!"

He squinted at the yellowing sketch. He could barely make out the shape inside the faded lines. The bottle, when it became clearer, resembled one of the old pharmacy jars in the English apothecary back home. "Why isn't it a photograph like that one?" He pointed to a stark black-and-white photograph of

Chanel No. 5 beside a cool white camellia. It looked the way the perfume smelled, clean and modern.

"Because Jicky was created in 1889. It was more common to do sketches. In later years, they shot only photographs. The drawings became a thing of the past. Pity. They were so pretty."

She slid a scent strip into a gently faceted flacon underneath the sketch, waved the strip in the air and smelled, a dreamy look on her face. She passed it to him.

"Jicky started it all, Elio. Before Jicky, perfumes were made from a single floral note, like rose or jasmine. Jicky was the first to mix all different notes. That's why it has so many gorgeous facets. It's fresh, flowery, spicy, oriental, animalic. A bit sassy, like a young girl. To me it's like a coming-of-age story."

"Huh?"

"The story of how a young girl, through a life experience, becomes a woman. It's transformative. Like Jicky. With it Aimé Guerlain created a masterpiece that transformed the perfumer from a tradesman to an artist."

She read from the inscription, but it was as if she repeated something she already knew. She seemed so comfortable in this space; there must be more to this *gita in Francia* than he had anticipated. "Who was Aimé Guerlain? Did he invent all the Guerlain perfumes?"

"His great-grandfather started, and Aimé kept up the tradition before passing it along. It says here that he was the first to use coumarin and vanilla. We sell his perfumes in our shop. You know them. Jicky, of course. And then his nephew Jacques's fragrances: L'Heure Bleue, Mitsouko, Shalimar, Vol de Nuit."

"Oh yes."

"L'Heure Bleue was created in 1912, and women still wear it."

"You don't."

"No. I wear other perfumes."

"I know."

She must have wondered why he suddenly became glum, because she started to explain herself. "You know, Elio, the Guerlain family believed that each perfume had to tell a story. Jicky, they say, was named after a young woman Aimé fell in love with. And Jacques created L'Heure Bleue after experiencing the light and the smells of dusk in Paris one particular evening. Shalimar was inspired by an Indian love story."

Elio was still waiting for an answer to his question. She paused.

"Those fragrances don't tell my story, Elio. That's why I don't wear them."

"But you wear gardenia."

She paused. "Only sometimes."

"Enough times."

He broke away and ran down a corridor lined with maps. He didn't care if she followed him or not. He turned a corner into an all-white room with tall, open windows and more pictures of perfumes: Nuit de Noel, 1922; Arpège, 1927; Tabu, 1932—perfumes created long before he was born and, in these tremendous advertisements, looking far more important than they did on the shelves of the Barati perfumery.

He spun around and found his mother standing in front of a photograph of Femme, the perfume she wore when she wasn't wearing the dreadful gardenia. She wore it on the days she and Elio did fun things together—when he helped her pull weeds at Castellina, or when they went into the Boboli gardens to steal flowers and eat *gelati*, or when he helped her make *strozzapreti*, the squiggly pasta she liked to serve with crushed tomatoes and *ricotta salata*.

His mother's Femme smelled of plums, flowers and smoky sandalwood. It made him think of the silk and linen dresses that fluttered around her knees on windy days. Her gloves smelled of it, and her shawls. It was his mother's scent only, and he liked that when she left a room, it would trail in the air behind her, making him feel safe.

"Created in 1944," she read, reaching him and kissing his forehead. "The year Paris was liberated, the year the allies blew up the bridges of Florence. Five years later, in the exact same month, your father brought it home to me, straight from Grasse, brought it into the hospital to celebrate something very important. Do you know when I wore it for the first time?"

"No."

"At three o'clock on the 25th of August, 1949."

He shrugged, though he knew where this was going. "So?"

"It was just after you were born, and before the nurse brought you in so I could hold you for the first time."

Another squeeze of his shoulders re-assured him, and she read the fragrance notes on the inscription: "Bergamot, peach, plum, jasmine from Grasse, ylang-ylang, sandalwood."

"All the notes you and I like, Mamma."

"And what did I teach you about bergamot?"

"That it opens up the scent. Makes all the other notes dance." He twirled around. "You told me in Greece."

But the mention of Greece sent a sudden pang through his stomach. He realized again that there was something very strange about this day and the way his mother moved from image to image. Avid. Pressured. Absorbing the didactics quickly so to school him.

"You know, Elio. On the day Femme was presented in the couturier's salon on Avenue Matignon, they sprayed the models, the curtains and the carpets with the perfume, and its scent took over the room. They knew then and there that this perfume was special."

"Like you, Mamma." He wrapped his arms around her waist. She stroked his hair thoughtfully.

"Elio, look here."

She pulled his arms away and held a finger to her lips. Beside them was a closed door. They looked around, over their shoulders and down the hall. Elio even ran to where the corner turned into another room. No one in sight. So they opened the door.

A burst of sunlight made them both squint. They stepped in and shut the door. A fragrant breeze entered through a single open window framed by billowing linen curtains. Like all the other rooms, everything was white and spare. In the middle of all this whiteness sat a gleaming mahogany desk. It was of an odd shape, semi-circular with three tiers of shelves. All along the shelves stood tiny amber vials affixed with white labels and arranged in precise clusters. At select points along the shelves stood pharmaceutical glass beakers filled with snowy white scent strips and, beside them, tiny metal contraptions that held scent strips in the shape of fans. Behind the desk and all along the back wall rows of roughly hewn wooden shelves held jars of odd squiggly things. Some looked like shriveled vanilla beans or dried herbs.

Elio stood, confused. Elena said nothing. She simply smiled. He walked to the polished wood surface. He touched the stool that seemed to be held inside the embrace of the desk itself. He squinted and leaned in closer to read the names, scripted to such precision they suggested a calligrapher's hand: coumarin, rose, vanilla, jasmine.

"What *is* this, Mamma?" It had to be something almost sacred.

She took a deep breath, pressed her hand to her chest. "Oh, Elio, we are so fortunate. This is *real* perfumer's organ."

It didn't look like a musical instrument. There were no piano keys or pipes, and yet its presence on this sunlit solitary stage in Grasse evoked a certain mystical awe. Elena motioned for him to join her as she pulled out the stool and sat down. She placed her hands on the organ, fingers spread, as if she were about to play the beloved baby grand in their living room.

A whiff of cypress brushed in through the window and across the three tiers of shelves. That smell always re-assured him. It was the smell of home.

"Let's smell some of these, shall we?"

"Are you sure we're allowed to, Mamma?"

"No." She opened a vial, slid in a scent strip. "They call this the perfumer's organ because this is where the perfumer

70

picks out oils—from all these tiny vials—and mixes them to create the perfumes we sell in our shop."

"But why is it called an organ?"

"Because a perfumer blends fragrance oils the way a composer blends notes to make music. "

When he furrowed his brow, she smiled.

"Like a song, a sonata, an aria, a perfume has to sing its story, doesn't it?"

He nodded, unsure where her thoughts would leap next.

"That's why you like it. When the notes play in your head, it tells you something that touches you right here." She gave him a ticklish touch on the chest and he laughed.

"The composer arranges notes into accords that please the ear. A perfumer arranges notes likewise to please the nose." She tapped his nose.

"All these vials in front of you, in each one is an individual note or an accord, synthetic or natural. If you sit here as a composer, you look at your notes, then you imagine which notes will help you create your composition."

He was still puzzled.

"For example, Elio, imagine you and I are perfumers and we work for a big fragrance house like Guerlain, Chanel, Givenchy, Estee Lauder, and our job is to make a fragrance that makes people think of the seaside."

"Okay." The vials looking back at him were suddenly making this very hard work.

"You're probably thinking of what's most obvious, the smell of the ocean maybe. But the air by the sea is filled with other smells. The woods around the beach, the stone and marble from the quarries, the yucky seaweed."

The strip she brought to his nose smelled briny and brisk. He jerked his head back. But in his head he could picture a beach with the waves rolling in, seaweed and dead fish washing ashore.

"This is a full accord. See the name on the label. It has some green and citrus notes and some synthetic notes that, combined, resurrect the smell of the sea. And they are in perfect balance, which is why you feel you're there when you smell them. I always think the air smells blue by the sea, a brilliant transparent blue," she says.

"More blue in Greece than in Italy, though."

She seemed both surprised and pleased by his comment. "If I were creating a sea smell for Greece," she said more softly, leaning in, "I would put in bougainvillea and the smell of salty fish. Instead of the smell of marble like at Forte dei Marmi, it would be the smell of granite, or crushed stone. The light in Greece is more transparent, more alive."

"The light in Forte dei Marmi is nice too, Mamma."

"But it's not the same."

"It's amazing that so much creation can come from something so simple," said a woman's voice.

Elio and his mother started and turned.

She stood by the open door in her crisp white lab coat. Her brown hair was pulled very tight, away from her tiny doll-like face and twisted into a chignon at the base of her neck. Her pale green eyes reminded Elio of the waters in Sardegna washing over white sand.

"I was going to offer you a fragrance lesson, young man, but your mother is doing quite well." She moved her clipboard to her other arm and extended her hand first to Elena, who clasped it with such eagerness Elio wondered if they'd met before.

"I'm flattered but I wouldn't want to miss an opportunity to have a true perfumer teach my son."

Elio had never, in his short life, seen his mother act so deferential to anyone, much less someone this petite and pretty and whose hands smelled of a flowery soap and not a perfume. Lily of the valley came to mind. As the women clasped hands, his mother's Femme mingled with the lily of the valley, one woman dark and caramel skinned, the other fair. One tall and sturdy, the other as fragile as a porcelain doll, yet they carried themselves the same way. The only other woman Elena ever responded to with such verve was the very young Marina.

But now the women were laughing and the younger one had introduced herself as Palma, a perfumer's apprentice well into her fourth year who intended to become a master perfumer one day, even though female master perfumers were a rarity. Elena praised her for her resolve. Wasn't it wonderful that women like Palma were taking up the mantle and pushing forward into this man's territory?

"Our younger generations will be different, however," said his mother, resting her hands on his shoulders. "I see a sensibility in Elio that I never saw in my brothers when I was growing up."

"So he has a perfumer's soul." Palma punched her fist against her heart.

"Yes."

Elio looked from his mother to Palma and back again. He sensed a secret message passing between the two of them. Minutes later he was on the bench, dueling fragrances from their wrists on either side, and he was having the time of his life.

His mother dipped slender white strips into the shimmering vials, which she then waved it in the air.

She brought it to her nose. "Luscious!"

She passed it to him; he closed his eyes.

"Take your time, Elio. A fragrance, like a fine wine, is to be savored slowly."

He smelled again. The scent was vague but tenderly herbaceous.

"Violet," she said firmly.

And he saw the small potted violets on the windowsill in his mother's bedroom. He remembered a sense of expectation whenever he would open and close the window. The scent could not be defined as sweet or fresh or anything remotely familiar. But it distinguished itself among the competing scents both inside and outside the house. He remembered that he would return again and again to smell the violets, and that whenever they were moved to the dinner table or the terrazza to get the sun, he would miss their presence.

"Some say violet is the most sensual scent there is because it comes and goes. Sometimes it's there. Sometimes it isn't," said Elena.

"According to our history, Napoleon was partial to violets," Palma piped up. "Violets were his favorite flower. Reputedly he gave Josephine a locket filled with the petals."

"How absurdly romantic for such an egotist!" Elena laughed.

"I would need a few glasses of *pastis* to share my theories about our past emperor. But what I have to say is not appropriate for young Elio's ears.

"I'm interested in how you decided to become a perfumer."

Palma shrugged. "It was my passion, and when you have a passion you have to follow it, don't you?"

His mother nodded. She'd always told him that one's heart directed one to where he had to go. And she would have that dreamy look in her eyes. The look Palma had as she spoke about her father's reaction when she told him she'd wanted to study perfumery. He was not happy. He'd wanted her to marry a doctor like himself and bring him a few grandchildren. Elio watched his mother and saw jealously there.

"I always loved flowers, of course. I had a garden," said Palma.

"Yes, I do too."

"So then you know what it's like, to dig in the soil that smells so luscious and then to smell the sprigs of spring. And the blossoms."

"Yes. Of course." Elena looked sad.

"So, Elio! Let's continue what your mother began. Let's examine what's called a full accord." Carefully Palma dipped a strip into a vial, then held it out.

When Elio hesitated, Elena took the strip from Palma. "You will know this," said his mother, sniffing slowly. She held it out.

He didn't know why but that moment made him sad. Maybe it was Elena's tone of voice, or the way she held that strip to her nose. The notes should have made her perk up. They were sparkling and uplifting. Instead she was pensive. And he felt her separate from him again, as if she were on the train on the way to Brindisi to catch the boat for Greece.

"Here, Elio." Palma handed him a second strip. He held it to his nose for a beat too long. Palma kept talking.

"The heart of this scent is composed of jasmine, Bulgarian rose and ylang-ylang."

She gave him the accord to smell first, then the three individual oils.

"Ylang-ylang is an exotic flower from the Philippines."

It was a sweet sticky scent, a bit powdery, but he could imagine his mother wearing it.

"You can imagine the heat of the tropics when you smell this, can't you, Elio?" His mother waved it in the air. "I read that the women of Manila once wore ylang-ylang to perfume harems."

"This perfume builds and blends from its head, from the shimmer of citrus and fruity notes, to its heart which is warm and seductive, but it's the soul that gives a perfume its tenacity." Palma handed Elio the third strip. "Tell me what you smell."

Elena was about to jump in and name them, but Palma stopped her with a single look.

Elio smelled. "Smokey."

"And?" She wasn't about to let him off easy.

"Sort of sweet. Creamy." He wished he could name it. It smelled so familiar.

"Doesn't it smell a bit liqueur-like?" Palma asked.

"Yes, like cognac," said his mother.

He smelled it again. It did smell like cognac and of something even more specific. Of rain-soaked nights outside their stone house in Castellina, of damp earth and wet tree bark, and of that feral sensation late at night when his mother would open the window to let in the smells of the outdoors. Sometimes she'd make him get out of bed so they could walk through the gardens and let the rain-splashed leaves and flower petals brush against them.

When they went indoors, his father, who'd also woken up, would be preparing hot tea from the dried chamomile flowers his mother had tied and hung upside down beside sprigs of lavender. After Gregorio poured the soothing floral infusion that permeated the room with a cloud of calm, he would stir in thick gobs of golden honey. Then the three of them would snuggle together on the sofa in front of the fireplace and watch the flames lick up against the charred stone. Gregorio would open up his dog-eared book of Italian folktales, the one his own father had given him, and read from it. Elio was his happiest then, cradling the steaming cup of chamomile in his hands, his parents' sweater-sheathed elbows on either side of him, the rain pattering against the windows and the lulling scent of sandalwood seeping in under the wooden doors. For that single hour, as the clock on the fireplace mantle ticked away, he believed his world would not unravel like the skein of blue wool in YaYa's tired hands.

"Sandalwood," he said solemnly and put the scent strip back in its place along the fan that radiated the one scent in the world he'd truly relied on.

"You know the fragrance now, don't you?"

He nodded and looked straight at his mother. "But it smells better on you."

Elena turned away quickly. Palma looked from mother to son and said nothing.

11

"THE TUSCAN IRIS IS OUR HISTORY, Claudio. There is no refuting it. No other flower can ever define who we are so clearly. Three petals, three personalities. Like the Tuscan. She or he is at once an artist, an artisan, a pragmatist. The Tuscan, especially the Florentine, is passionate but restrained, and it is that restraint, that discipline, that melds the right and the left brain together and yields complete magnificent works of art."

"And centuries of civic conflict," says Claudio dryly.

"Well, yes!" Elio waves his hand in the air. "That's in our nature too of course, but we come by it organically, in our botany *and* in our history. For example, the three petals, the three faces of we Florentines if you will, cause us to fight sometimes, like the Guelphs and the Ghibellines, even today. Eh!" He shrugs. "Those battles will never end. But, as artisans, we know that good things come from disagreement. Why should we agree about things? When they had to decide where to put the *David*, they argued for weeks. Inside, outside, inside the Loggia, outside in the piazza, *blah, blah, blah.* So! For awhile, and poor Botticelli was dismayed that it would not be with Santa Maria dei Fiori, it was outside there in the piazza and then, eventually, it ended up there, inside in the Accademia. So! Everyone won and everyone lost! But it is now in the best place. You see!"

One of his hands flails about. The other digs his walking stick into the earth. It's easier on his knees. He doesn't risk a fall, and he can raise his head up towards the sun.

When he was small he'd imagine himself on a magic carpet of sunflowers or grain, and it would swoop him along under cobalt skies just below the radar of the American fighter planes and within viewing distance of the cypresses standing like sentries outside their house. If he tells Romina and Claudio this, they may think he's too inclined to dwell on the past, which is true.

"This one is lovelier than all the rest." Claudio cradles a white iris in his palm.

"Don't you have irises like this in New York?"

"Somewhat. In Chelsea, not far from my place. I go there early in the morning to buy flowers for the restaurants. They have irises but they don't smell like this. There's structure to this flower, a certain dignity."

Elio's pleased by the words but won't say so.

"So, Claudio, when you are here in Florence, you can find them on Via Pellicceria. Donatella always saves me the freshest ones. *Almost* as nice as mine." He stares down at the icy blue center of the iris in Claudio's hand. Giacciolo, they once called it, because its color was as cool and transparent as an icicle.

"The irises at Donatella's smell sweeter than those in New York. But these have even more character somehow."

"Ah! Now you know! No soil on earth yields flowers such as this. Where else would you have such perfume?"

"Grasse." That pompous young woman is behind him, eyes as fiery dark as his own. Ah well, she is his daughter after all, and all the lovelier in the long white t-shirt with a black dancer splayed across the front. A New York City dance group, she'd said, but not ballet, as she prefers modern dance, the kind one does in bare feet and on a barren stage.

He looks up in time for his daughter to snap his picture from her smartphone.

"*Perfetto.*" She shows him the photo. While looking at it, he admires the red leather satchel that drops from her shoulder. She'd picked it out last year as her birthday gift because its usual shape could easily hold her camera lenses and tripod, shawls from India, and all sorts of tiny treasures she liked to pick up from the artisan shops along San Frediano.

The smell of the soft leather takes him to the neighborhood of Santa Croce and the Scuola del Cuoio, where he'd asked the artisans to fashion just that bag for Romina, one that expressed all her eccentricities. He often shops for leather there, where the Florentine tradition took root and flourished. And it owed a debt of gratitude to the Gori and Casini families who knew that Santa Croce was the best place in the city for the tanneries to thrive. It had the necessary proximity to the river, the support of the Franciscans and the Gori family's undaunted commitment to train the orphans of the war as craftsmen so they would have a livelihood.

The owner had invited him on one occasion to observe the process, and he watched a young Korean man press a thin sheet of gold leaf over a dark green book cover imprinted with the Tuscan iris. The man brushed the surface of the gold leaf first, using a wide brush to cover the entire sheet. Then with a small engraving knife and using the lines of the imprint as a guide, he cut away the gold leaf so it settled into the form of the iris. Finally, with a small sponge, he wiped away the gold flecks, leaving the gold pattern firmly imprinted inside the leather. Elio left without thanking her and without saying goodbye. To this day he still wonders why he was rendered so speechless, and so impolite. He had watched many artisans at work and they all took his breath away, even today. But that young man, miles from his home country, working at a craft kept alive by the devotion of families like the Goris, and the intransigent dreams of the young, affected him in ways he would never be able to explain.

"Where has your mind gone to?" Romina moves the satchel to her other shoulder, slips her arm into his. Her Calyx plays well against the violet-like scent of irises spread out before them. He never imagined that this year's crop would be so bountiful. He was not and would never be the gardener his mother was, but growing irises took hold of his heart and never let go. He could make a life of this, no question. The honesty of this natural world awakens a part of himself he can summon only when he is away from the venerable palazzi and the ubiquitous *pietra serena* of the city he loves.

His mother would say that Florence was the more somber of the famous Italian cities. Even Milan with its steel gray clamor and pallid winter skies had the brazenness to sequester its past and usher in the irreverence of modern design. It is the world's fashion city, even though fashion's artisan roots reside in the city of Michelangelo and Michelozzo and Gentileschi and Masaccio. Without them there would never have been a Ferragamo or a Prada, a Cavalli, or a Patrizia Pepe.

"For an artist you don't know how to stay in the moment."

"Eh, *stellina*. You know me too well. My memory is so bad that when I can seize on a past recollection I have to grab it." He clutches at the air.

"Grab this instead."

The bouquet of irises she sticks under his nose jerks him back to the present. So much so that now he digs down into the earth, ever so gently with his hoe so as not to damage the roots of the white iris Claudio held earlier. Dirt kicks up around his mud boots and no one stands back. When one is with the earth, one should embrace its messiness. Like families, like relationships. Because even the iris does not carry its precious scent in its leaves, but in the muck-covered root now in his soiled hand.

"This orris root, *ragazzi*." He speaks with emphasis now, insisting they listen. "The orris root was to Italy what jasmine was, at one time, to France. Today, it is far too expensive to use in perfumery. Even artisans like Villoresi use it only in bespoke perfumes for the very rich. *E una tragedia*."

"There is no comparable synthetic substitute for our iris paste," says Romina

"None whatsoever?"

"None, Claudio. And there never will be. Do you know that my mother would give me the orris root to chew on when I was teething?" He laughs, aware that his daughter is rolling her eyes.

"Yes, yes, it's true. Years before this became a luxury substance, it was something we simple people used for practical purposes. For our toothpastes, our powders, to just grace a tiny vase on our windowsills." He picks away part of the stem and holds up the flower. "Or to give to a pretty girl on her birthday."

He hands the flower to Romina, who slides it over her ear.

"Did you put orris root in your perfume, Papa?" She takes his arm and points up the hill at Sofia, waving for them to come in.

"No!"

Romina stares, surprised by the vehemence.

"I wanted nothing to do with Florence back then! Nothing! I was a young man, full of passion, in a new country. France was far more liberating than anything I'd ever known."

Romina stops him. "How about lily of the valley?"

Elio's face grows warm.

She reaches down into the tall grass, pulls up a single lily of the valley, holds it to her nose. *"Diorissimmo.* The first perfume you ever gave me. I was only sixteen."

And there was a reason. For a time, it was my lucky flower.

"It must have been amazing to be in Grasse back then, Mr. Barati, when they were still using fresh jasmine and mimosa, and lily of the valley from what I hear."

"To simplify is one thing, but to stylize is something quite different."

"Now where did *that* come from, Papa? You've lost me again."

"*Oof!*" He shook his head, as if waking up from a dream. "I was quoting the great perfumer Roudniska when he spoke about Diorissimmo, a scent that is so deceptively simple. This lily of the valley, which he crafted with green hyacinth and rosewood, speaks in a strong and measured voice. It is many things, not always what you want it to be, but it makes its presence felt."

Hearing the melancholy in his own voice, he changed the subject.

"But! You are right, Claudio. It was wonderful in Grasse, wonderful perhaps because I was so young. You see, my darling Romina, for you it is nothing to go to Bangkok or Johannesburg. Back then to leave the country was an adventure. It was frightening, titillating. Many were critical. Why should you leave your country, they would say? Why would you venture north when we have everything everyone envies right here? How could you leave your father after—"

Romina pointed up the hill at her mother standing patiently by the wide oak door.

"It's almost time for Mamma's *spuntino*. We can continue this over a cup of the jasmine tea I brought back from Thailand, and Mamma's delightful *amaretti*. No one makes them as well as she does. Very moist."

She looked at her father pointedly. "But I don't want to lose the conversation. You never really told me what it was like to be a student in Grasse. And, from the look on your face, I know there's a lily of the valley note in your perfume."

12

HE'D LEFT HOME THAT AUGUST MORNING only thirty minutes after the sun broke through the mist over the fetid Arno. He'd looked into his father's room but didn't wake him, having said ample goodbyes in the evening. On impulse he took the bottle of Gregorio's lavender aftershave from the dresser and slipped it into the pocket of the British raincoat Elena bought for his father after the war. He tied the belt tighter. It would keep him suitably dry and it was fashionable enough for France.

Downstairs he stepped silently into the mist and closed the heavy wooden door behind him. Clutching the handle of the battered leather suitcase taken so often on Elena's jaunts to see Costa in Greece, Elio hurried down the steps and past the potted fig tree. Its liquor-like morning scent was as heartening as a slap on the back telling him he should keep walking, and never turn around.

Inside the deserted Piazza della Signoria, the drizzle became a steady rain. He didn't open his umbrella. It felt good. He felt almost giddy as he glanced up at the bell tower of the Palazzo Vecchio, admiring how self-contained it appeared. In spite of its civic stature the Palazzo did not overwhelm. Instead it presided over the public square with a quiet dignity and an intimacy atypical of municipal buildings elsewhere in Italy. Even the imitation *David* in front of it seemed to relax its pose. He could afford to do so. After all, his superior twin inside the Accademia had the far more daunting responsibility of impressing tourists year after year. His mother's voice again played inside his head.

"Why did they remove *Judith and Holofernes* from the piazza, Gregorio, to replace it with this hulk of a male? Because of sexism, that's why. Because Judith reminded them of the brilliance of Artemisia Gentilleschi, the only female Renaissance painter we ever hear about!"

"There was more to it, Elena. Yes, sexism played a part. I do not disagree. The *David* was a magnificent male specimen, and so they wanted him there, inside the Signoria, in full view to represent the secular civic life of the city and—"

"And, and, nothing! And in the end what did they do? They moved him inside anyway, where he participates in nothing!"

The words of that argument resonated with the patter of rain. All those rows his mother would draw Gregorio into about the city. Elio walked to the center of the piazza and laughed out loud, grateful he could do so even though she had hurt him.

Having paid homage to the *David* that once was, he walked past the Loggia dei Lanzi where *Cellini's Perseus* now stood alongside the Giambologna *Rape of the Sabine Woman*. Sinister and violent statues that ironically reproached him for leaving. He shrugged, pushed past wet café chairs still tilted against tables where raindrops pooled. Awnings fluttered in the misted breeze.

He turned, walked under the damp stone arches of the Uffizi and double-backed toward the river. He passed Ponte Vecchio, delightfully devoid of crowds at this hour, goldsmith shops boarded up, the Vasarian corridor in darkness, the Medici portraits smirking across it at each other. What would Cosmio be saying to Lorenzo? His Lungarno walk stopped at the ever-graceful Ponte Santa Trinita. More than any other of Florence's five bridges, this one made him pause. His mother had told him the story of how it was reconstructed with stones raised from the Arno after the war. She told him it was also rumored that Michelangelo had influenced Ammanati's designs for the original bridge and that the plans had been stored in a secret vault inside the Uffizi. How true the story was mattered little, especially on that morning when the chill swept over him, possibly from fear. And it was because of that chill that he ventured off track and walked straight onto the bridge, in the opposite direction from where he needed to go. He walked halfway across, paused and looked east toward Oltrarno where Santa Maria del Carmine beckoned from behind its small piazza. The Masaccio frescoes. Would he come back again to see them? Would he return for the holidays? Should he have called Marina one more time before leaving? He hadn't because he knew he would miss her most of all. She had been with him in his darkest moment on another gray day, much like this one, seven years ago.

Perhaps it was the sludge inside the river, the endless expanse of lavender sky, or the sense of himself all alone on the bridge, suspended and removed from his city, that sent the first shot of regret through his entire body. He revisited in that moment all the impressions of the night before. His father's bony hand pouring the grappa, the fire licking inside its charred home, his mother's sheet music still open on her piano. He could turn back, of course. His father would embrace him and then...all would continue as before.

He straightened his back, gripped the suitcase handle, and turned back, away from Oltrarno. But again he took a detour, around the Palazzo Spini Feroni, up Via Pellicceria so he could once more cross Piazza della Repubblica, where he and his friends would gather after class for hours at a time, showing off new *motorini* and checking out pretty young tourists from America or Sweden or France. His father's friends at the restaurant Paszkowski and Caffè Gilli had yet to set out their chairs.

He pressed his nose against the cold stained glass and stared at the table where he would often sit with his mother She liked all the coffee desserts that the waiters would willingly give her at no cost because she was so pretty, and because she caught the attention of the wealthy businessmen from the Hotel Savoy across the street. He would not go past the perfumery on Via della Vigna Nuova. For some reason he felt no nostalgia about it.

The streets grew narrower and darker as he walked away from the piazza, but soon a sliver of white light between the buildings along Via dei Calzaiuoli told him he was steps away from the Piazza del Duomo. He picked up his pace, entered it and looked up at the burnished dome and the now muted colors of its campanile.

When he was a small boy, his parents told him that all Florentine life led to and emerged from the Duomo. Florence's streets had been arranged in the shape of a star, to protect it from invaders. All the roads led to Santa Maria del Fiore at the city's northern center and the illustrious Duomo crowning its walls. That meant that you could never get lost, no matter how far you wandered from the city's central point. That meant too that there was always a central point drawing your heart.

But there was more to it, and it came to him sharply that morning. It was a labyrinth of discovery. Once you wandered away from Florence's piazzas and its larger main streets like Via dè Tornabuoni, its tributary streets grew narrower and darker, bordered on either side by the familiar *pietra serena* or the dark terra stone shaped like interlocking pillows. And just when you could no longer tolerate the shadows, when you longed for the freeing effect of sunlight, a silvery gleam would flash between the stone buildings and you knew that in a moment you would be in the center of something magnificent.

He walked around the Baptistery, the Duomo and the Campanile, remembering how often he'd race around them on his bicycle, mother alongside. They would whip past Alberti's gilded doors, down Via dei Pecori toward Palazzo Antinori, where she would stop and let him share a glass of wine with her, and then onward to Piazza Santa Maria Novella.

A surge of self-confidence took him there, faster than he'd intended, certainly faster than he'd walked all morning. And soon the ancient Gothic church with its gorgeous re-fashioned façade approached him. Its pistachio, raspberry and mint colors shone brighter in the cool gray morning light than they ever had before. He hurried past the antique shops on Via dei Fossi and in seconds he was inside the piazza. Beyond the church was the train station. He stopped for a *macchiato*. The

Officina Profumo Farmaceutica would not open its doors until mid-morning, so he couldn't buy any of the potpourri before leaving. How could he have forgotten? Elena would be shaking her finger at him. A smile spread over his face. Yes, in the midst of all this separation anguish she would be reprimanding him for just that.

Inside the first class compartment, he stored his coat, in the overhead rack and leaned his head back against the linen-covered headrest. He stared out the window as they pulled away, slowly and then faster. The gray rails sped past below the tender hills, now shrouded in a silver fog. The Duomo pulled away too, rising above the weave of terra roofs he imagined jumping across when he was a boy.

What did she see on that morning seven years ago, after she'd said goodbye to him forever? Her train was moving south so what she saw would have been different. She would not have had the time to watch the noble cypresses glide away, along with the warm earth colors of his province. No, she would see the pines of Rome and the palms and the barren lands further south along another sea, more savage perhaps, more closely linked to the Aegean. He closed his eyes and saw her lovely face leaning against the window. He saw himself as a ten-year-old son pulling away on the platform, wondering if the train could turn back, if she would change her mind like the heroines in the movies, if she would pull the cord, make the train stop so she could run back to him. That was something his mother was entirely capable of. But she chose not to do it. He saw her wide black eyes in his reflection in the glass, the same as his own. And then he closed them.

13

"TOPOLINO, WAKE UP." She stroked his cheek in a way that felt strange but he chose to feel encouraged. Soon the three of them would have breakfast together in the dining alcove with its window overlooking the piazzetta. The sun warmed his face through the floaty chiffon curtains. It all felt right until he took a deep breath and recognized the scent. Gardenia.

"Topolino, topolino, *caro*," she said. "Come with me to the station."

He pulled the sheet over his head. "No! Where are you going?"

"I'm going to Greece," she said, in a firm voice.

"For how long?" It wasn't even summer yet.

"I don't know."

She'd always known before.

"Yes, you do."

Gregorio didn't take her to the train station. They didn't even have time for breakfast. She brought him his *caffè latte* while he was still in bed and wrapped a warm brioche for him to eat in the car. Rosaria would drive them in her navy blue Cinquecento with the white leather seats. Marina, who had just turned seventeen, slid in next to him. She slipped a melting bar of chocolate into his pocket and held a finger to her mouth.

"We can eat it while we wait for the train," she said, kissing him on the forehead. He usually brushed her kisses away with his hands. He was much too old. But on that day he did not feel so old anymore.

Elena slid into the seat in front.

"Are you going to see Costa?"

Rosaria shot Elena a reproachful look.

Elena's shoulders stiffened. "No, Elio. I'm going to see YaYa."

"I hate Costa."

"That's not why I'm going to Greece, Topolino. You have to trust me." She looked quickly at Rosaria, who averted her eyes.

"Costa looks like one of those scary guys in the Uffizi." Elio thought of a particular painting inside the Vasarian corridor. It was of a thin, pale-faced man dressed in black. He looked like he had a secret, he looked evil.

"He probably does, but all those people are dead. So you don't have to worry." She reached over to cup his chin in her hands. He jerked his head away.

Marina held his hand on her lap and kept squeezing it from time to time to reassure him she was there. But he wanted to be up front with his mother. If these were the last few minutes they had together for a long time, why wouldn't she want to be near him?

Last summer before she left, they celebrated the night before. She and Gregorio cooked green lasagna with béchamel, stuffed tomatoes, and lamb coated with oil and rosemary. She mixed some lemony American soda with his wine and toasted him. Then she ceremoniously took out a pencil and some paper and wrote down their list of requests. Gregorio asked for ouzo, Elio, for YaYa's sticky honey pastries.

They gathered in the living room and Gregorio read to them from the familiar book of Italian folktales. Elena let him lean against her on the sofa while she played with his hair. Hours passed and they'd still be listening to the calm, even pace of Gregorio's voice as he read about creatures who inhabited woods and palaces, who served up sumptuous banquets, who learned and taught lessons that survived generations. There were giants and knights and princesses and grandparents. Each story spun itself out like an expanding spider's web, taking them outside their city to the duchies of Milan, Mantua, Naples and Venice.

Someday he would travel to all those places, but he had to go to Grasse first.

Finally, at midnight Elena poured two small glasses of *vin santo* for herself and Gregorio and asked Elio to unwrap the vanilla and almond *cantuccini*. Elio had to dip the first one into his mother's glass and eat it before his parents could do the same. The three of them dipped and ate until their heads spun. Then Gregorio opened up the wooden box and threw a handful of wrinkled playing cards on the table for a few rounds of *scopa* before they went to bed at around one o'clock. She left early the next morning, but there was never a question that she would be coming back.

Marina's pat on his knee made him start. They'd arrived at the station. Immediately his eyes started to fill.

"*Coraggio,*" she whispered.

His mother opened the back door to take his hand and lead him out. He slapped it back. He was old enough to get out on his own. If he were old enough to be left at home alone with his father, he was certainly old enough to walk to the train.

He looked at her eyes, holding him steady in their gaze, as he got out and stood beside her. She took his limp hand and they walked together toward the platform, Elio behind, resisting the pull of her hand. But the tears covered his face, dripped down onto the collar of his jacket. Everything in front of him was a blur. Behind them the figures of Rosaria and Marina grew smaller, the beloved hills of Tuscany rising up so high over their heads. If Elio made a scene or if he walked more slowly, she could miss her train.

"I know you're angry because you're reminding me of your father," she said in a voice too jovial for the occasion. They stood only a few feet away from the gleaming steel tracks.

"I'm *not* like him!"

She put her arm around his shoulder.

"I want you to promise me one thing, Topolino."

"I won't promise anything unless you promise to stay."

"I can't promise that."

He shrugged his shoulders and pulled away, folding his arms and turning so his back faced her, but he couldn't stop the sound now chugging far behind him. Try as he might to wish it away, the sinister black locomotive rumbled toward them.

"You have to promise me one thing, Elio."

Her hands were still on his shoulders. He didn't turn to face her.

"You must continue your studies and be as diligent as you can," she said. The tracks shivered. The train spewed smoke from its wheels.

"Your father promised me he would honor our agreement to send you to Grasse. You need to do your part now and be the best student you can be."

Her voice broke. He turned and let her embrace him hard against the rough weave of her coat. Her hands pressed against the back of his head. And now they both cried, not caring about the sound of the train screeching to a stop, or the dark exhaust blackening the air.

He was still crying when he felt her lips on the top of his head, when she gave his hand to someone. Marina pressed his teary face against her waist. He heard Elena's familiar footsteps moving away from him, taking her gardenia-honey scent with her. He felt the sweep of her red coat. He turned and watched as she placed her hand in the stationmaster's palm and stepped up on to the train without turning around on the top step to say goodbye. She vanished behind the dark gray steel of the train car.

He looked up and his heart jumped as she waved to him from the train window. Now she would shout something. She would shout that she'd be back soon. She would tell him not to cry. She might even change her mind and get off the train. Instead she cupped her hands around her mouth and shouted:

"Goodbye, Elio. I love you. You must keep your promise." Her voice melted into the rattle of wheels and the chug of the engine, the train pulling away, its steel cars flashing in the sun, streaming past, she leaned out the window, letting her hair fall forward, and reached her arm out so far it looked like she was going to fall on the track.

He couldn't run toward her. Nor could he wave. He stood still, hands at his sides, as the train pulled further away.

HOURS LATER, on the connecting train from Genova to Nice, he watched the Ligurian coast swerve past. Craggy rocks, yellow and pink villas trimmed with limestone, wrought iron gates bolted shut. It felt strange to ride on the edge of the terrain. At home he'd always felt protected, by hills and rolling fields and an expanse of rich, fertile land that stretched forever. Even in Volterra, and along the Versilian coast, closer to the sea, he didn't have a sense that this was where the earth of Tuscany stopped and gave way to open waters. Now he felt himself on the outside of something that was moving away from him too fast. Jagged cliffs punctured wispy clouds. Tree-shaded villas and the perfumery hothouses of Sanremo sped past. The skies grew bluer as they rode west, around the curve of the Italian Riviera, into France.

But it wasn't until he entered the gleaming café car, appointed with white linens and crystal glasses from Germany, that it all began to talk hold.

He poured himself some red wine and held the glass up to the light to look at the violet glints inside. He swirled, sniffed, took in the berry notes and then he drank. He sat back as the waiter placed a dish of *steak frites* in front of him, broke off a piece of bread, and refilled his glass.

A shockingly blue sky startled him when he opened his eyes an hour later. He looked away from the two empty carafes on the table. The café car was completely empty but the train hummed along, curving brightly with the shimmering interplay of sun, water and sky. So how did one create a fragrance? Should he start with the colors, smells and sensations of nature? Perhaps a fragrance should be inspired by a place. Elena told him that the earth, stones and smells of a place were never mute. They conversed with you. They were the grandest symbols incarnate. The character of a Florentine, or a Tuscan for that matter, was intrinsically molded by the region's architecture, art, and nature. The smells, colors and textures of a place made you what you were always intended to be. Maybe that's why she had to go back to Greece. She had always belonged there.

That wouldn't happen to him. He was ready to leave Italy. His perfume would be inspired by something outside of it. He could take ideas from music, like the Miles Davis piece he and his father loved listening to; or maybe its genesis would emerge from an emotion, a sensation that snaked under his skin and took hold. Or something that cut through, like a surgical knife, leaving a scar. A scent didn't have to be pretty or even romantic. It had to provoke.

Winds whistled shrilly outside. The *scirocco* coming in from Spain. They were heading west. Elena would be listening to the same wild winds at home, only she would call them the *meltemi*. When he was a boy he thought she was talking about something good to eat. What did she look like now? He stood up, unclipped the window and slid it down so he could feel the wind whip against his face, feeling it just as she would, on the island of Paros, inside a different sea.

14

"I THOUGHT AT THE TIME THAT I WANTED something gorgeously French, like—" Elio turns in time to see Sofia enter from the kitchen, balancing a platter of sweets, and jumps up to hold the door. Claudio pours the tea and a sweet jasmine vapor wafts over the coarse wooden table now strewn with platters of apricots, dried figs, cheeses, jars of apricot jam and chestnut honey. Romina moves them artfully around a square glass vase filled with white lilies, pink tulips, purple hyacinths and lavender, Elio straightening in her wake the central hyacinth sprig so it peaks up from inside the curved petals of the lilies. Flower arranging is an art too, and today the cool, airy colors play off against the sun burnt terracotta tones of the house interior, and off one another like brushstrokes in a painting by Renoir.

"And?" Romina has clasped her hands on the table and Claudio sits down. They crowd around to listen to Elio's story about the twenty small brown vials lined up in front of him. A yellowed sheet of paper at his elbow shows a diagram of his perfume in its most primitive state, when it was merely a scattering of names set inside random triangles with odd drawings of flowers, herbs and people. He looks around for Sofia, who's gone back into the kitchen, and picks up where he left off.

"Well, it's still a primitive formula. Needed more work. I was young when I started and full of dreams—you can imagine."

"Yes, I can," says Romina. It throws him off but he continues.

"I wanted to create something as gorgeous as the South of France. Maybe—" He clasps Claudio's hand because it's the closest to him. "Maybe I was like the Impressionist painters, when they went there and never left. You know it's the colors and the light, and the flower smells. Different from here. Our *paysage*, as they say, is sensual. It is Tuscany. But in some ways we are more rigid or too pragmatic, perhaps a bit more masculine in the conventional sense. Provence is lush, more feminine, and braver, a place where even the vulgar has a refined sensuality. So if I am Renoir, Monet or Matisse, or even Gauguin, I see the landscape and I long to idealize it, make it a spectacle in hues that dance on the page."

"That's a beautiful image, Papa. You should be the painter, not me."

"*Oof, stellina.* I know my limitations."

"I'm not so sure," says Sofia, with that mischievous smile as she pats his shoulder.

"Humph. Your mother always has to make a comment, even if she doesn't know what she's talking about." But he smiles too.

"I've been there and I know the landscape is lovely, Papa, but I don't much like French fragrance. It's just too pretty, and the perfumes, the older ones and the newer ones, are just too sweet. Except for the one you gave me for my birthday. I do love that one."

"L'Heure Bleue. And Chanel, well..."

"Chanel, especially No. 5, will always be modern. Even I would wear it."

"Your mother, at one point or other, has worn them all. My mother wore Chanel Gardenia. Interestingly enough, the most prominent note in that scent was orange blossom, the flower she refused to carry on her wedding day. But make no mistake. Those vintage perfumes were powdery but they always carried a bite, like French women."

The room grows quiet. The two women glance at each other, so he concedes. "Italian women too. But think of Hélène Rochas. She grew the fragrance empire her husband set in motion. She believed women should always have an air of fragility, but be very strong under the surface."

"I disagree. I don't like anyone or anything that's fragile," says his daughter and then pauses, holds up her hand. "Except maybe for the jade in this ring."

Claudio, who probably gave it to her, clasps her hand and kisses it. Elio looks away.

"Woman who play at being fragile rarely are," says Sofia. She winks at her daughter and drinks from her teacup. "Delightful," she gushes. This is the second-best time of day for her. The first is at night when the stars come out and she goes out to her telescope to look at them for hours at a time.

"Didn't Rochas create Femme for Hélène?" asks Claudio.

Elio eyes the bottle of China Martini on the dark wood bookcase across the room. "Correct. Another great scent that is not as traditional as it appears. My mother wore that too." Beside the bottle is a picture of his father, with a sprig of lavender beside it. He tilts his head at the bottle, looks at Sofia, but she barely has a chance to say no because his cell phone rings. He pulls it from his pocket, smirks at the number on the screen and throws it across the room where it bounces on the sofa. Romina and Claudio laugh, but Sofia shakes her head. "Enrico?"

"Who else? Who else would ruin this gorgeous spring day and interrupt my eating one of your wonderful *amaretti*." He grabs another.

"Elio, you can't keep putting this off. At least talk to him." Sofia plants her elbows on the table and gestures with the rationale air of an astronomy professor. "This is a process. Listen to what he has to offer. You are free to say yes, to say no, to come out with another plan. But until you know precisely what he is offering and make a decision, you will do nothing and you will remain stuck, one foot in one place and one in the other and you can't move."

"Not true!"

She leans in close and looks him in the eye. "It is true! You have one foot in Florence and the other here in Castellina, where you are the happiest, although you won't admit it. I love our shop, Elio. But I think it's becoming too much for you."

Romina and Claudio glance at each other cautiously. Romina picks up her teacup.

"And, quite frankly, Elio, I think you're bored with it."

"Absolutely not! Besides, Sofia *cara*, this is not just about you and me, and this is not the time. We have this pleasant young man here from New York. He's going to leave soon and who knows when we will see him next, maybe not for six months or a year." He ignores the expression on his daughter's face. "And Romina has her application for the Accademia, where she will study for the next four, maybe five, years. It's such an honor to be accepted, and I can't unsettle her now with the possibility of her family leaving a place she knows—"

"Wait! Wait a minute!" She slams her teacup down, pauses, but not for long. "Truth is, I *wouldn't* be unsettled by your selling the shop. It wouldn't bother me at all. It would be a *relief.*"

"A relief?" Elio looks around, astounded.

She purses her lips and swings her head around to stare at the wall. Claudio grabs her hand.

"What she means, Mr. Barati, is that you and Mrs. Barati should do what is right for the both of you. Romina's an adult, she will make her own life here or elsewhere—"

"Elsewhere?"

"Oh for God's sakes!" Romina throws her hands up in the air. "What *is* the problem with *elsewhere*? I'm not talking about outer space. Do you honestly believe I would *never* aspire to leave here?"

Sofia doesn't seem as taken aback as he is. She sips her tea quietly.

"Or are you *that* clueless?" She's shaking now, as if she's about to cry, but her bite is sharp. The resentment hits him hard because he doesn't deserve it. Has he not given her all the love and praise he's capable of? Is she not the luckiest young woman in the world, heir to a family business, inhabitant of a city tourists gush over, a beloved daughter of parents who have denied her nothing these twenty-three years and who have, quite the contrary, sent her off around the world at their expense time and time again? Would she even be able to contemplate *elsewhere* if she had never been to Indonesia, South Africa, Morocco, all paid for with money earned in the damn shop she now rejects.?

"She's right, Elio." He doesn't look at her but he knows Sofia's eyes are serene and her hand steady, probably placed just beside her English teacup. Romina's energy is palpably different

"I've applied to go to graduate school in New York. They have a program in installation art that I'm interested in. But it's more than that, I want to live there."

"That's wonderful. Which school?" And Sofia is up. She lifts the teakettle from the stove. Elio removes the lid of the ceramic teapot and watches as she pours in the boiling water. Mellowing Indian jasmine vapors urge him to breathe deep, listen, consider what she has to say. He takes a deep, more labored breath and laughs a cruel laugh.

"What in God's name is installation art? Are you going to be an artist or a carpenter?" Nervous laughter comes now, but when he looks up at Sofia, hoping for a co-conspirator, she tells him with a single look that he should watch his tone of voice. Well, if he's sounding bitter, so be it.

But his daughter can match him any day.

"Sure? Why not be a carpenter? More gratifying to build things than to sell perfumes all day." She raises her arm towards the open wooden shutters. "How satisfying it must have been for the architect to build this house, stone by stone, to lay the foundation inside the earth, to paint the green shutters and put in the wooden beams above our heads. And the peach stucco outside. I'm sure he was trying to match the hues of our sunsets that you speak about with such fervor, Papa. No, a builder is not an artist at all. He merely constructs."

"I didn't say that, *stellina*."

"No. You implied it. And you apparently have no respect for what you have no desire to even *try* to understand."

She flicks her palm up before he can muster the will to speak in his own defense.

"I'm going to New York, Papa. I *will* study there. If I'm accepted I will go to Parsons School of Design. If I'm not I will work in a gallery and keep trying until I get in, or I will apprentice myself to an artist. I don't need a degree from the Accademia to call myself an artist. I just have to create good art."

"And how do you define good art, you who live inside the greatest city of art in the entire world and think it's incidental or irrelevant? How do *you* define it?"

"Art is something that wakes you up inside. And it exists everywhere, not just on the walls of a venerated Renaissance gallery. It's in our gardens, in our streets, in our sewers; it's in the eyes of beggars in Mumbai and the gowns of divas at La Scala. That is what installation art is. It creates art from the commonplace, the irreverent, and sometimes the luxurious. Art is a living thing, and you find it in the oddest places—if you're willing to *see* it!"

"*Oof*, she is your daughter, Elio!" Sofia has that twinkle in her eye now.

"For better or worse," he mumbles and shifts in his seat.

"Like every decision we make in life, *caro*. When we win we always lose something, and when we lose we always win something. *C'est la vie*. And you should applaud your daughter for her courage. It's not easy to bring up these things, especially to you."

"That's not true. And nothing is definite yet. I think you're crazy, Romina, to sacrifice a space at the Accademia for something so indefinite in New York, of all places. You have heard nothing from either school...."

"But, Mr. Barati, she has already told you. Whatever the outcome she is going to New York."

"You be quiet! This has nothing to do with you."

"Elio!"

"Well, he is not a member of this family. This is—"

"*My* decision, Papa."

"Influenced by him."

"No, influenced by me. My choice. My life."

She stands up and shoves her chair underneath the table. "And you insult me by even insinuating that I would make this decision based on Claudio or any other man. If I hadn't met Claudio in New York I would still have done this. I've been wanting to leave here for years. You just never heard me because you were never willing to listen."

Claudio stands up beside her. Elio stares at the blue etchings on the teapot, figurines of farmers tilling fields and ladies riding carriages, an English pastoral landscape. He traces the figures.

"I apologize for offending you, Mr. Barati," says Claudio, with a courtesy Elio would never have expected from Claudio, the adolescent. "I'm simply trying to support Romina in what she's trying to do. She's very talented."

"I know that! Why do you think it was *me* who encouraged her to go to the most prestigious art school in the world?"

"There are many routes to becoming an artist, Mr. Barati, not all of them conventional. There is a lot to be said for on the ground experience, especially today. I have contacts with some very well respected galleries in New York. Romina would have a place to display her work. I promise you."

"Why, do you think I'm not willing to pay for her studies? Why just last week I spoke to Professor Morelli at the Accademia about her application!"

"You did *what*, Papa?"

"Stefano knows me. We have a respected name in Florence...and you know, in life you always have to know someone." He turns to Sofia, who buries her face in her hands.

"So you decided to intervene on my behalf."

"Yes! Of course!"

"Because this great talent I presumably have was not enough to get me in."

Sofia gives him a *you've done it again* look. She doesn't understand either.

"*Oof!* Don't be crazy now. I just wanted to give a hand."

"It's not a hand. It's an intrusion. And an insult."

She takes her Indian shawl from the back of the chair, wraps it around her shoulders.

"And why is it not an insult when *he*," Elio points a shaky finger at Claudio, "when *he* offers his contacts, but an insult when your father does?"

Sofia sighs and stands up to kiss her daughter and Claudio goodbye. She kisses each of them on both cheeks and gives her daughter an extra hug. Elio traces the design on the teapot yet again.

"I won't even dignify that with a response, Papa."

15

MIMOSA. ORANGE BLOSSOMS. Hibiscus. Irises. Honeysuckle. Oleander. Delicious! Irreverant! Marvelous! He'd been right to insist on coming here! He would never go back to Florence! Never!

On that fall morning in Grasse, the seventeen-year-old Elio ran out without even a sip of the *café au lait* the hotel proprietress followed him out the door with. No, no, *Martine bella*. I have far too much to see before my first class starts. I must be on time, even early, to make *una bella figura*. But in the meantime I want to explore this gritty new town that is filled with salacious promises. I felt that last night as we drove through damp liquor-scented fields and as I looked up at the town of Grasse sinking into the marshy hills. I smelled beauty and eroticism everywhere, I saw flowers and knotted branches of trees and the sinister tinge of the sky, and I wondered what I would do when I arrived, what I would dare to do that I'd never done before, because I was free and this town, this new country would forgive me no matter what. I have no history to explain here, no parental expectations to stay my hand, my body or my voice.

I want to see the girls, and sample the food, because I am very hungry but not for anything familiar. I want those croissants we Italians consider too buttery compared with our more precise *cornetti*, and that sweet French butter my mother used to baked cakes with, and I want to smell the musky perfumes of girls more liberated than the girls at home.

He brushed past a slender woman in a purple sundress carrying a red leather tote. Her smell, amber and leather, mixed with the smells of bread and pastries, and even though she was clearly older than him and probably married, he would have done anything to sleep with her. He picked up his pace and ran after, even though the tiny heels of her open-backed shoes kept twisting right and left along with her hips. She wore no stockings but her muscular legs were gloriously tanned and the strap of her dress kept sliding off her shoulder. No tan line. He felt his heart pound and had to duck inside a storefront when she turned her head to dodge a small child on a bicycle.

"Eh alors!"

She flicked her arm in the air and the boy came to a screeching halt, jumped off in time for her to clasp his chin and plant a kiss on it.

"Pardon, Maman," he said in all earnestness and Elio shook his head. But her scent still played in the air around him, along with bursts of morning sunlight, and he watched her glossy ponytail swing as she and the boy walked to a fruit stand and she squeezed white peaches to put in his lunch basket. As she leaned over, she gave Elio a full view of her tiny breasts and the gleam of her young bronzy skin. A gold band flashed on her left hand, but she wore no other jewelry except for an ankle bracelet, oh so sexy on this morning where the scent of violets became a promise for what was possible.

There would be others like her and they would be single, and he wouldn't mind if they weren't. He was miles away from the probing eyes of the Florentines and he had every intention of doing whatever he wanted. He laughed, winked at the proprietress of the fruit stand who smiled back, and leaped back into the street where he let himself become distracted by the flower-strewn path leading up into the Place aux Aires and the noise of the morning markets. Flower merchants in tattered clothes jumped from the backs of trucks spewing gas fumes and went about setting up stalls. Hammers drove nails into paint-stripped wooden planks, canvases floated mid air and landed on makeshift tables. Merchants yanked enormous terracotta pots filled with flowers, herbs and plants of every variety from the beds and lined them up along stone walkways, against tree trunks, up stairwells. Ah, the smell of rosemary and basil in the early morning, before one even began to cook with the herbs themselves, unless they were to be sprinkled inside an *omelette,* not laid flat and flipped onto a plate like a *frittata* back home, but folded over in a neat little pocket, from which oozed a creamy sharp cheese that would so satisfy him right now.

The coffee the pretty girl served him was thin and bitter. How I miss your espresso, dear Luca! He paid her no attention as she placed a blue plate with the heated croissant and a dollop of raspberry jam on the point of a white napkin trimmed in blue and folded into a neat triangle. And he ignored her even though she kept looking over the glass pastry case at him. An attractive older woman next to her greeted everyone who came through the door. This was most probably a family-owned business like the Barati's perfumery back home. Poor girl. She should try to move away.

He became even more aware of the buttery smells of the place, the thick cream and blue crockery, lace curtains pulled back behind window boxes stuffed with geraniums. He'd expected the smells to be different and sumptuous in this gritty little town with its unabashed sensual energy and doll-like shops displaying sugary French breakfast cakes split in half and oozing jams, teeny petits fours dotted with candied lavender flowers, sexy potted violets, bitter hot chocolate in thick ceramic cups. Linen shops displayed the prerequisite sheets and bedding in the background of bay windows where the front was devoted to racier lingerie than he'd ever seen at home. Flowers popped up everywhere, under arcades, behind courtyard gates, inside the crevices of rocks, as bold, as uneven, and as irreverent as the spirit that pervaded his new country to the north.

Of course the two handsome young men, obviously twins, at the counter, were distinctively German with their high cheekbones, casual attire and long legs. One spoke in that pitch-perfect French only their brethren could master with such precision. His brother lit a cigarette with an antique lighter, kept brushing a swath of blonde hair off his forehead so his bold blue eyes caught the attention of the girl's mother, who flirted with him while Elio felt an instant twinge of embarrassment, for her not for himself.

"Are you finished?" The girl pointed to his coffee cup. He started.

"I'm sorry. I didn't mean to interrupt."

"It's all right. I'll have another."

Why did he say that? The second cup would probably be as bad as the first.

"You're a new student here, aren't you?" The tremor in her voice helped him relax.

"Yes." Was his Italian provincialism coming through? He looked down at his tie and the gray V-neck sweater that matched his pinstriped shirt, at his pleated trousers and polished shoes. Everything on him was glaringly new, clean, pressed. Compared to others in the café with their open shirt collars, worn jackets, and scuffed shoes, his dress seemed that much more cautious.

"I thought so because I haven't seen you here before."

"Well, it *is* the first day of class." He flicked open his newspaper.

There! Her mother was trying to get her attention. Turn around, will you?

"I read *Le Monde* too. My mother is very liberal in her politics. She thinks you should have some of our fresh fruits. You seem homesick." She giggled.

"I'm not actually."

He said that to no one because she'd already run off to retrieve the plate of grapes, apples, berries and figs a woman named Berthe handed to her with a sympathetic smile at Elio. He knew her name was Berthe because one of the Germans called her that before she lit his cigarette for him. Elio grabbed his tie and tried to loosen the knot. He raked his fingers through his hair to loosen it up like the French actors did.

"I would be nervous if I were you." The plate made a noise as she put it down; the chair scraped the wood floors as she pulled it out. Aside from the large mole on her neck she wasn't bad looking. She reminded him a bit of Leslie Caron.

"After all, you're going to study at the most famous perfumery school in the world." She looked across the street at the ochre stone structure set back from a wide-open iron gate where a man in a gray suit greeted students as they arrived, mostly in pairs, holding briefcases and portfolios, and shaking hands with a confidence Elio so wished he had. The girls wore breezy dresses and sandals with small heels but no stockings, and some even wore trousers. Some of the boys wore jackets but others wore sweaters or cardigans or leather coats like the Germans. The ease with which they moved baffled him. He shook his head. From what the girl had just told him, it was no use pretending.

"My name is Nathalie. You're from Italy, aren't you?"

"How can you tell?"

"You're so well dressed, and you are the handsomest man here."

The two Germans elbowed each other and pointed at him.

"By tonight, after your first class with Monsieur Lefevre, you will be fine. That's what all the students tell me. You will need to relax after that first class of course. I can offer you a Pernod if you come by after." She looked down at her starched white apron with strings that wrapped twice around her waist because she was so thin.

"Nathalie!"

One of the German boys waved to her from beside the counter. He pointed to Elio and then to the building across the street. "Are you going there?" he mouthed.

Elio nodded, embarrassed he'd not taken the first step. But the German's handshake was warm and firm, as was his brother's, and Elio was relieved that he didn't choke on the Muratti they offered and lit for him.

"Hello, I am Jan and this is my brother Tomas. Our family owns a perfumery in Hamburg—Dumas. Maybe you have heard of it."

And so the conversation began, with Elio telling them all about Profumeria Barati, which they had heard of, while his eyes stung from cigarette smoke, and their telling him that they chose to study perfumery because it was either that or mind the family shop forever.

"And it's so much more prestigious to be an actual perfumer than a salesman," said Tomas, ignoring little Nathalie's adoring gaze from behind the patisserie display. Elio looked down. She would probably never have the same opportunity. He flashed a smile in her direction, a subtle promise that he would come to see her after the first class.

Jan jabbed his elbow hard, stood up and pointed at the school. He grabbed Elio's briefcase and handed it to him. "Come on or we will be late."

The wiry gray-suited man swung the gate out further and gestured for everyone to hurry inside. Students clamored forward as did other people in white lab coats, many carrying clipboards.

That evening he would sit across from Nathalie, Muratti in one hand, a Pernod at his elbow. He would no longer cough with each puff, nor would the Pernod burn his throat. A fire would blaze under the scorched stone mantle as Berthe, dressed in sequins, poured cognac and bitters for the doctors from the hospital, and Elio would describe the airy, almost clinical classroom that smelled faintly of dried lavender, the gleaming desks set for four, in even rows, polished wood surfaces set with textbooks, metal trays of amber colored vials, tiny pipettes and snowy white scent strips twisted like helixes inside glass beakers. He would stare into her dazzled eyes and describe the spare wooden shelves along the back of the room and the rows of jars filled with grotesquely shaped masses.

"One thing looked like a shriveled fig, the other like this hideous waxy blob and then there was this bean thing. They were all awful looking. I was able to identify one, it was vanilla bean and another smelled creamy sweet, so I knew it was sandalwood."

He would sip the licorice-scented Pernod, flirt with her a little. He would tell her about Paola from Rome, who wore her hair cut short like a boy's and dared wear trousers instead of a dress, and then he spoke about the robust girl from Corsica with coarse olive skin and honey colored eyes who kept tripping over everyone's briefcases when she walked down the aisle. The German twins didn't speak quite as perfect French as he'd thought but they were generous enough to share bites of their brioches. It seemed they couldn't stop eating but that had to be because they were so tall and it took more food to fill up a tall person than a short person. He would tell her about Chiara from Sardegna who had the most organized briefcase and pearl-tipped fingernails. Everything inside the briefcase was straight and even and she pulled out a slim wooden box with sharpened pencils. And then there was Elif from Turkey, whose boyishness he found oddly attractive, but he didn't say that to little Nathalie.

He would let Berthe bring him a goblet of cognac that smelled woodsy and earthy as he cradled it in his palm. He would sip the amber liqueur and tell Nathalie how alert everyone was, cracking open the covers of their textbooks as they stared at words they had never seen before and looked at sketches of the chromatogram created by Archer John Porter Martin and Richard Laurence Millington Synge and formulas that reminded them all of how they had struggled to pass high school chemistry. Did she know—?

Surprisingly she did. She also knew the myth of Catherine de Medici in Grasse and she told it with great nostalgia, urging him to come again tomorrow when she would take him to the grand terrace overlooking the fields of lavender and rose, because she wanted to feel important too. He would describe to her how all twelve of them looked around the room at their classmates with expressions of sympathy and support. How they'd each wondered what the others knew and if they were less prepared than anyone else. And he told her he felt proud to be among them, as they were all so smart and so prepared and, it appeared, as intimidated as he was.

But he didn't tell her how he felt in that moment when all he could focus on was the wide, unlined brow of Master Perfumer Jean Claude Lefevre. Ice blue eyes surveyed the room, lips formed questions that demanded quick, intelligent answers and twitched with sarcasm when responses didn't match expectations. Why did they choose to study perfumery? Where were they from? Did they think they could make the sacrifices?

The living art form of perfumery, Lefevre declared, required a discipline many of them would have difficulty achieving. Did any of them smoke? If so, they should stop. If they didn't, they were not dedicated enough and were more than likely to return home with nothing in hand, not a certificate, not a diploma, nothing. A social life was important. After all one could not control one's libido, and shouldn't if he or she wanted to become a serious perfumer. Sex they should indulge in, most definitely, not only for inspiration but for physical well-being. Emotional connection was a different thing. It got in the way.

The professor paid no attention to their discomfort. He bore it as a simple nuisance in the face of his own brilliance. He often smiled at Chiara, who was always the first to raise her hand, but perhaps it was also because she was the prettiest girl in the class, with pale skin and light red hair that curled around her face. When the sun came in through the window and washed her in light she looked like a Renaissance painting.

Jean Claude seemed to care little for Elif and listened impatiently as she introduced herself and gave her reasons for coming. He curled his lip and took her in from the top of her small head down her boney frame to her boyish shoes. She was far too androgynous and perhaps too different ethnically. He liked to provoke the Germans because he had a wicked streak and because he was French, and the French would always spar with the Germans, and vice-versa, Elena had told him once. The maestro probably thought of himself as suitably mischievous, but in fact he was just cruel. Towards Elio, Jean Claude displayed cautious curiosity. He made no comment when Elio introduced himself and explained his passion for perfumery. He nodded, looked away, then scanned the room with those cold blue eyes again. And the further the eyes moved from him, the more Elio felt the chill.

"I still wonder what drives all of you. You have all you would ever need. Do you not? Your families have businesses or careers that at least allow you the luxury of coming here to study."

Elio's face burned. He looked over at Paola, who was about to cry.

"No need to humiliate the students to make a point, Jean Claude."

The voice came from the back of the room and as she moved forward, with the same sultry grace as her voice, the scent of lily of the valley brought him back to the perfumer's organ seven years ago. He swung around to see an older, but still attractive Palma strut down the aisle clipboard in hand, eyes lit, head swiveling from side to side so she could take in every visual detail of her students.

"It's a logical and fair question." The professor slid his hands into his pockets and narrowed his eyes. "I'm sure you agree that the practice of any art requires vast amounts of sacrifice if you plan to be good at it. It requires a devotion that can and often does border on obsession. Some of the finest master perfumers were terribly eccentric. They were madmen literally. Art leads to a certain madness in brilliant men."

He ignored the expression that crossed Palma's face.

"That eccentricity came from their devotion. There is no in-between. If you boys in the back, Jan and Tomas, if you honestly believe you can become perfumers and still run your father's shop, you are wrong. At some point you will have to make a choice, and if you are as privileged as we all know you are, you will make the easier choice. And that choice will not involve your becoming even a perfumer's apprentice. *That* would involve delayed gratification."

"But since they are males, the gratification would be less delayed than it would be for the young women in the room." Palma sat up on the desk. "Even so, I'm delighted to see there are so many of you breaking ground. Chiara, Paola, Elif, welcome. In fact, welcome to all of you. And I don't necessarily agree with our esteemed professor. Times change and some of our younger students find ways to accomplish with less sacrifice than their older predecessors."

Jean Claude glared at her, but for only a second since he was distracted, as Elio was, by her smooth, tanned legs as she crossed them.

"Well! My associate and I have a difference of opinion. Only time will show who is right. Now! Let's get started! Palma, I will defer to you when the time comes."

"I'm sure you will." Her smile made her prettier, or perhaps Elio had been too star-struck as a boy to notice the fine lines around her mouth and along her brow. The luminous green eyes, the tight chignon, the small features all seemed coarser than he remembered, and while she was gracious, there was an edge to Palma who listened to the professor ramble on with a lesson she could probably have delivered with far more finesse.

"A perfumer smells. That's what he does all day long. He needs to know all the important smells, where to find them and how to distinguish them clearly from others. So! Let's do just that!" Jean Claude passed out several tins and jars and had them smell and comment on each one. One tin held a lump that looked like a decaying potato and smelled nauseating.

Ariane from Corsica jerked her head back and recapped the tin. "*Oof!* I don't know what this is but it's awful."

"Ambergris, one of the most disagreeable of scents, but also the most important. It's a substance coughed up by whales and used in perfumery as a fixative. Not all scents are gorgeous or seductive. In fact, many are not, but they add structure and depth to the fragrance."

He opened a glass vial on his desk, pressed several blotters together to dip inside the liquid, pulled them out. Fanning out the strips, he walked around the room and handed a blotter to each student, the wet, fragranced tip pointing up.

"The perfumer's skill is one of passion and concentration. To smell, first close your eyes, bring the strip to your nose and inhale. Leave everything around you and live inside the scent you are holding."

Elio did as he was told and he was once more beside the woman with the red leather tote bag, and he could see the way the sun cast a sheen on her chestnut ponytail and the way it swung as she walked.

"I need everyone's attention. I understand this scent might inspire reverie but we are here to work." The words hit Elio as hard as the strap Sister Maria used on the back of his hand in math class whenever he would day dream. And for a minute he felt as if Jean Claude was staring only at him.

"I want you to concentrate on this scent, think about all the different fragrance elements, fleeting wisps of scent that come into being, disappear and then reappear again. Reflect on how they interact in this composition, like guests at a party, people that make themselves known and then become wallflowers, guests who sparkle and give verve to the event, others that slink behind everyone else with suggestions and complexities that slip in and out of view ever so slowly as you move about the room. That's it. As you smell, imagine yourself moving about in the Gallery of Mirrors at Versailles on an evening when all the women are in strapless dresses of taffeta and the men wear snow-white shirts. Know that some are pleasant, others are not, but they all portray a dimension of human character, part of the character we work to show and to hide, depending on where we are in life."

Elio sniffed. He looked around.

"Don't tell us what you smell. Tell us something we don't know. Tell us how the scent makes you feel," interjected Palma, "or what it makes you desire."

"Something sweet, a cake with lots of icing, or *crème brulée*."

"Not bad, Chiara. But you can do better."

"I want to be with my girlfriend."

"Close, Jan. You might give us more description." She winked at him flirtatiously and smirked at Jean Claude.

Elio looked down at her silvery sandals and wondered how she could wear something so coquettish with the serious lab coat she'd left unbuttoned.

"I see myself in a silk dress with very deep décolleté," said Paola, who'd probably never worn such a dress in her life. "And perhaps I would be dancing at the Mardi Gras ball in Vienna."

This was taking too long. "It's Shalimar," said Elio a bit too heavily.

A look passed between Palma and Jean Claude.

"Our young Italian is correct." Why did he make the word *Italian* feel like an insult. "And what is it that gives Shalimar this warmth, this glow that makes it so recognizable. Anyone?" The maestro didn't wait for any responses. He picked up the infamous tin. "The brilliant mix of notes that include among them this awful ambergris. It's repugnant to smell alone but when it is aged and dissolved with just a tincture of alcohol and used in the base, it gives this fragrance its sexy velvety feel."

"The vanilla is also prominent," added Elio, surprised by the tinge of arrogance in his own voice.

"Right again. Many perfumers say that vanilla turns this perfume into an outrageously low-cut dress. So you were right too, Paola."

Jean Claude gave her a suggestive smile, which he didn't mean, and flexed his shoulders. Maybe a bit of ego for a master perfumer was to be expected. But as Elio reflected, lily of the valley infused the space beside him. It seemed to lock him in, denying him an escape. He felt emboldened by it. Palma moved around the room, placing a single tin on each desk. She nodded when he looked up at her and paused to study his face before moving on. Her scent followed and Elio's eyes did too. He liked the way she moved, fluid but focused, and when she smiled a single dimple deepened along her right cheek.

He opened the tin half filled with a white waxy solid, brought it to his nose, stroked it with his fingers. There was no mistaking what it was.

"It seems Mr. Barati already knows the name of our wonderful substance."

"French jasmine." Elio's voice betrayed his embarrassment. Was his face so easy to read? And in this case was it a good thing that he knew the ingredient? It had to have been obvious to the others.

"It's different from our jasmine back home," Elio said, showing off that he knew the difference. Then he frowned, unsure if it seemed he deferred to the master, implying the inferiority of Italian jasmine.

Jean Claude's smile confirmed the latter interpretation. "Yes! French jasmine is still the finest in the world. Its odor is so particular it can't be duplicated by any known synthetic."

Palma held up a photograph. "You see the flowers are so light you need over four thousand of them to make just one pound of pure jasmine absolute. Once the first blossoms open up in early August we know we have only a hundred days to harvest all the flowers we'll need. Just like the rose, the jasmine has to be picked before dawn. See the workers in the photograph bent over to pick the blossoms so carefully. It's hard work."

She put the photograph down on the desk and stared at it. She finally looked up, first at Elio and then at the others.

"In sumner, our nights are fragrant with the smell of jasmine because the night wind sweeps down from the hills and carries the scent across the fields into the center of Grasse and as far west as the city of Cannes." Jean Claude stiffened at the dreaminess in her voice. "Indeed, you smell it as far down as Corsica."

"It's perfect then that jasmine, with rose, would be at the heart of Shalimar," he said. "Together they are the exotic center of the fragrance. It's not unlike a meal. You start with champagne, which is the sparkle, the lift, the invitation." He twisted his hand in the air, eyes joyful. And then he looked at

Elio. "Of course in your land you would drink Prosecco, inferior but not bad." He winked as if to say this is a joke.

"Your bergamot, your white flowers are your champagne. They are light. They waft away. But now your fragrance, like your meal, needs something more palpable. Indeed it is that note that makes your heart pound. It is that lush, dark red wine that is like velvet on the tongue. This is the center. This is the heart and your mid-note needs to reflect that. That's why Jacques Guerlain used jasmine, with rose. Together they are the exotic center of the fragrance."

"And how does the meal end?" Palma prompted him, a bit suddenly.

He cleared his throat. "How else but with a glass of cognac, warming in your hands." He mimicked holding a glass inside his palms.

"And that leads us to what is for me, and for many perfumers, the most exciting part of the fragrance. Beyond the heart is the soul, where the true message resides, only it doesn't surface early, does it?" said Palma.

At a look from Jean Claude, she started to pace the room, much like he did, and stared directly in the face of each student. Elio felt his own heart pound.

She must have heard it because she backed away and spoke to the entire room again. "No. The base note, the soul, only emerges after it has been on the skin for thirty minutes. It's like a conversation, a relationship, sex. There is flirtation at first, a lightheartedness, something that bubbles, like champagne, and then there is the revelation, what one learns about the other intellectually, emotionally, intimately, there is touching and there is seduction, connection. Then the heart is full, like Jean Claude said, lush and provocative, like a glass of Bordeaux, and it is only after that fulfillment that we have the sensual core, we revel in that person, our senses take hold and explode like so many fireworks, but only for a minute before we touch upon something far more profound, and perhaps more dangerous."

"Ah, so cognac is more profound than Bordeaux," taunted Jan.

Everyone laughed, more out of relief and perhaps nervousness. It broke the tension between Palma and Jean Claude because they laughed too, but Elio was still thinking of the cognac and its warmth and the smell of sandalwood.

"The sultriest, most sensual notes are always in the base note of a fragrance, in its soul, because that's where our own more feral and truly human selves reside. It's who we are when all our defenses are stripped away. That's why perfumes parallel life. Because we only get to the soul of the fragrance after we first open up our minds to the lure of the top note, then expose our hearts to the mid-note, which is the fragrance's heart, and to the complexity of human connection."

He felt her hand touch his shoulder. Thud.

Elio ducked down to grab his textbook from the floor. His face felt hot, and when he looked up everyone was staring at him.

"Yes, let's move on," said Jean Claude. "This is an important session because today we will begin to learn perfumery according to the teaching principles of the great Jean Carles. First, you will learn and memorize contrasting odors. The next day you will learn others. And so on. Then after some weeks you will progress to differentiating related odors. And then to identifying simple combinations of scents, from the simple to the more complicated."

Elio had no idea who Jean Carles was, he told little Nathalie, but at the time he was glad the attention was diverted back to the lesson and not to the awkward boy who had dropped his ten-pound textbook onto the floor.

Jean Claude simply ignored it and went on to talk about greatness in perfumery, to tell story after story about great perfumers, most of them French and male, although not exclusively. He talked about Edmond Roudnitska, Bernard Chant, Guy Robert, Josephine Catapano, and paid homage to the visionaries who guided them: Coco Chanel, Hélène Rochas, Robert Ricci.

"The designer Robert Ricci saw fragrance in this proverb that guided him for most of his life: *Let reason speak, but listen to the heart.*"

"And he could well afford to do so," added Palma, "because it was his mother Nina's reason and vision and heart that created the fashion house of Ricci."

16

HE CAN'T RESIST. He jabs a needle multiple times into the cream-colored paper bag embellished with the blue and gold emblem of the Officina Profumo Farmaceutica di Santa Maria Novella.

"Elio! Can't you wait even a minute!" Sofia shakes her head and Anna, the saleswoman, laughs, her tiny glass earrings dancing under the light.

"No! I can't. It's too beautiful."

"I thought this was *my* birthday gift?" With eyebrows raised, she holds a basket filled with scents and balms.

"And I want you to enjoy it immediately." He holds up a finger to make a point, and his point is not just for Sofia. It's for the crowd of young Japanese women who now turn their heads. He switches to his heavily accented English for their benefit. "All these flowers, herbs, berries, woods, are collected by hand and soaked in essence to macerate for thirty days in terracotta jars sealed with wax. We still use this ancient method established by the Dominican monks in the thirteenth century, in the time of Dante and Giotto. Imagine!"

"Thank you for helping me with my job, " says Anna to the crowd gathering around them because Elio's voice is so loud. But he's all the happier because she has flattered him.

"*Foglie, bacche, petali di fiori dei colli fiorentini,*" says Anna, because the women also understand and speak Italian. This takes Elio by surprise. His is not a language spoken frequently outside his small country.

"What are you laughing at?" asks Sofia.

He shrugs impishly and peeks inside the basket on Sofia's arm. There is the iris toothpaste and pomegranate soap, some colognes, some milk soaps, the Crema Arnica she rubs along her knees and ankles after a long bike ride or a run along the river. The running is not good for her joints, even though she is so much younger than he is and at forty-five still has that glowing skin that drew him to her on that train nearly twenty-five years ago. She'd sat across from him, her astronomy book open on her lap, as she underlined with the straight edge of her ruler and a very sharp pencil. Her long braids kept brushing against the page, and one time when she flung one back, her calm celadon eyes met his and she paused. She held out her hand to shake his the way a girl from a Swiss finishing school would do, only she told him she was studying at the University of Bologna where her father was a leading professor of astrophysics, and there was something about her confidence when she offered her hand that told him something was to happen between them, and as he reflects on it now, she had that quality he sees more and more in Romina. It has matured into something different that eludes him, even now as Sofia speaks in Japanese to the youngest woman in the group, the girl with the long lustrous hair like Romina's. It moves like a sheet of black lacquer molding to the movements of her back but always in a long, even motif—barely a renegade strand, with that assuredness that, yes, her mother has passed on to her. And with which he can never firmly argue.

Sofia studied Japanese and Mandarin at the University and seems to have a head for the technical aspects of language learning. Her remarkable memory, grown sharper with age, makes her capable of remembering all those characters and drawing them on a page with such meticulous precision it makes him wonder why she ever married someone as untethered as himself.

So now he looks up at the angels in the frescoed ceilings, at the ornate wooden cabinets, softly lit inside to shine through the glowing fragrance liquids. The sweet scent of flowers and prickly herbs and essential oils wafts around the grand room from which massive wooden doors open all around. So many other lovely rooms veer off from the central hall, in this, the world's oldest pharmacy, founded by friars who distilled flowers and herbs into essences, fragrant waters, elixirs, as sensory as they were curative. Each potion, from the oddly named Vinegar of the Seven Thieves, a whiff of which revived anyone about to faint, the antihysteria water, which did calm and soothe, to the orange blossom water Sofia sprinkled on their bed sheets in early spring, derived its alchemical properties from a complicated but revered ancestry, and from a time when herbs and flowers were cultivated primarily in the cloistered gardens of monasteries.

To Elio the Farmaceutica's name would always be synonymous with things that heal, and with the nature-infused scents of his homeland, scents even Sofia wears when she is not wearing the more rarified fragrances of the grand perfume houses of France. Regardless of who we are, we are still tied to our soil, and to what we grow.

Elio looks round the grand room, thinks of the da Vinci man whose arms spread out. The hallways that radiate, much like the rays of the star outside his shop, and like the streets around the Duomo, are his appendages. We all have a center, from which our desires fan out, always in the shape of a star.

17

"SO THAT IS YOUR THEORY, ELIO?"

Paolo brings sparkling pink Prosecco to his two guests. The visit to the Officina Farmaceutica is always followed by brunch at the JK Place across the street. Paolo manages the boutique hotel where he now exhibits the photographs of Massimo Listri. Massimo, with a calibrated architectural style, has photographed all the grand libraries of Europe. To stare at them as one passes the geometric black woodwork of the hotel's library, before settling into the dimly lit fireplace lounge with its neoclassical bookcases, gorgeous art books, and whimsical artifacts, is to almost walk their very halls. Such is his gift of perspective, a talent so refined as to impress Brunelleschi. While the photograph stills the setting, there is movement too, and that movement is on the part of the observer since there are no people in any of Massimo's shots. But that's another theory Elio will not bore his host with now. Instead he leaves Paolo to happily show photos of his beloved four-year-old on that infernal iPad everyone seems so enchanted with.

"*Un tesoro.*" Sofia clasps her hands over the photograph of Silvia in a yellow piqué sundress outside Marina's linen shop. Of course Sofia's nails are beautifully manicured with their new enamel by Chanel. It's selling out and it suits her, because she is *molto particolare* as the Italians say of anyone or anything unique. And the color is particularly enhancing as she's dressed in white and taupe, and the taupe-silver shade on her toes sets off her silver sandals and her incipient spring tan. He often wonders how she puts herself together with an almost artisanal hand, and in so little time. He really should answer Paolo, who waits politely for his response

"Yes, it is one of my theories, Paolo. Everything in our city radiates out, like the rays of a star. The Duomo is at the center. All our roads, our experiences branch out from it. Yes, it was part of de Cambio's master plan, to build the city around its most celebrated structures. But it makes sense to start from the center and branch out, as long as the heart beats strong enough to keep a pulse throbbing along all of those streets."

"I think the heart is not beating strong enough in some respects," says Paolo thoughtfully. "The shops at the end of those streets are not artisan shops any longer."

"Aha! I say that all the time to everyone. They sell garbage. Garbage."

Sofia looks from her husband to Paolo, who nods, more in deference than agreement.

"I like the metaphor with the Duomo at the center, but of course I see it differently."

Elio throws his hands up in the air. "Of course she does."

"I think we are more like a circle. Our walls kept expanding as you know, almost with every city architect hired by the Medici or otherwise. So, yes we did expand, we did open our arms so to speak, to the new and the undiscovered, but we have always been inside ourselves. The walls are not porous." She holds her arms out curved in a circle. "We are still our own universe."

"I hope so!" Elio holds up his glass, just the right provocation for his charming host to refill it. He picks up a distinct scent of amber in the air and takes a deep breath. Gorgeous. He feels so happy here.

"And here's a toast, to walls that become more porous because of places like JK Place, and because of your *profumeria,* Elio, which is never afraid to introduce what many find shocking. The advertisement of that nude girl is your window is stunning. *Salute!*"

"Sofia's idea. She insisted it would bring in some younger customers and it did."

Paolo spoons some peanuts into his palm.

"I like to think that's what I'm doing here with Massimo's work, and the work of other less famous artists and photographers, and with this hotel that is not like a hotel, not in the traditional sense. This is more like a grand house; its architecture, its bones are old, but we fill the inside with the new, the more modern Florence. After all we are outside Diladdarno with all the contemporary galleries. No one thinks..." He stops to correct himself. "No one outside Florence thinks of Florence as a center of contemporary art, but look what we have around us..."

He spreads his arms out as if addressing a room of admirers. Some of the guests meander, holding large art books in their hands or maps of the city with major attractions drawn in 3D.

"We nod to the classics in our city." Paolo's arms are out again, only this time he holds his glass in his hand. Elio's eyes dart to the velvet cushions. "But we are starting to embrace the contemporary as well. Like Bonan when he designed this place. Like Massimo. Still, we have a long way to go."

Sofia steeples her fingers, her diamond and sapphire wedding ring flashing. "That's not entirely true. The Frederico Gori exhibit at the Strozzina last year was superb. Our photography museum across the street has had record visitors. The exhibits at Marino Marini are more out there than ever before. And Poggiali e Forconi is marvelous. Marvelous! There is a fresh wind blowing. Our young mayor—soon to be prime minister, for example."

"When he's not causing traffic jams like he does with all those street closings. *Per la Madonna*. It is a catastrophe!"

Elio agrees with Paolo but also admits silently that he does like strolling along Via dè Tornabuoni without the cars, though dodging bicycles and motorini requires some agility, which he still has.

"Romina, Claudio!" Paolo is up, shakes their hands, his manner as crisp as his shirt

Heads swivel, hands shake. Simon, the butler, brings another tray of Prosecco. Romina gives her mother a black and white knotted scarf and a braided silver bracelet from Luisaviaroma in a glossy white bag with black print. Sofia casts the scarf over her head, slips her hand in the loop and twists until it's a braid, and all of a sudden she's ten years younger, still the chic married woman she is proud to be, but something else too, a savvy modern woman who could, very easily, be or become single, take a young lover, and walk the streets of New York without missing her husband or home one bit.

Paolo pours more Prosecco, Claudio talks to Simon in his native language, Spanish. Elio didn't know the vagabond was trilingual and this bothers him too. He wonders if his polyglot wife notices. Obviously Romina's impressed because she too uses a few Spanish words, and charmed Simon is all too happy to talk about Peru, his home country. Glasses clink again over voices that light on spontaneous subjects and weave together the narratives in ways that make absolute sense even though each one is coming from a different place. Claudio waxes on about the hospitality business and how tourism to New York has altered his menus and the hours he keeps his restaurants open. For the Brazil crowd he needs to stay open very late, which wrecks havoc with his staff, but he can't turn away the business, and the Brazilians tip generously and look so gorgeous inside his digs, he has to accommodate. Paolo admits he's enjoying all the multi-cultural families that come to JK for global reunions. That's why he labels every dish on the breakfast menu with translations in a number of languages. "Last week I had a family from Malaysia with grandchildren in Australia, Scotland and America. I heard every English and American accent known to man," he laughed.

Sofia asks Paolo about the clear glass vases that hold a single floral bulb. She wants a few for the shop since votives can be a fire hazard now that she and Elio are getting older and inclined to forget things. Romina says she no longer uses scented candles as she and Claudio stay up very late and can become forgetful too. So she opts for the fragrance diffusers, like the amber-scented ones Paolo has placed around the reception area, their thin wooden stems poking up from clear glass bottles.

Elio feels his collar grow hot. He wonders how late Romina and Claudio do stay up. To cover his embarassment, he fills his own glass.

Romina grabs at her own silky hair from time to time, lets it fall. Claudio gives her a look when she tries to answer her phone so she puts it away. Her toenails are painted an emerald green and she wears filmy harem like trousers with a denim jacket, an odd mixture, but she can carry it. She has her mother's elegance, but her own quirky style, and every time she lifts her glass, he sees both a hip young woman and the ten-year-old girl who would dip a wand into a plastic bottle and blow bubbles through it with such glee it makes him laugh to this day.

"Papa," she nudges his knee and digs into her handbag. "I have something. Since you never come to visit me, I'll lend it to you!"

All eyes are on him.

"*Grazie, stellina! Grazie!* But where did you find it?" He holds the CD in his hand. *A Kind of Blue* by Miles Davis, one of their mutual favorites, and a piece that will always remind him of the night before he left for Grasse as a young man.

"Wonderful choice, Romina," says Paolo.

She taps her father's knee again to get his attention. "We have to listen to it together, Papa, but at my place. Now you can't refuse me." She tilts her glass at him and casts a conspiratorial glance at Claudio. It washes over him again: she is someone different from the girl he knew?

"Ah, the scent of amber and the voices of good friends. Salve!"

Elio welcomes Michele's voice and the clasp of both his hands. His violet shirt is rolled up at the cuffs, which even Romina must notice because it makes his violet-blue eyes pop. Does Elio notice a flicker of attraction between the two of them? Romina always does seem to flush a bit when he kisses her on both cheeks, and the hug is longer than it is with others. It's a hug that says something beyond the obvious. Perhaps it's a reiteration of a childhood pact, that they are always there for one another, that they are part of the same family, but not so much that a liaison, however short, would be prohibitive. It is, he thinks, an understanding between them that Elio and Sofia are getting on in years, and that when old age makes its demands with increasing obstinacy, the two of them will boost each other up and have a laugh over a Campari spritz, and they will swap music and share each other's iPods, and speak with affection about the childish prickliness that returns to us all with the onset of years. Perhaps with age also comes a certain childlike wonder and sense of abandon. Would that that were true. That is one sensation Elio would welcome but he doesn't feel it yet. Michele jokes with Romina now, touches the many bangles that jingle on her thin arms.

Sofia hugs him as she would a son. "I feel the same as you about this amber scent, Michele. It is rapidly becoming my favorite."

"It is because it reminds you of this place. Wakes up pleasant memories." He sits down and rubs his thumb and forefinger together to simulate amber's textural qualities.

"Hmm. I wonder who taught you that, Michele," Romina winks.

Michele raises his glass to toast Elio. The others follow suit.

"Wait a minute! I thought I did!" Romina places her hand on her hip.

"Touché." Michele touches her glass with the tip of his.

Another sign. There has to be some heat between them, and behind that wistful expression that suddenly crosses Michele's face. He's far too good-looking, far too in love with her, and would it not be nice for them to hook up and run both the profumeria and the café? She could still be a star student at the Accademia…

Elio's daydreaming misses the shift of mood that washes over the room as Michele puts his glass down. He clasps his hands and looks down at his feet, then around at the group. The conversation stops.

"Elio, you know. But is everyone here aware that Marina is very sick?"

Sofia shifts so fast her handbag falls off her lap and lands on the floor. She stares at him. He can't move, so Paolo picks it up and places it on the coffee table.

"It's cancer, pretty far along." Michele nods when Sofia touches her breast.

"One or both?" she asks.

He swallows hard. "Started in one and now..."

"But it's not so far along!" Elio realizes he is shouting, perhaps in his own defense because he's told no one, not even his wife. It doesn't matter which it is. He's been found out. Sofia, to her credit, will not reproach him in public, but her disapproval is sensed by everyone. Are they intentionally avoiding his eyes?

"I had no idea," she whispers, conscious of other people in the lounge.

"I saw her on her bicycle in Santa Croce yesterday. She seemed herself," says Romina, shaking her head. Claudio clasps her hand. Elio wishes he'd thought to do that first.

"What is the prognosis?" asks Claudio.

"She may go to Verona for treatments and maybe not."

Why did she tell Michele and not him? "Why not?"

"She says that if she has a short time she doesn't want to spend it in doctor's offices and hospitals. She has better things to do."

18

He'd arrived too early because it was still light. He realized his looming error at the patisserie as the woman placed his pastries in a white carton and tied it with a ribbon People ate later in southern France. Quite logical since it was so warm here and no one seemed to be in a particular hurry, like in Castellina, where dinner began with a walk through the garden to pick herbs and lettuces, and a stop in the cantina for wine and oil. Gregorio and Elena would start cooking whenever they were ready and sometimes they finished dinner after midnight. He couldn't remember there ever being a clock in the kitchen, only in the bedroom with an alarm they often ignored.

He didn't want to appear too eager, he was still her student after all, and ten years her junior. He had found it odd that Jean Claude would assign her to tutor him personally, especially since he seemed to bristle at the attraction he observed. The maestro had once stated, in his elevated French, that he denoted a frisson of tension in the room and raised his eyebrow at Palma, who gave it back to him in her inimitable way: re-directing the class to a lecture topic on the composition of base notes.

He squared his shoulders, lifted up the door knocker and let it go.

"Perfume is not an accessory. It is something one should live," she'd said in class, echoing Jean Claude's lesson, but with an expression that suggested something more.

Through the door he smelled garlic roasting slowly in olive oil, and whiffs of oleander and hibiscus in a garden not too far away. He should probably run and come back later, but it was too late. He looked down at two thick terracotta pots filled with sage and rosemary on either side of a thick straw mat. Maybe she wasn't even home. Maybe she was having an *apero* with Jean Claude after class.

He hadn't heard her footsteps, so when the doors suddenly swung open, a bright interior light pushed him backward. She looked surprised as well, standing barefoot in a long skirt, a damp dishcloth tossed over her shoulder. Even though her hair was still pulled back in the same unyielding chignon, she looked attractively unkempt, even lovelier than earlier that day.

"Elio! I hadn't expected you so early!" She wiped perspiration from her forehead with the back of her hand.

"I thought I'd come early to help you." He quickly thought of an excuse.

"There's very little to do, but come in, please. You can help me make the salad, and I have some fresh fish we can roast very quickly. Do you like fish?"

"Yes." He lied.

He followed her down a long white hallway lined with photographs toward a kitchen that opened up, through large glass doors, onto a stone terrace overlooking her garden. From where he stood he could see the white oleander pressed against the outside wall of the house, but he stopped short in the middle of the hall to look at photos of what looked like Palma as a young girl. He thought it odd that she was alone in most of them, except for one where she seemed very young, no older than thirteen. The man standing beside her with his arm on her shoulder stared blankly at the camera. His face was heavily lined and he had jowls. He could have been her father or her grandfather. She smiled broadly, but not genuinely, her hand holding just the tips of the man's fingers. They stood in front of a small fishing boat, the sea and a sunset behind them.

"Oh, Elio, I'm so sorry! Just put those in the refrigerator so they don't spoil!"

He'd been standing with the cream-filled pastries in his hand. The woman at the patisserie had just filled the cream puffs and the chocolate covered éclairs and she'd told him to please keep them cool. And here he was gaping at a photograph of his teacher in front of his teacher.

Once inside her kitchen he was briefly overwhelmed by the sharp smell of blue cheese. It reminded him at first of dirty socks, but then it mellowed into that tart milky promise cut up in squares beside a long loaf of French bread, the stench offset by the fresher smells of green tomatoes, wrinkled black olives soaked in oil, salad greens and the new fall fruits heaped in baskets on the long wooden table. He smelled the salty, dry codfish on a grill layered over a bed of woodchips and pine cones.

"Here! You can help with the salad." She handed him two tomatoes and a bunch of basil. On the table in front of him was a thick wooden cutting board, a tremendous bowl, a knife, some washed frisee lettuces and small bulbs of shallot. The smells were not unlike those of the Barati kitchen in Florence, so he quickly got to work. He tore up the frisee with his hands, sliced up the shallots, chopped the basil with some parsley and mint. He dropped everything into the bowl, drizzled olive oil and red wine vinegar over the leaves, added salt, and then looked around.

"You can use your hands," she said, as she flipped the codfish on the grill. "We do the same here. Although I do like to mix a little mustard in my vinaigrette."

"Too late for that," he said.

While she minded the grill, he walked to the sink, washed his oily hands and then looked around for a towel. In front of him, small ceramic pots held familiar herbs: basil, parsley, oregano, mint, sage. Three large sunflowers rose out of a tin vase. The sunflowers made him start. Near the vase, in a silver picture frame, was a recent picture of Palma at a gala in a black evening gown. He squinted to look more closely at the man with her.

There was no disputing it. The tall, imposing man in the tuxedo was Jean Claude.

The grill sizzled as Palma turned the fish over and sprinkled it with coarse pepper and dried oregano. The herbs smelled spicier than those back home. What was it about the expression on her face? As puzzling as in the earlier photograph. Jean Claude's hand rested at her waist while he looked squarely into the camera, a commanding presence. One of her arms was behind him. The other crossed in front of her and rested on Jean Claude's hand.

Her elbow dug gently into his ribs. "Here." She handed him a flute of champagne.

"Thank you." He took it, turned his head and drank it down.

She seemed amused. "You must take your time or it will go right to your head. Would you like another glass?"

"No...er no, thank you."

"All right." She slid her arm inside his. "Let's sit down to dinner then."

They took their dishes and the bowl of salad to the table on the veranda outside. Below, a small oval pond was surrounded by flat rocks and clusters of flowers. After putting down his plate, he returned to the kitchen to pull a round bread loaf from the oven. Slicing it, he covered it with linen to keep it warm and brought it to the table.

"You are an excellent assistant. I didn't even have to ask you to do that."

He felt himself blushing so he quickly picked up his napkin, unfolded it and placed it on his lap. "It's just something I'm used to doing. "

"Welcome to Grasse," she said, lifting a glass, already filled with a clear pink rose. She clinked her glass against his. She then lifted up a heavy platter of cheeses, prosciutto wrapped around breadsticks, thin slices of salami and a pile of vinegary green olives. "Antipasto?"

He was so hungry he heaped more food on his plate than he could possibly eat. When he saw the spare portions she arranged in small, colorful mounds around her plate, like paints on an artist's palette, he felt like a barbarian.

But Palma was suddenly too distracted to notice. She looked up at the sky and around the garden as if noticing something for the first time.

"Elio. Do you see what's happening?"

He looked up at the deepening violet sky and down at the garden, now wrapped in a smoky, blue hue.

"Close your eyes and smell the flowers! Do that right now!"

He closed his eyes. Although he'd detected all the smells in the garden as soon as they entered, he'd not felt their presence fully until now. Now he experienced every scent diffusing slowly into the freshness of the night air: the green notes sparkling over the pond, the luminous vapors of jasmine from a tree in the very back of the garden, the muguet blooming softly on the earth below the terrace.

"I have never smelled jasmine like this," he said, looking around for the deceptively delicate white flowers.

Where was it coming from, that single jasmine tree so far off? No, this felt too close, and too vibrant, as if it were virtually touching his hand. He shivered, got up quickly and walked to the jasmine tree. He picked one of the flowers off its stem, crushed it inside his fingers and brought it to his nose.

"It's the most unforgettable scent," said Palma, having followed.

He lowered his nose into the nest of flowers and branches and thought for a second that he was becoming drunk.

"I'm also wearing the oil," she said, finally turning her head.

A playful smile spread across her face.

"I've been working on this scent for a few months now. It's almost there." She held her arm up.

He took her wrist in his hand, lowered his head to her skin and, in an instant, he felt as if he wanted to stop breathing. It was the most beautiful perfume he'd ever smelled.

"What do you think?"

He took her wrist and smelled again. The scent was even more amazing the second time.

"Jean Claude and I worked on the muguet note for three or four months. It was hard to get the right balance. If you use too much...the smell is a bit too sharp. Too little and it's weak."

"You don't use real muguet?" he asked, bending his head one more time, just because he wanted to, and because he didn't want her to see his face.

"Muguet is always synthetic. Some floral oils cannot be extracted. The enfleurage process is only for the most delicate and precious flowers like jasmine, rose and jonquil. It doesn't even work with lily of the valley." She laughed, grabbed his hand and squeezed it. "You see? You come for dinner and you get a fragrance lesson."

He didn't laugh. Her playfulness discomforted him.

"How long have you been working on it?"

"This composition? For a year now. Actually, it's Jean Claude's perfume. He was given the brief by a *parfum* company up in Paris and he's been struggling with it for—"

"For a long time?" His voice rose high and sharp.

She paused. "Well, yes, for about a year or so before he brought me on board."

"Is this the first project you've worked on together?" He was burning up inside.

"No." She looked at him quizzically. "For about three years now." She slid her wrist under his nose again. Only this time he smelled interference from the fish she'd handled. She understood so she went to the pond, dipping her hands in. "Come here."

She stood very close to him while he held her wrist to his nose again.

He smelled the jasmine, even warmer and more pronounced, a mix of fresh-cut florals, something dry and woody with a creamy sub-note, probably sandalwood. The musk was sharp and aggressive but amber oil rounded its edges. He was still a fledgling student but he knew a brilliant composition when he smelled it. This was what Jean Claude was capable of. No wonder Palma adored him.

"There's some amber in it."

"Excellent. It's still in its initial stages. I'm working on a new type of amber synthetic, something subtle and suggestive. Nothing overt. But subtlety is hard to accomplish."

"So Jean Claude likes subtle fragrances?"

"Jean Claude like complex fragrances. He likes to push the limits of the art. He thinks life is dark and dangerous and complicated and a fragrance should be the same."

"Funny, I don't see him that way. He seems pretty conventional to me."

"He is in some ways," she said thoughtfully. "But that is being far too personal for a student."

The buzz from the champagne made him press for more.

"Jean Claude's been my mentor since I was fifteen. You'll hear it whispered about that we were lovers once. It's true. I'm not ashamed of it, but it's over now." She looked amused at the look of shock on his face. He wished he could have controlled it better. He wished she had been less forthright, less desirous of showing him what a provincial young man he was. She was as calculating and aggressive as the scent of jasmine snaking through the air around them.

But there was one more thing he needed to ask.

"So you're no longer lovers, then?"

"I told you a moment ago. It's over now. So let's finish eating before the fish gets cold." She led him back to the table where they picked up their knives and forks and began to eat without speaking. The silence felt so awkward he had to break it.

"This is very good," he said.

"I'm glad you like it, and you should eat it all because fish is very good for you. But, enough talk about perfumes and work. Tell me about your family. How are your parents?"

Uncertain what to say, he drank from his wine glass before answering, glad that she was distracted as she paused to refill it. So he started to talk and lost total control; she'd been so candid, why not him? He told her everything, about Elena's Greek lover and the times she'd left so she could be with him. He told her how much he'd hurt as a young boy, and how he'd hated her for so many years. His father was a defeated man because of it and would never marry again. But Elena had made him promise to send her son to perfumery school and Gregorio had honored this.

When he finished Palma steepled her fingers in front of her nose.

"I really liked your mother, Elio. And I'm not surprised she left your father."

He picked up his fruit knife and turned it around in his hand.

A soft wind grazed the leaves of the jasmine tree. A dog barked in the distance.

"He's barking to protect our mushrooms from your Italian brethren who sneak over the border to steal them."

"We grow the best *porcini* in all of Europe."

"Hmmp. Or so you believe. Elio, you're her son and it's hard for you to forgive her. My father's never forgiven me for leaving Marseille. Some people are able to suppress the burning desire to do something so impractical, so against the wishes of one's family, friends, the world, but I couldn't."

He opened his mouth to object. She stopped him.

"You're thinking it's different for a mother to leave a son. But you're mistaken in thinking she went back to Greece because of this man. He was only a symbol or the catalyst, if you will. Your mother and father were never a match, even if they were deeply in love. I knew that when I met them. Your mother had a dark renegade quality, which is why I liked her instantly. If I could select a fragrance for her it would be Tabu, for all the obvious reasons. Your father, a good man from what I saw, could never have given her the life she wanted. If she bore it at all, she did it for you, for as long as she could. And it's because of her that you're here. She saw that you were as alive as she, that you had an artist's talent, and she wanted you to indulge that passion with everything you had in you. Could you see yourself running a perfumery in Florence? That kind of life is too confining to you, the way being a doctor's wife in Marseille would have been for me, the way a life married to your father was for her. She did what she had to do to save you *and* herself from that."

"Perhaps." He played with the knife in his hand.

"Thing is, Elio, you have to do this for you, not for her."

She tossed a pebble into the pond beside them. Rings of water spread out around it, deepening at first and then melting away until the waters were as still as glass.

"You see how much friction a stone thrown into its pool of passion can generate? It isn't always there for you. Opportunities come. They are moments that open up like the rings you see here, and then they melt away." He caught the remorse in her voice and saw in a few seconds how she seemed to grow older, the regret carving lines into a face that earlier had seemed as fresh as a girl's.

But he was undeterred. The opulent jasmine began to overwhelm him. It was telling him to put down his fruit knife and to act, soon. He had never so wanted an evening to continue forever.

She grabbed his hand.

"Have you ever heard the story of Jacques Guerlain and why he created *L'Heure Bleue?*" she asked.

"Yes."

She moved her chair closer to him.

"It's wonderful story, and one you should keep in mind as you create your own fragrance, and as you go about life." She stroked the back of his hand and looked out into the garden. "It was a real phenomenon of nature that captivated him. How at dusk flowers release their final bust of scent before the world is hushed. Everything smells lusher, more provocative, more sexual, as if something powerful and illuminating were about to happen. He explained it in a favorite quote of mine."

Elio lifted a strand of hair from her cheek and slid it behind her ear. Her hand was still on his.

"He said, *It's that special moment when the sky has lost its sun and has yet to find its stars.*"

And then she kissed him.

19

SOFIA DOES KNOW HOW TO EXPLOIT a birthday, he thinks as he follows her, shopping bags in hand. She has an eye—for the exquisite and the expensive, even the inexpensive, and when he adds it all up, it puts a dent in the family budget. Not one he minds totally because she always looks *impeccable* as the French would say, with an emphasis on the *a*. The buttery soft handbag from the San Lorenzo market was cheap enough and complements her tan shoes. She has so many handbags, so why did she need this one? But if she hadn't bought the handbag she would bought something else of equal beauty: an *objet d'art*, ceramic platters from Deruta, silver wine goblets from Brandimarte, maybe even another pair of tortoise-shell reading glasses in a woven case from Laura's Scuola del Cuoio. Or she would spend it on him, like a choice bottle of Brunello di Montalcino from the San Filippo winery, just because she feels the need from time to time to indulge Elio with a gift. It's always either the wine or a belt handmade at Monaco Metropolitano in Oltrarno. And he raves about each gift, but still, he would prefer to save money.

But not this very moment. The red satin shoes she's trying on are stunning beyond belief.

"*Bellissimme,*" he says to Maria, who makes handmade shoes *su misura*. He respects that one so young would not only embrace and learn a traditional craft, but make it relevant and so downright sexy.

"You see, Elio, I make sure that every curve of the foot sits inside its proper place. The shoe has to hug, but not confine."

She sits on a stool beside Sofia who stands in front of the full-length mirror. Maria's brown eyes are fixed on the shoe as her finger traces the curve of the arch. "You have to feel secure inside a shoe, as if you're wrapped in a blanket that gives you comfort without stifling you. And there has to be balance, so she can walk elegantly and safely, even when the heel is high."

"And if she twists her ankle?"

"Sofia wouldn't, but even so, she is agile enough to regain her balance quite quickly."

"I've never twisted an ankle." She studies the reflection of her legs, which now seem even longer, in the mirror. She does this whenever she tries on shoes, but she usually looks up at him from time to time to engage him in some way. She doesn't do that this time.

He should have told her about Marina.

"This leather feels like a glove, Maria."

She sits down, slides the shoe off her foot and places it, with its companion, on a glass countertop. She picks a brown leather pump. What is she doing? The agreement has been all these years that she buys one pair of shoes from Maria on her birthday. *Basta!*

But now she has five gorgeous choices lined up on the grey carpet in front of her, a set-up that will guarantee the sale of not one but two pairs, possibly three. He tallies the cost in his head. A few thousand euros. *Per la Madonna!*

Maria picks up each shoe, run her fingertips over its surface as if caressing the skin of a lover. She invites Sofia to touch it too as she talks about its shape, the elegance of the last, the suppleness of the leather, how its lines complement the latest collections. Sofia can wear the crocodile pump with her suits, the gladiator sandal with her shorter dresses, the jeweled pump for their wedding anniversary, when they will go, yet again, to Capri.

He stares, transfixed, because he's seen both Romina and Sofia employ this strategy in their own shop. They would never show a perfume without its companion body lotion and bath powder. And then they place yet a second scent in front of the purchaser, one that is perhaps in the same fragrance family, but lighter or deeper in intensity; one perfume for day, one for evening, another to recall a special moment, or to transport the wearer back to a favorite place.

He eyes the ruby satin pump Sofia is now smoothing her hand over. How many men bought perfumes to facilitate seduction? Would a pair of shoes be more enticing? Women did seem to have an arresting fascination with them. Beyond comprehension. They could be in full conversation along Via delle Belle Donne, aptly named, and stop dead in their tracks at the sight of a Gucci black leather boot, molded to cover the knee, with a single buckle and a killer heel. It happens in all countries of the world, he's been told, and for the moment he can't say he minds it. Sofia's eyes glitter for the first time today. She slips her foot in the shoe and he admires how slender her foot is, how it is so well taken care of, like everything else she is and owns and wears. This same woman, rendered powerless when a gorgeous shoe is put in her hand, would never sell a woman a lipstick without a lip pencil, blush, mascara, etc., etc. And she would never let a man who asks for a fragrance walk out with anything less expensive that the parfum.

"When you buy a new dress, you always need to add at least one special and new accessory, be it a pair of shoes, a bag, a piece of jewelry. That is what style is about," she will argue. "A lipstick is the same. And when you have bought color for the lips, then you need to consider the eyes." So that unsuspecting customer will now watch as Sofia opens a palette of eyeshadows, matches a kohl pencil, and voila! The Profumeria Barati shopping bag is filled with products, samples and tissue paper, and the woman is all the happier.

But it's the men he feels most sorry for. When they come in for a fragrance to give as a gift, Sofia will always show them the *parfum.*

"A fragrance gift should always be precious. The *parfum* is the most concentrated and most precious rendition of a scent? And when a man can't afford to give diamonds or rubies, or gold, he has to choose something of a high perceived value. *Parfum*, if you think about it, is one of life's most affordable luxuries."

"Look, Elio." He jerks his head back from the silvery indigo sandal Maria has placed under his nose.

"He was daydreaming, Maria." Sofia holds up the sandal, lifts up the rhinestone-studded strap that wraps gladiator style around the ankles. "A work of art, Maria. Takes your breath away."

"I'll give you a discount if you take a second pair."

"Done. And if I do a third?"

"Have you lost your mind, Sofia?"

"No. Put this and the first pair on our account, Maria."

Why won't she look at him? And isn't it just wonderful that Maria is so quick to walk away and pack up the two chosen pairs, thereby leaving his wife to ponder further the tempting row of shoes in front of her?

If Elio's day is to get any worse, it begins now with chimes from the outside door. Sofia greets the portly customer with a lot more deference than usual.

"Enrico! What a surprise!"

Enrico pauses just beyond the door, looking from Sophia to Elio. "I'm actually surprised to see your husband here. Maria isn't one to give discounts."

"So now you're a cross-dresser, Enrico?"

"You never lose your spry sense of humor, Barati. In another life, perhaps. In this one I am merely the messenger." Enrico pulls his wallet from his back pocket, searches for his credit card. Maria gestures for her assistant to come out carrying six bags of shoes. He hands over his card, grabs up three shopping bags in each hand.

"Francesca will be very happy. I stretched the front of black pump a bit," says Maria. She swipes the card and hands it back to him to sign.

Elio and Sofia glance at each other. Elio would never have imagined Francesca with this man. Neither would Sofia apparently. She has to despise Enrico as much as he does, but one would never guess it from the way she smiles as he kisses her hand.

"It is always a pleasure to see you, Sofia. You grow younger with every birthday."

"In some respects yes, in others no."

"I think that on a special birthday such as this one your husband would take you on a trip. To the Maldives perhaps."

"I would love it but Elio thinks it's too long a flight."

"Not if you fly first class."

Elio wants to rebut but it would open up the discussion about selling the shop. Instead he gets up and walks outside. Sofia will know where to find him.

20

HE WAS RELUCTANT TO GO HOME for the Christmas holidays. He and Palma were working intently on his first fragrance submission, to be presented to Jean Claude after the winter recess. But he hadn't seen his father for fifteen months. Gregorio's letters had been vague and noncommittal, a lot about the shop and life in Florence, about Marina's pregnancy and Luca's arthritis, and the new red Fiat Cinquecento he'd just bought because it was easy to park in the increasingly more crowded city center. He never referred to his health, although in the one photograph he sent last summer, he appeared to have lost a lot of weight.

True, the time passed far too quickly and France was beginning to feel more like home. But that morning as the train pulled out of the station, his connection to Grasse seemed to unravel with it, like a thread that you pull until it becomes so thin it breaks. It snapped just as the train rumbled past Nice towards glittering Monte Carlo, and he smiled when they crossed the border into Italy, where the rocks of Liguria and the umbrella pines welcomed him home.

Gregorio hugged him hard, lingering in the embrace in a way that made Elio suspicious. But he had no time to ponder because, for the next few minutes, he was hugged, kissed and pulled at by Angela, Luca, their four boys and any other neighbor who passed by. He had barely survived the honking of horns, the shouting from windows as Gregorio drove him home from the station. It seemed as if all of Florence knew of his return.

As they entered the house and closed the door to the rest of the city behind them, Gregorio wrapped his arm warmly around his son's shoulders. His arm felt limp and bony. Elio remembered it firmer.

He sat down in the chair his father proudly pulled out for him and looked around, feeling like a young boy again about to have lunch with his parents, only this time there was only one parent. The house was as spare and immaculate as ever. Polished wood, marble floors. A new glass chandelier hung over the huge oak table. A terracotta vase held spiky white chrysanthemums. There was a basket of fruit, a plate of almond biscotti, a silver tray with a bottle of *Rosso Antico* and miniature glasses. Tiny pots of violets, his mother's flower, sat on the windowsill, the same as when Elena was there. The familiar aria from *Turandot* played from the phonograph. The shelves on the wall were lined with jars of tomatoes, artichoke hearts, green olives and porcini, all grown, harvested and preserved by Gregorio's own hand. A straw *fiascho* sat on the table, filled with red wine from Gregorio's cantina. And, best of all, the comforting smell of hearty minestrone—carrots, celery, cannellini beans, zucchini—simmering on the stove. But it was the basket of sliced Tuscan bread with its thick, floured crust and deliciously unsalted center, set beside a bottle of the family's own olive oil first pressed from the groves in Castellina, that made Elio spread his arms out and clasp his hands. It felt so very good to be home.

And his father's happiness could not have been more palpable.

"I'm happy to set the table for two tonight." He folded two linen napkins, and placed them beside the thick yellow ceramic plates and wine tumblers they had used in the family for years. No frail long-stemmed wine glasses or delicate porcelain here.

Elio finished three bowls of minestrone, three glasses of wine and half the loaf of bread. Afterwards, his father's specialty was placed on the table, veal with potatoes, roasted in olive oil and rosemary from the family *orto*. Gregoria tossed the arugula and fennel salad, heaped some of it on his son's plate beside the veal and sat down across from him.

"There! What do you think of my cooking?" Beaming, he used his napkin to wipe the perspiration from his brow. He'd worked very hard on this meal. This had always been characteristic of their home life, the joy the three of them took in preparing, sharing and enjoying the good and honest food they grew themselves.

Elio realized he was thinking too hard and eating too fast.

"So delicious I can't even talk," he finally said, wiping his mouth with a napkin.

Gregorio's cooking, always very good, had clearly improved. He used more spices, the balance of oil and vinegar on the salad was just right. The veal was tender and slightly rose in its center, so moist the knife slid through with no effort.

Elio had barely finished when his father swept their plates away and put them down inside the sink. He came back to the table with two small bowls of jiggling *panna cotta*, garnished with sprigs of mint. He had left Grasse and entered heaven.

Afterwards he told his father to rest and offered to prepare the moka pot for coffee, something he'd always done as a boy. He made coffee stronger and more flavorful than anyone else and it had always been during the post-lunch espresso that he and Gregorio talked at length about the most life's most provocative topics. When Elena was there, they would launch into heated discussions about local politics, and after an hour or so they'd fall lazily asleep.

"I thought you might prefer French coffee now."

"Not a chance. Our espresso and Luca's is the best. He has the Marzocco, though, so I defer to his expertise. How is he?"

"His joints hurt but he never complains. He says he can better predict when it rains now so he always remembers an umbrella. We'll go and see him as soon as we finish here. Let's go by the shop first. I know Marina wants to stop by. She is looking like a mother already," Gregorio put his arm out. "She's quite large, so we all think she'll have a boy and name him Massimo."

"Do you still see her often?"

"Every day! Nothing stops her. You know they're expanding the shop?"

"Yes, again! She wrote to me."

"Ahhh!" Gregorio flicked his fingers. "You have to see it. Since Marina took over, it's all changed. She knows how to make money, that Marina. She never lets a customer leave without spending twice what she wanted to. And she's found some new suppliers! She has exquisite taste! In the window you'll see blankets from Scotland, linens from Ireland. Now she's looking at importing some silks from the Far East. She never stops. It's incredible."

Elio pictured the small and intimate shop under the apartment she'd lived in with her parents. He didn't know if he was ready for all this change, but he was ready to see her.

"Alessandro next to her sold his trattoria and retired."

"So soon? Alessandro's still young, like you."

"Eh! Not so young, Elio. Running a shop is hard work, especially a bar where you work late into the night. And now business is harder than ever before. He made money when he sold it. So he's retired and in Arezzo. His children are at the university and his wife is glad to have him home more often. But they fight more than before, she says." Gregorio laughed, the lines around his eyes deepened.

"Do you still go to Castellina?"

"Yes!" Gregorio's face brightened. "Wait until you see the house. I repainted all the rooms and put out window boxes. You see how I polished the wood here?" He pointed to the gleaming table and the window frames. "Well, I polished all the wood trim and the mahogany staircase and even the marble there. You need sunglasses to look inside. It's so bright."

"And the garden?" Asking this made Elio realize how much he missed it.

"Your mother was the master gardener. Me, I'm just an amateur but I try and I like it! I can't make curtains but I

146

bought some nice Belgian lace ones from Marina. Oh! You have to see the linens she gave me. Each bed in all three bedrooms looks like it's ready for royalty!"

"And the shop? Isn't it getting to be too much for you?"

"Eh! We'll talk about that another time. Hurry up so we can go there and I can show you what I've done."

Inside the profumeria, Carrara marble floors beamed up white and translucent, their edges disappearing into even whiter walls. The air smelled of new perfumes and soaps, pine boughs and cedar, everything fresh and ready for the Christmas season. And in the window, strips of beveled glass held the famous antique atomizers, colored jewels refracting light.

"My God, Papa. This is amazing."

Later his father would tell him his eyes had opened up the way they did when he was a small boy standing before a *gelateria*.

Vases of chrysanthemums enveloped the room in a green, wintry sweetness. A perfumery had to have flowers, real ones with green pliable stems and spiky petals that littered the countertops when they grew tired.

He was still looking at the shelves filled with holiday baskets and gilded boxes when Marina's full, marvelous face appeared in the window. She was wearing a sweeping red cape and a woven scarf knotted tightly around her neck in tones of yellow, gold and teal. She was inside before he could open the door for her.

"You are chic as always, Marina," he said.

"And you! You are all grown up." She took his hands. "Listen. I just stopped by for a minute because I *had* to see you. I must hurry to see Doctor Li. She's going to be delivering my baby." She patted her stomach. "She's the best doctor in the city so I can't miss my appointment but I'll stop back on my way home," she promised, sliding her hands into a pair of tan kidskin gloves that smelled like Florentine leather, the way he remembered it.

"I'd like that."

"Gregorio. You're not going to take him visiting today, are you?" She frowned as a customer opened the door, letting in a whiff of the cool, dusty air. "He just came home. They'll eat him alive, he's so gorgeous." The customer graciously moved to the far shelves, eyes signaling willingness to wait.

Marina pressed her palms against each side of his face. "I'm sure he has stories for us." She winked. "He writes so seldom so he probably has a girlfriend."

"Stop, Marina." He looked down at his feet.

She frowned, studied him.

"Hmm. You're too preoccupied to be in love."

"As if you would know."

"Maybe I don't. But I suspect, because you're still far too serious." She pinched his chin, a bit too hard. "You are becoming more and more like your father."

He bristled. He was an internationalist now, with friends from countries his father had never even dreamed of visiting; he was earning a university education, becoming a perfumer, and Palma loved him.

"Not really," he said coldly and was suddenly sorry. He didn't even need to look over at his father to know he'd hurt his feelings.

Marina squared her shoulders.

"Well! I need to hurry. Will see you before you go back." She re-arranged her handbag on her arm.

"Join us for an aperitivo. Meet us tonight at Gilli." Elio could see the hurt lingering inside Gregorio's eyes as he hugged her. He felt awful.

"Another time. Not today." She kissed Gregorio on both cheeks. "Tonight is for you and your son, alone. You're both invited tomorrow for *pranzo*. Don't forget. *Arrivederci*."

Later that evening in his room, he found boxes filled with presents from his father. He slid silk ties from long flat cardboard envelopes; opened boxes holding linen shirts, gabardine trousers and a lizard belt with a silver-plated buckle tucked inside a felt drawstring bag. A new cashmere blanket was folded down at the foot of his bed. The linens smelled of lavender. Why had Gregorio done this? What did it mean? What kind of a son was he anyway? He'd left his father alone here, to care for the shop, the family business and everything else that he didn't want to be bothered with. He'd been allowed to pursue his career dream single-mindedly, without anything being demanded in turn. Was this right? And for whom?

21

ON CHRISTMAS EVE THE NEXT DAY the perfumery was closed. Elio and his father spent the morning visiting churches to look at nativity scenes. In Santa Maria del Fiore the crèche was made of travertine, the figures of the wise men and the Christ child of unpolished stone. In some of the smaller churches the robed statues looked as if their garments were made of satin. Large bouquets covered the marble steps leading to the altar and the straw-covered manger inside. Lighting a few candles, he knelt and prayed for Elena, wishing her well wherever she was. He would never see her again and had no desire to. Too many years had passed.

Then he looked up again at the crèche and studied the fine detail in each carving, how the robes of the wise men seemed to be made of something far more fluid than clay or stone, how the faces seemed to change expression as he walked around them, how their skins varied from pale cream smudged with rose, to burnt caramel, to the subtle peach gold of Tuscan skin, to deep brown. The colors played in his mind, with the smells of church incense, rough-hewn wood, and melting candles.

As they moved out of the churches into the Piazza del Duomo, his father said, yet again, but it felt fresh this time around: "Do you see? They say this city is somber, that we lack the colors of Rome and the textures of Genova. But see, those tiles look black and white from here, but up close they are really deep with color, red, green and white. How truly special this city is!"

Elio thought he saw tears collecting in his eyes.

That afternoon they filled baskets with all the traditional Christmas sweets. Gregorio had made them all himself, he boasted, with no help from Angela. He'd made the batter for the thin *pizzelle*, warmed the toasting iron, spooned the batter on when the iron was steaming hot, and pressed it closed, making perfect star shaped *pizzelle* with each pressing. All the while watching his new television set from America. Luca had purchased it through a relative in Boston. It took eight hours to make nine hundred *pizzelle*, which he filled with a paste of figs, walnuts, almonds, honey and orange peel.

"Can we throw in some fragrance samples?" Elio asked.

"They're expensive."

"So?"

"All right, all right. You're a university student now. You're smarter." Gregorio winked.

Elio couldn't help wishing for a less practical world. "Okay. We won't overdo it. But when I create my fragrance, I'm going to strew the streets of Florence with samples and get as many people as possible to try it. Is that a deal, Papa?"

He expected Gregorio to laugh, and he started to, but the gray, deep set eyes grew moist again.

"Then I'll be even prouder of you than you are of yourself," said his father quietly as he pressed his son's shoulder and looked away.

The afternoon rounds were less tedious than Elio anticipated. Everyone in town wanted to see him, and they couldn't logistically honor every invitation to lunch or dinner, so it was easier this way. A stop for an hour at each house, where they never stayed too long since everyone fasted in anticipation the fish dinner that night. This did not completely deter the mothers who, dismayed that they couldn't feed Gregorio's son a full dinner, insisted he drink a cordial and eat some *cantuccini* before leaving.

As soon as they got home, tired and a bit inebriated, they went upstairs to Luca's. Without being asked, Elio sat down at the kitchen table in front of the empty clamshells and a bowl of filling. Using a small spoon, he stuffed the washed shells with a paste of breadcrumbs, chopped clams, garlic and parsley, dribbling more olive oil over the tops before placing them on the baking sheet. Gregorio went down into the cellar to help Luca decant the wine into flasks. The four small boys set the table, while Angela drenched the salty fish smelts in flour before tossing them into a cauldron of crackling oil. Slinky black eels thrashed in the sink, oblivious to their fate. A basket of mottled persimmons, their skins bursting, nested beside a platter of bow-tied dough ribbons, coated with honey and rainbow-colored *confettini*, a bowl of *torrone,* chocolate nougat and roasted hazelnuts, and another platter of *pizzelle* with almond paste oozing from between the vanilla-scented wafers.

"This is my favorite meal of the year," he told Angela, brushing away a swiggle of filling from the side of a clamshell.

"Mine too. When your mother was here, we could cook a *branzino* in sea salt and eat it for lunch, just the two of us. She knew how to cook fish." Cooking fish was a science, his parents and Luca and others would say over and over again. The Florentines knew how to cook their boar and *bistecca fiorentina* but fish—that was the specialty of the coastal towns. Along the Maremma, one could eat fresh fish, and in Liguria, one did even better with the *branzino*, whose eyes seemed to talk to you. You can always tell a fresh fish by the eyes, his mother claimed.

Angela lit the slim white tapers on the table while Luca put Christmas music on the phonograph. The church bells in the piazza started to chime, on the hour, as they sat down to the first course, the clams Elio had filled, along with a glass of Prosecco.

"Let's toast our brilliant young man," said Luca, holding up his glass, the red veins in his nose more prominent than before. "We're honored to have him with us this Christmas."

The smells from his plate were all too tempting, but Elio drank the dry and bubbly wine. What was Palma doing tonight? She had no family to go home to. But that didn't seem to matter to her. "I'm accustomed to being alone for the holidays," she'd told him. "Just me and my cat."

The second Prosecco made him almost giddy, but he put his glass out for yet another.

"Not too much," his father warned. "We have a nice Chianti Classico from the cantina."

"*Oof!* Let him drink what he wants, Gregorio. I have lots of wine there. What do we save it for? When he finishes perfumery school, though, I want him to bring us some French champagne to celebrate!"

But Elio did not miss the masterful French wines tonight. The Prosecco was simpler, more transparent. Less complicated and more Italian.

"We will one day celebrate his graduation from perfumery school." Gregorio held up his wine glass, hesitated for a minute, avoiding his son's eyes. He cleared his throat before continuing. "And the successful selling of Profumeria Barati."

He was the only one who drank to this toast. Angela put down her wine glass. Luca held his suspended in mid-air.

"What? Papa?"

"I said what I said." Gregorio folded his arms and sat back in his chair. "I'm sorry. This is not the time to talk about this, but—"

"Of course it's not," said Luca. "This is the Christmas vigil."

"You're right, Luca. I'm wrong. But now I must finish what I foolishly started. Elio has not been here for over a year. He doesn't know what's happening in Florence so we can't blame him. But he's old enough now. He's eighteen. And he should know what I'm thinking."

Yes I should know, Elio thought. But I wish I could have enjoyed my first Christmas at home without this. Damn his father. He was a stupid as ever.

"This is no longer the city where I can grow the business, or even sustain it." Gregorio leaned over the table, resting his folded arms.

"Why not?"

Gregorio sighed impatiently. "We spoke about this yesterday. And I know Luca's been telling you how much more difficult it is to do business these days. The small, family run perfumeries are being squeezed."

"Yes, Papa, but—"

"Let me finish, Elio," Gregorio held his hand up but he didn't look at his son. "You seem to think and some others seem to think." He raised an eyebrow at Luca, warning him not to interrupt. "Some think this is a temporary condition. I don't. Times are changing and we need to change with them. The chains will grow bigger and more powerful. They will be able, because of their size, volume and financial resources, to offer specials and discounts galore. We small businesses can't compete. I can't join the race with the fervor and strength it requires." Shrugging, he threw up his hands.

"It's that bad?"

His father laughed a discouraged laugh.

"My son, you are an artist. You have this idea that the perfumery can run by itself on good faith alone. But I am a business man and I know when it's time to get out."

The room grew quiet. Angela whispered something to her oldest son who stood up, gestured for his brothers to join him, and they left the room quietly.

Gregorio tipped his head toward her. The Christmas music on the gramophone was beginning to annoy Elio and the wine was making his head throb. Maybe he'd been wrong about the merits of Prosecco. French champagne never gave him a headache.

"But why sell it now?" It was the safest question he could ask.

"Not now, but some day."

"Some day means many years from now."

"Maybe. You can't imagine, nor should you be able to imagine how hard it is."

"But it's successful," he argued.

"For the moment. This success is making me very tired, Elio. I'm too old."

Elio wanted to reassure his father that he wasn't getting old but he couldn't in good faith. It was obvious that Gregorio was not in good health.

"Why don't you hire some people to help you?"

"Angela *bella*, to supervise them is even more trouble." Gregorio pressed his palms together as if he were praying. "You know how young people are today. They're too spoiled to know what it is to work hard and to build relationships with clients and vendors. Those relationships are what keep Profumeria Barati strong. Without them, the competitors win."

"And you don't think they win by your closing the shop?"

"Look, Elio, I'm not going to do this tomorrow. We're just talking here, that's all."

Luca tapped his forearm. "Your father gets these ideas every now and then. I don't take it seriously when he says them."

"He's talked to you about this?"

"Yes, yes, sometimes, when we play cards. When he has a few glasses of *grappa.*" The two men laugh.

"But he never brought it up to me. This is the first I hear of this."

"Why would I? You're a university student now. I don't want you to worry about this business. And besides, we're just talking. I've always been the pragmatist in this family. Think about it, unemotionally, for a minute. Who will run the shop when I'm gone? Not you. You are capable of greater things. You will become a perfumer."

"But you're not going to die tomorrow."

"I know. But, one day, and that day is approaching, I will want to retire. And then I will have to sell the shop. Sooner or later it will happen. I've already been approached by some chains who would be willing to pay a healthy sum for my business."

"What do you mean? Whom have you been talking to?"

"That's of no concern of yours. All you have to worry about now are your studies. We agreed to that when you left."

Angela stood up, took away his plate and put another in its place. A plate of *branzino*, filled with herbs, baked in rock salt. When the salt was removed Angela drizzled her own olive oil over it and sprinkled parsley from her garden.

"I cleaned all this fish myself, Elio. It's all right if you don't eat the pasta. But if you refuse this, I'll be offended."

His father patted his arm. "It's Christmas Eve. Let's just enjoy the meal. I'm not selling the shop tomorrow. It's too soon to talk about this."

Elio picked up his fork. Then why are we?

22

HE FOUND OUT WHY A FEW DAYS LATER. His father suggested they drive to Volterra early New Year's Eve morning so they could celebrate with friends up north.

"We can eat dinner at that small place where they make the best *bistecca fiorentina*. Remember? You were just a boy. It's the restaurant with the terrazza near the Pinacoteca, where your mother took you to see that fresco by Giotto."

Elio barely remembered it, although he did recall wandering into a cloister and walking through a studded door where he and Elena discovered a roomful of paintings. One was of a Madonna, her hand raised in a blessing. The halo around her head was of resplendent gold.

"Just think, Topolino," she'd said. "In most countries you have to go into a big, serious museum to see art like this. Here, you can just walk into a small *pinacoteca* or a cloister and see a work of art that takes your breath away. This is a real Giotto."

The recollection became even more vivid as his father drove around the interminable, twisting streets toward a turreted city with sienna walls partially hidden in a misty morning fog. The road grew steeper and windier as they continued their steady climb toward the city in the clouds.

They finally pulled into a small square outside the Palazzo Inghirami, which housed a museum of alabaster sculptures and reproductions of Renaissance tapestries. Beside it, the windows of a ceramic shop displayed the yellow and blue pottery of Cortona, the terra and blue patterns of Deruta, and a few large terracotta bowls. He liked the combination of yellow, terra and blue. They made him think of the Tuscan sun and the sky and the ruddy terra roofs that stretched like a quilt outside his bedroom window.

But before he could go into the dark, arched corridors that led to a row of artisan's shops, the smell of espresso drew them to a terrace café. They could look out beyond the wall encircling the medieval city, past the valleys, to the Versilian coast. On a clear day one could see Corsica. But this wasn't a clear day. Elio kept staring and drifting away into his own thoughts as Gregorio pulled up two chairs, ordered coffees and brioches.

He stirred his *caffè latte* and looked out over the trellised fields at the towers of San Gimignano, the hills separating them from the sea and the few houses sprinkled like white islands over the wheat and sage-colored fields. There had only been a slight dusting of snow, just enough to soften the hues of terracotta, and glitter on the branches of silvery olive trees. He'd missed the November harvest two years in a row.

"What are you thinking about?"

"Nothing. My project for school, I guess."

"Good. For an artisan, work is your life. It's your lifeblood, your passion."

Yes, it is. Even now the smells surround me and I'm happy, I'm transported. The espresso smell in the cold air takes me back to winters when you and Elena would walk me past Santa Maria Novella to the café where I would ask for gelato even in winter. And the smell of dried earth under snow—well, that resurrects all the times we came here to buy alabaster from Simone because Mamma loved the hard, veined, white surface, so perfect and imperfect at the same time, she would say. Volterra sounds like earth rising up, flying—*volare* and *terra*. Even if that's not where the name comes from.

What if he could create his fragrance here, after he graduated? There were a few fragrance houses in Tuscany, not as illustrious as those in France. They didn't create or manufacture alcoholic fragrances, perfumes worn by celebrities and chic women. Their trade was in scented soaps with an olive oil base, in fragranced lotions of apricot, sage and lavender.

He watched Gregorio puff on his cigarette, content, the smoke swirling around his head, eyes narrowing as the sun broke through the fog.

"I'm sorry you have to be here alone, Papa."

"Why? I have Luca, Angela. I don't have my son, but..." Gregorio opened his palms and spread his hands. "But you're a man now. You can't stay here with me. For what? You will be a perfumer. And after that you'll marry and have a life of your own."

"I know, but I still miss home sometimes."

"We all miss you too, but you're no longer a child."

"I can move back home after my studies are over."

"Don't you have to work as an apprentice?"

"True." There was no way around the apprenticeship requirement, and it was the part of his training he most looked forward too. "Maybe I could apprentice to a perfumer in Florence?"

"Elio, please! I raised an intelligent boy, not a foolish one. You have a year and a half of study left. But then you'll be an apprentice. After that, you may go to Paris, or Rome, or to America. You may come back to Florence, but maybe not. You have to go where your vocation takes you. Where the world's best perfumers are working. You don't know where you'll have to go to accomplish what you want, and you can't let me be the reason you don't do it."

Gregorio was pressing the fingertips of both his hands together. The ironed cuffs of his shirt slid forward from under the sleeves of his sweater. A gold link bracelet, the one Elena had given them for their first anniversary, slid over his wrist. His cigarette burned in the ashtray.

"I didn't tell you before, but I have a girlfriend," Elio said suddenly.

"Hmm. Good!"

"You don't seem surprised."

"I'm not. I would be worried if you hadn't fallen in love at least once by now. I hope you do again. Many times."

"Why many times?"

"I think, perhaps, it's better to love many times so when it's right you know it."

Elio frowned.

"What I'm saying is that sometimes you fall in love when you're young and it's a mistake. A mistake you pay for the rest of your life."

"So, you're saying I can't know if this is the love of my life."

"Exactly."

His father's words, though, fell flat, especially since Gregorio hadn't dated a single woman since Elena left him. Part of the reason was simply practical. The Catholic Church did not recognize divorce and would not allow him to remarry as long as Elena was alive. The other reasons were less apparent. He'd never asked.

"Papa, what about you? Why haven't you seen anyone all these years?"

"One woman was enough for me. I didn't have good luck then, I don't imagine I will again. What can I say? I lost all interest in women after Elena. I don't know why," he shrugged. "I'm not like other men, maybe. Not like Luca. His first wife died and he found another only six months later, a young and pretty one. And he's always looking at women—like her." He pointed to the waitress. "See how pretty she is, but she's pretty for you, not for me." He put his hand on his chest and shook his head to imply that Luca was crazy. "I am not going to fall in love with anyone and certainly not a girl young enough to be my daughter. But one thing, Elio—maybe more than one thing." He took his son's hand into a dry and scratchy palm, leaned in close, eyes inches away.

"First, do not become distracted. Your work comes first. Remember."

If his father only knew how hard Palma drove him to achieve.

"But, more important. When the time comes, and I don't think this is the time. This is your first girlfriend, not your last. Wait for that. But when you do fall in love, make sure she truly loves you with all her heart. You have to matter to her more than anything else. Or—" He hesitated.

"I'll be careful, Papa."

"Good!" Gregorio rubbed his shoulder. "Now! We need to talk about something else. Something less cheerful, but equally important."

"What? Not about the shop again."

"It *is* about the shop, Elio. But it's mostly about me."

Elio's eyes settled reluctantly on his father's face.

"It's about me because I'm not well."

Elio released his breath as if after a punch.

"This is life and we have to confront it. What else can we do?" Gregorio paused to puff his cigarette. He put it down on the ashtray again with unsteady fingers. With his other hand he gripped his son's forearm and looked away.

"I have emphysema. It's a disease of the lungs."

Elio rallied. "Have you seen Dr. Li? Another doctor?"

"*Oof!*" Gregorio waved his hand in the air, trying to bring in some humor, but his eyes betrayed him.

"I've been to Dr. Li, who sent me to a lung specialist at a clinic in Rome. I was in the hospital a full week for tests."

"You went to Rome? When? Why didn't you tell me?"

Gregorio turned abruptly. "Shh. We don't want to disturb everyone in the restaurant. I didn't tell you because I didn't want to disrupt your studies. What for? What could you have done?"

"But, Papa..." He was panicking. "What did the doctors say?"

"The emphysema is very serious. My lungs are thick with scar tissue so it's becoming more and more difficult for me to breathe. So..."

"So, what? Tell me."

"So, Elio, I have to make plans. I have to sell the shop while I'm still somewhat healthy and lucid enough to do what I need to do. I have to find a buyer. It may take me a year, but I will sell it." He paused. "Elio. Please don't make this hard for me."

Gregorio regained composure.

"Look. No one knows for sure what will happen to me. I've had this illness for many years. The doctor says that perhaps if I retire and rest, that I could buy myself some time. The air in Castellina is better than in Florence. I have the garden. I will have enough money from the shop to pay for a woman to come in and take care of the house, cook for me when I no longer can. Luca is planning to retire soon too. He and Angela and their children will be able to help me. I don't know how much time I have left, Elio. It could be a year, maybe more if I'm fortunate. No one really knows."

"No! Papa! You can't be serious!"

His father reached over and clutched both of Elio's hands. "It's fate. What can we do?"

Elio pulled away and grabbed a folded handkerchief from his trouser pocket. "Who else knows?"

"Only Luca and Angela."

"You told them before you told me?"

"I didn't want to disrupt your studies. It was the right thing to do. So don't bother being angry with me, Elio."

"I'm not, Papa. Really, I'm not." He meant it. "When did you find out?"

"I saw the doctors just about a year ago."

"And I didn't come home for Christmas." He hated himself and Palma. It was all her fault. No. It was his.

"Again, what could you have done? Given up your studies to stay with me and take me to doctors, which I'm capable of going to myself. And for what? Your sacrifice would not have given me my health back. We both would have suffered. No, one of us is enough." Gregorio laughed as if he were less afraid of his own death than his son's sadness.

"Is there any possibility the doctors could be wrong?"

"I don't think so."

He glanced at the cigarette in hand—the villainous cigarette stealing his father—and stubbed it out in horror. "What can I do now to help you, Papa?"

"It's too late now, it no longer matters. What does matter is how I'm so proud of you, Elio. I'm proud of your talent and your stubbornness. Yes, your stubbornness. Or, maybe I mean determination. You went after your dream with such ardor. Your mother was right. One should always live that way, with passion. And—" He tilted his head to make a concession to the beautiful, passionate woman both of them missed so much. "Maybe with a little bit of danger. Life is far too short to live any other way."

He shrugged his shoulders, raised his squinting eyes to the sun, and then looked around, again, at the fertile landscape beyond the café walls. Elio longed for the simpler, less conflicted life of his father.

"Do you know, Elio, that some people will live entire lifetimes without ever seeing this inspiring province of ours, without taking time to smell its lavender, look up at its cypresses, see the *chiaroscuro* light as it changes. Some will never feel that beauty inside them as I do. Some will never have a son as capable and as devoted as you. I have been truly fortunate, I really have."

He squeezed his son's hands tighter than before while the Tuscan girl took their plates away. Her lilac and rose perfume trailed behind her. Elio squeezed back, his eyes misting over again.

23

HE WOULD HAVE BEEN AT MARINA'S before Sofia if he hadn't stopped at the shop for his bicycle. And he still might have averted a catastrophe had it not been for the *delinquente* scrawling graffiti all over the side of the Neptune fountain in Piazza della Signoria.

"*Maledetto! Delinquente!*" Elio yelled at the teenager. This time heads turn. *About time.* "Do you know who created that fountain! Ammanati, one of our greatest Mannerist sculptors!"

The boy turned, pedaled faster, and dared to snub him by holding his phone nonchalantly to one ear. Elio pedaled after. They raced past the leather and jewelry stalls of San Lorenzo. The boy cut people off and flew into the Piazza della Repubblica. Elio kept yelling, whipping around a corner.

Maledetto!

A Yorkshire terrier rushes out from Francesca's blasphemous wine shop that sells New World wines. Elio presses hard on the hand brakes, only he's grabbed the one for the front wheel first. A jolt, he falls forward, lands hard on his side on the cobbled pavement. The pain's excruciating. The petulant Yorkie licks his face. People gather around, chattering, but he hasn't the will to open his eyes or tell them he is fine. How very stupid. An old man chasing a young boy who did nothing more than scribble across a fountain. Tomorrow the city workers will simply wash it clean.

Elio feels his head on the ground one minute. The next it's cradled in a woman's hand. Her perfume is delightfully fresh and warm at the same time, notes of anise and vanilla, of root beer. It makes him smile in spite of everything. How he can find good humor in the situation, he doesn't know, but he does. She calls out to her Yorkie: "Pirandello, Pirandellito." She has to be just like the fragrance she's wearing. Coarse, curly hair brushes his shoulder, and he hears her Argentinian-accented Italian. Of course he doesn't have to see her colorful Peruvian skirt, or hear the hundred silver bangles that clang against her arm. He can only guess that the *carabinieri* hate her because she's a foreigner, has no regard for Florence's conventions, is not what they'd call a lady. *Dear Francesca, would that I cared so little too. But I don't have your charm.*

"Come on. Don't just stand there! Help me." She brushes unruly hair from her face and stands until the police bring Elio to his feet, then she ushers him into her wine shop. She pours him a glass of Malbec and passes a plate of crostini anointed with a piquant olive paste. He takes a bite, looks around at the monochromatic décor that looks nothing like anywhere else.

"You should not be riding like a madman, Elio." Bracelets rattle as she uncorks yet another bottle.

"That *delinquente* deserved it." He arches his back. "Ayy."

"He's just a boy."

She stands behind him, rubs his shoulders, runs her long fingers along the sides of his neck. "You are very, very tight. Giancarlo, some music, please."

Her son, the brother of Claudio, who's been stacking wine glasses into a dark metal cabinet, presses the white circle on his iPod and strains of salsa fill the room.

More whiffs of anise, delicious, fill his senses, as well as a bright and balanced lime sweetness that makes the floral bouquet less floral, less conventionally feminine. He knows it.

"You're wearing Quand Vient la Pluie by Guerlain."

"Your memory is always amazing. I love how it's contrary to its name—*when the rain comes.* Maybe it's something about the softness in the air after the rain. What do you think?"

He shrugs. He wants to say, but doesn't, that he's never been touched by anyone who wears it so well.

Fingers press along his collarbone, he releases his shoulders. Pain travels in tiny footprints along his spine. Where did the boy go? Who else saw Elio make such a fool of himself? He's done that quite a few times today. Now she is pressing hard all along his back. She pulls off her bracelets, drops them noisily on a counter strewn with torn sales receipts.

He stares at the back wall as she continues to knead. It's covered with framed amateurish paintings, likely by the young artist lovers who came before Enrico. There is one, though, that stands out—a watercolor capturing the transparent play of shapes and tones, as sharp and lucid as stained glass. He squints to see and it is the Bridge of Sighs in Venice. Romina painted her own rendition of it years before; when he teased her for her fascination with watercolor, she ignored him. She was only fifteen but firm even then in what she wanted to do. So he and Sofia would go shopping while she set up her easel and painted. Precision was her strong point, every line flowing into the next, every nuance of color reflecting the green of the canal in front of her, the gray light of early March, the whiteness of the mask worn by a reveler for Carnevale, and only she could re-imagine the texture of the stone of the bridge itself so that it hovered both solid and weightless. Yes, so perfect. And wait, this *is* Romina's watercolor, the one that once hung over her mantelpiece, where an enormous flat screen television has taken its place.

"A birthday gift from your lovely daughter."

"I recognized it."

"Not right away. Are you sorry she gave it to me?"

Elio refrains from answering, dipping his head. *Keep pressing there along the base of my neck. My stress collects there, makes it hard to turn my head at times. I can feel it happening every time I argue with Sofia, or my daughter. That seems to be happening more lately. Then there's the business. And of course, when your new lover Enrico enters the picture my blood pressure soars.*

"No. Well, maybe. I'm surprised she would part with it."

When she smiles, he smarts. "She's quite the romantic, your Romina. Don't look so surprised. She's a lot like you. I told her I loved the Lord Byron poem. You know the line in the poem where he talks about standing on the Bridge of Sighs, as if at a crossroads. There's a castle on one side and a prison on the other. Romina said she admired me because no matter what circumstances I find myself in, I will always choose the castle, or perhaps something more. I would never choose a prison."

He looks up at her wearily. He's drinking too much and too fast.

"Not even the prison of my impending old age."

"You're still young, Francesca."

"Oh yes. In here! But I'm fifty years old." She pats her heart. "That's why my lovers are under thirty, except for Enrico. But he is an exception. He's amusing. But it is also why I choose wines of the new world versus the old."

He stares at his glass. "Interesting."

"Your daughter noticed that too about me."

"She's perceptive."

"More than you know."

He feels his shoulders drop, but she clasps both hands on either side and forces them back up. "*Forza!* Up with life, as you say here in Italy! I think my younger son is less perceptive too, that he has no intellectual curiosity and no substance. We think we had it at their age. But we didn't."

Maybe you didn't but I was always my mother's son. Elio's mouth tightens at the lie, so he softens it. *Though maybe I was frivolous too at times.*

"Try this vintage, Elio. It's from a new grower. He told me he loves the whimsical nature of this wine, which he created for his wife." She dims the lights. The wine glints like garnet. He loves the décor here. White, black, clean straight lines, nothing ornate, but still warm. Paintings are the only shots of color. Romina once told him that Francesca has a third son, Davide, an architect who lives in New York with his male partner. Elio remembers him as being handsome and somewhat quiet, but enormously talented, and as eager to leave home as Romina.

"No more wine. I won't be able to bike home in a straight line."

"Leave your bike here. Where are you rushing to?"

Now she has drunk too much too, something that makes his eyes widen because she flips through the iPad, stopping when tango floods the room, and sways about, away from him, in her own world, seeing her castle. Her fragrance wafts in and out with her movements.

"Think about it, Elio." She sits next to him. Her eyes are light hazel, almost golden, tinged with green. "You know I belong to many human rights organizations. I advocate in person, by email, in whatever way I can. Injustice pushes my buttons."

He didn't know. Nods anyway.

"But as hard as I work at this, when I can because of the business, I am struck by how many young people around the world are engaged by all these humanitarian issues. They do more than talk philosophically in cafés. They act. Look at Egypt, at the protesters in New York, in New Delhi, here in our city, see how young people rise up all around the world to join the struggles, whatever they may be; revolutions, human rights, the stupidity of war. They don't want the culture we have made for them. Yes, Elio, I see the expression on your face. So much of what we've done is good, especially in the arts, in architecture, and yes, we have instituted laws and democracies, inspired by the Greeks and Romans, blah blah blah, but we've also given them a violent world where the resolution for strife is always war, where women are disenfranchised, depriving the world of economic prosperity. What was it Mao Tse Tung said? Women hold up half the sky? He said that how many years ago? And look at how we deplete our planet of everything because we are so greedy. What will we leave for our grandchildren? This is what keeps me awake at night!" She gulps down her wine and refills. She's gorgeous right now, her cheeks pink, eyes glowing.

"It's time for a new paradigm, Elio, and they know what it is. We don't, even though I sometimes think I'm in sync. I'm really not. I don't grasp at solutions as efficiently as they do, I don't use social media, I don't delve and discover. I skate on the surface. But they dig in. They see the opportunities. Like the girl who created a canvas handbag called FEED to fight hunger. So simple, Elio! So simple! We would have made it complicated! Even worse, we would have looked to our politicians to fix the problem. These young people don't wait. If politicians don't act, *they* do, and it's marvelous and threatening all at the same time! I love to watch their little fingers on their keyboards and their smart phones. They do so much so fast. And so what if they scribble their messages on our fountains and our buildings? It's only stone! And it can be washed off the next day! These young people are going to the other side of the bridge." She points to Romina's painting. "Because the side you and I are on *is* the prison—a prison of our own limited thinking. Didn't Einstein say that the definition of insanity was doing the same thing over and over again and expecting a different result? Well, that's what our generation has *been* doing, *continues* to do, and *won't stop* until we die off! *Ecco!*"

"*Ecco!* Let's try the special vintage now." He holds out his glass.

24

WHEN HE ENTERS MARINA'S SHOP, he isn't prepared. Not for Marina's words or Sofia's silence. He knows that he provokes them just by entering, and true to form, Marina locks the door behind him, shaking her finger at a tourist with huge Ferragamo shopping bags. The woman holds her hand out to ask—when will you open? Marina shrugs. Maybe later. Maybe never. Go away.

The woman leaves and Elio feels a sharp pain in his lower back. His clothes are still covered with street dust, and he is in obvious pain, but neither woman pays attention. He decides that the tourist with the Ferragamo bag was the lucky one.

Does he detect the scent of narcissus from the embroidered linen sheets in the window display? Lilies stand straight up in a glass vase. Marina's watch is thrown haphazardly beside it. Cups of chamomile let off steam, on a mosaic table in between two chairs. Sofia is already seated. Marina joins her on the other side and picks up her cup with careful formality. Though it's uncomfortable for his back, he sits down on the ottoman.

"Sofia and I were just catching up," she says, sipping.

Sofia glances disapprovingly at the dirt on his trousers.

"I had to apologize for not coming here sooner, Elio, because I had no idea of what Marina was going through."

He nods. Marina should defend him for keeping her secret. *If* it had ever been a secret.

When Marina says nothing, Sophia continues, "I would at least have gone with you to the clinic, or tried to see if I could help in some way. I know some very good doctors there."

"I have everything under control, Sofia. You know me. I don't talk. I just do."

"It helps to talk to friends—"

"*Oof!* Stop fussing about nothing. So Elio forgot to tell you? No one died." She laughs. "Not yet of course."

Sofia frowns. Marina leans over and slaps her knee.

"You all want to protect me from the inevitable. It *is* inevitable, Sofia. Both you and Elio have to come to grips with that."

"It's *not!*" Elio suddenly sits up. Big mistake. Another shot of pain.

"Oh really?" Marina's sarcasm cuts deep.

"Really! It's not inevitable if you go for treatments. Instead you have this crazy idea that you can do what you want and it will magically go away!"

The pain shoots through him. He arches his back, gets up and walks around the room into the children's area where tiny waffle-weave robes wear appliqués in the shape of sailboats and sailor caps. He touches one and his eyes fill.

"It may be a crazy idea, but it's my crazy idea." Marina stares pointedly at Sofia. "And don't you even think about reprimanding Elio for what he's just said. You think the same thing."

Sofia crosses her legs with her inimitable air of authority. "But, Marina, you have to agree that at least you need to give the treatments a chance."

"Give the treatments a chance? *Not* a chance? How's that? I will not spend a single moment of my now-shortened life throwing up from chemotherapy, getting my arms poked with needles, or whiling away useless hours in a doctor's office. I'm done!"

She raises her hand to keep them from talking. Then she stands, pulls two of her most expensive sheet sets from a white armoire and places them on the table.

"Here! Gifts for my friends. This is what I intend to do. Give things away. What I take with me, wherever I go, are my memories, the time I have had with friends and my children. Do whatever I want to do until I close my eyes and say—*Basta!* Ask your daughter. She gets it. Why won't you?"

"Romina is only twenty-three—" starts Sofia.

"And she has more common sense than her parents."

"Now, Marina, that is not right."

"Sofia can hold her own, Elio. But consider this, that when Romina looks at the two of you, she sees two people stuck. What are you both doing? Your business is a disaster and you're doing nothing about it."

"That's not true."

"Not true? Come on, Elio. Sofia, don't stick up for him." She puts her hands on her hips. "Why don't you do a website, like every other successful retailer in Tuscany? For God-sakes, even the *nonnas* selling olive oil in the hills of Chianti have websites. Why are you not out there marketing, promoting, doing something new to let people know what Profumeria Barati is, for heaven's sake? Okay, okay, you finally show a *naked girl in the sun* ad, ten years after everyone else has done it and moved on. You think the commercial world stops for you?"

"It's more complicated than that, Marina."

"Oh, come on, Sofia. More complicated how? You're selling perfumes and lipsticks!"

Elio feels his face grow hot. "We have traditions, values. We don't do what the others do."

"What values, Elio? You make money one way and they make money the other way. It's all the same. You're still a merchant and still a salesman. They just do it better than you."

"You think that charlatan Enrico is—"

"I do." She smiles, sashays over to a Chinese armoire, takes the bottle of Fernet Branca and pours herself a glass. "Fancy some, either of you?"

They shake their heads weakly. Elio looks down at the floor.

"Glad you both think you're so rich you can afford to hold out. It's not complicated, Sofia. It's actually very simple." Marina glares at Elio, sits down again, drink in hand. "Either you are committed to your business or you're not. If you're not, sell the damn thing. Go off to Castellina, move to Morocco, or go trekking in the Himalayas. But do something before one of you gets sick like me and it's too late."

If only Marina had sent him away along with the Ferragamo-toting tourist. Because what she delivers next is a litany of everything he has done wrong: he closes the shop for the daytime *pranzo*. All his competitors are open. He never offers discounts. Yes, he is not a chain store, but people don't have money for luxuries these days, not with unemployment so high, and the economic woes of the Euro Zone, the recession in the United States, and an overall feeling of malaise. "In times like these one looks to save money, and yes there is the *petite* indulgence, a precious perfume by Guerlain, a set of linen sheets, a glass of *vin santo* discounted by a dear friend. How often do you go to Forte dei Marmi now, Elio? You did so often many years ago. Now you won't leave your shop. Neither can I, because we need to seize the business when we can. You still close in August and go to Castellina. But your competitors stay open, and clients who would have come to you, tourists who would have discovered you, go elsewhere, and they forge relationships there. They may not be the same as those they would have forged with you. But what is the same nowadays?"

Marina shook her head sharply. "We are entering a new period of Enlightenment. Not the age of Voltaire, Rousseau and Diderot. This is the age of economic enlightenment. The good idea is the one that makes money. And don't tell me it's a sign of the times. It's a sign of all times. Think the Medici were all about art and honor? They were about their own legacies. Get inside your own skin and you'll find that your loyalty to the family business is more about fear than it is about anything else. Who are you doing this for, Elio? Can you tell me genuinely that it's for Romina?"

25

"IT'S GOOD, ELIO." Palma didn't look up from the fan of scent strips in her hand.

It was quiet outside her window except for the intermittent chatter of strollers walking up to the cathedral for midnight mass or the muted roar of a vespa sliding across snow. The clock ticked quietly on the mantelpiece, and a flickering fire continued to cast out embers like fireflies that then died on her living room carpet. Nina Simone played in the background, and the colored lights on her tree would have made even bad news palpable.

"Good in what way?"

Nina's voice reached out with long coaxing fingers to steady his pounding heart. It started to melt the tension between his shoulder blades, dull the edges of her faint praise. It didn't work. He wanted more. He wanted specifics and declarations. He wanted her to gush over the notes he'd so brilliantly included and re-imagined, notes they had experienced and talked about together—the bougainevillea along the white stone houses in Saint-Jean-Cap-Ferrat. The quirky briny nuances he had worked so hard to perfect, blended inside the smells of the stony beaches along the Promenade des Anglais in Nice. The mimosa, so well rounded as if to recall the flower itself stroked across a beautiful woman's arm. The mimosa had been one of his first impressions of Grasse and he'd balanced the oils to re-create just that moment, of life opening up before him, of leaving Florence behind, of finally shaking loose from everything that had held him down. Perhaps this one note, and the way he'd constructed it, was his way of showing that he'd indeed left his provincialism at the border. The middle accord was deliciously creamy and deeply floral. There were no halting steps. They flowed as smoothly as a sonata, calibrated and precise, like Palma herself, like the manicured fields around Grasse.

"It's different from anything out there right now, Elio. That's what makes it special. You have a rare gift for giving fragrance dimension. Well done." She put the scent strips down on the mantelpiece where the candles lit her face with a strange pearlized light.

She tried to walk away but kept returning to the scented papers splayed on the stone, smelled them with eyes closed, did everything she could to keep from smiling. He became distracted by his reflection in the mirror behind her. Such a contrast between them. Visual more than verbal, but there all the same. Always there. And now her composure, another difference, now began to irk him. He tapped his hand against his trouser leg. The snow outside fell more heavily; lacy flakes swirled around the Belle Époque street lamps outside.

It was Christmas Eve, almost an entire year after Gregorio's announcement that he was sick. Elio hadn't gone home because Palma insisted they continue to work. As Jean Claude's protégé and as Palma's lover, Elio didn't have the same holiday privileges as his classmates. He had other privileges, which he exploited. And he'd wanted to remain here. No one had forced him. No one to blame.

His guilt was assuaged by a letter from his father who had decided to visit with old friends in Rome, where he'd gone to university. *It's amazing that the Via Appia still holds magic for me. And the small streets around Via Margutta, they are more commercial now. Perhaps I will go up to Monte Pincio this evening, to see the city lit up from up high.* Funny how Elio could hear a melancholy voice in the architectural script. Re-reading it, he secretly hoped to read into it something else, the possibility that the warmer climate and the spirited nature of the Romans might help his father heal, that the treatments in Verona were miraculously clearing up his lungs so he could breathe again like a normal human being, that he would never smoke again, that his longevity would be guaranteed. Not likely. But there was no reason to feel guilty given that Elio would go home soon enough, at Easter, in time for the iris festivals. More importantly, tonight he'd finally brought something to show Palma. His composition.

This was her Christmas surprise—these three vials representing the three accords, three scentstrips arranged along a metal fan so she could smell from top, middle and base accord and back again, so she could breathe it in, amidst the competing scents of chrysanthemum, candlewax and mulled wine.

"The topnote is perfect. It's immediate, fresh. It captures you like a brilliant discovery. Then it becomes warm and gradually more floral. And the florals are feminine in a bold and modern sort of way. It's traditional but tradition is its root, not its dynamic, if you know what I mean."

He shook his head, but he liked what he'd heard so far.

"It's not unlike your city, Elio. Think about it. Florence is rooted in tradition, in its Renaissance heritage. You see it all around you, in its architecture, in the Duomo and the arcades of the Vasarian corridor along the river. But it's also modern. You have the most modern vespas. Their sound is young, feisty, not laborious like our old ones. Your fashion has an edge and a sharpness we have yet to acquire here in France. There's a buzz in Florence. But that's where the scent falters. I was hoping for some of that in your middle accord."

Elio faltered himself for a moment—grabbed the table, the chair—grabbed at anything that would help keep him upright. But Palma didn't notice, or decided not to notice.

"You probably couldn't help including some cypress. Because of the mix, we don't know where it's coming from. And maybe we don't need to know. A fairly commonplace oil but you've re-directed it somehow. Interesting. I think you're close to figuring it out."

"There's nothing commonplace about cypress. And this isn't a fragrance about Florence."

"I beg to differ."

"On which of your two flawed observations?"

"On both counts."

"Right. Like you would know. When was the last time you were there, Palma? You don't really like Italy, remember?"

"One never forgets the smells of the Lunigiana, even when one is a visitor." The raised eyebrow reminds him, yet again, of his place in the hierarchy. "Your creation is good, but it isn't there yet."

He glared at her in such a way that she started, looked away.

"You can't pretend that this surprises you."

He felt every part of himself stiffen and he couldn't speak. Turning, he walked to the fireplace mantle, grabbed his scentstrips, crushed them hard inside his hands.

"You know that wasn't necessary, Elio." She sighed impatiently as if she were in the company of an impetuous child, and this angered him all the more. Then she did something he'd never seen her do. She opened the cigarette box on her coffee table, took out a cigarette and lit it. Elio tried to wave the smoke away with his free hand. He let the crumpled scentstrips drop to the floor. She smirked and paced. Her back to him. Smoke swirling around her head. She stopped. Finally...

"It lacks complexity. That's it." She turned to him and puffed again. "I was trying to figure out just what it's missing and I have it now. The topnote is perfect. It's alive. It has energy. It reaches out to you. The middle note is nicely rounded."

"Yes, it is, and it's damn good." He so despised that involuntary tremor in his own voice.

"But it initiates too soon. It's not distinct. Common is the word, whether you want to hear it or not."

He wanted to jump out of his own skin. In this moment he hated her, and he was about to hate her even more.

"And your base is lovely but rings shallow, Elio. After all our hard work I expected something better. That said, Jean Claude will applaud your effort."

"Effort? This has been my *life* for almost two years!"

"And it has to be your life for far longer than that." She squashed the cigarette into a lovely crystal ashtray that should never have been used for that purpose. "You will never become a perfumer if you can't take criticism. Your composition lacks gravitas. Pure and simple. And that's a death sentence for a fragrance. Without grounding and authority, it doesn't exist, no matter how lovely at first breath."

"Gravitas? Are you joking? This is good. Really good."

She looked at him pointedly. "You wanted my impression. This is it. I'm sorry."

She sat down on the sofa and patted it so he would sit down. He obliged her and hated himself for it. She stroked his thigh and as he felt the desire well up he wanted to push her away, but he needed her. He knew that. So did she.

"Hush. It's your creation and he'll respect it as such. He'll also respect that you've given it that much thought. But now you need to go to the next step. Write up the formula, bring it to the lab where the perfumers will make the oil. They'll submit the formulas to us periodically so we can smell them and suggest changes."

"We?"

"Every fragrance is a collaborative effort, Elio. No one is denying you a say. This fragrance will be, ultimately, your creation. But Jean Claude and I, all the perfumers on staff, will collaborate on its development. You know that a composition evolves. It's like the first draft of a novel that's fraught with possibility. But it's not, by any stretch of anyone's imagination, the final, polished work."

"I know how it's done, but what does *he* have to do with it?"

"Do I have to say the obvious?" She paused. "Because he is who he is."

"And I'm better than *he* is."

It seemed to happen in slow motion, even though his heart thumped so loudly it resonated in his ears. He gathered up his vials and the scent strip fan and threw them clumsily into his briefcase, as if to destroy every last vestige. So what if they broke. He felt her hovering around him. He snapped the briefcase shut.

"Elio, you can't do this without the guidance of a master perfumer and a reputable school behind you. You wouldn't have gotten this far without Jean Claude's support."

He put on his coat, grabbed his scarf, shrugged her hand off. No, not now. Not tonight. Never again. She reached out again and he pushed her hard into the sofa and spoke in a calm voice. "I've learned everything I need to learn from that man. And from you, quite frankly. I created this fragrance in my own mind and with my own expertise, and he's *not* taking credit for it."

He knew little about where Palma's heart was at the moment. She baffled him. But one thing he did know. His composition was far better than the one Palma and Jean Claude had been working on together.

As he moved toward the door, she said something about being patient, about recognizing his talent and learning to mold it through the tutelage of someone with far more experience. She was still talking when he slammed the door, briefcase tight against his chest. He'd found her out. Or perhaps he'd always known. But why did it suddenly feel so liberating to have one's suspicions confirmed? He didn't know, but kept walking to the end of her street, around the corner and into the Place aux Aires. Nathalie's café was dark. The white field of snow glistened peacefully under the streetlamps. A group of boys threw snowballs and one hit Elio square in the back. He dropped his case to the ground, gathered up a mound of snow that stuck together very well, and flung it back. It missed the boy, hit a tree, and had all of them laughing.

A light snow tickled his face. For some reason it made him smile.

26

HE WONDERS IF IT'S THE FIFTH SHOT of grappa that does it. Or the incipient dots of rain on the window glass, or the grayness outside. Michele presses a prosciutto and arugula *panino* for Enrico, sitting at a back table with his iPad. Behind him is a wall of photographs, some Michele's, many Romina's. There is the white Bow Bridge in Central Park with pink-speckled trees in the background; yet another of the Bridge of Sighs at sunset; and then the Brooklyn Bridge and the Golden Gate Bridge, more majestic and solitary than the other two. Michele doesn't photograph bridges. His shots are of ski mountains, the craggy Dolomites sheathed in snow, skiers gliding down into bowls or an infinite expanse of moguls, pillowy mounds of white. And then of course there is the one of a woman's hands holding a small bowl of what looks like a spice—saffron perhaps. Her caramel-toned wrists wear bangles of gold, coral and turquoise. Her fingers wear stone-encrusted rings and open out in a gesture of generosity. This must be one of Romina's photographs from India.

Enrico frowns from time to time because he's not adept with the iPad. Elio stifles a giggle, and because Michele's back is to him, he refills his glass. Not noiselessly, so Michele had to hear him place the bottle back on the counter. Still he doesn't turn around. Instead he grabs an orange, cuts it in half to make a spremuta. Elio downs the grappa in one gulp.

And bam! It's back! The flood of memories, the searing regret. Why can't he step back in time and change it all! If we can do so much with technology, why can't we conquer the distance to the past. It rains outside. Not a soft reflective rain, but the scolding slap in the face. The kind that says, *Ha!* You thought spring was coming, that life would lighten up. But I am nature, I am life, and I still have the upper hand. People make plans and God laughs, they say. This morning just as you took your suede jacket and new Ferragamo loafers out of the closet, I bring on the rain. Just as you thought you would have a few days of wandering through your iris fields, I make the wind blow so hard it breaks their stalks. I, Mother Nature, have never been predictable and now with the climate change you humans have brought about, I reserve the right to be as petulant as an adolescent, and laugh about it.

Michele presses the last orange and brings the glass to Enrico. Elio sneaks one more. Grappa feels so good going down. Like a drill through your insides, Elena would say. Enrico and Michele are now talking about that infamous soccer match when Italy beat Germany and so easily gave it up to Spain.

Yes, it's shameful but who cares? How can they talk of such trivialities when everyone is hard at work. Well, even he, Elio of the shop that never closes except at lunch time and August, is taking the afternoon off. The only people wandering about are tourists because the Florentines have enough sense to stay inside during such miserable weather. He sees them stop by his perfumery, cup their faces against the glass. It certainly looks as if someone should be inside. Everything is lit. There are fresh flowers in Romina's vase and Elio's suede jacket hangs neatly on the back of one of the stools. A collage of photographs—Romina's doing—flash intermittently across the computer screen. He stares for a minute, feels a headache coming on and turns away.

Old age is supposed to erode our memories, or at least weaken their power. If it succeeds in making us forget where we put our checkbook, why is it not as sanguine against the regret that wells up whenever a sleeping image returns to life?

He rubs his aching forehead, checks his reflection in the gilded mirror behind the bar. That mirror, his mother's, had been in their shop until Sofia decided to renovate. It was too antiquated for the more contemporary look she wanted. So out it went, and Michele, also renovating at the time, was willing to give it a home over his newly modernized bar area. He liked the old with the new he said, and that was it. Done.

It works. A classic ornate piece inside a spare minimalist space. You can smell the citrus when you walk into Michele's bar. Like an aesthetician's cabine at the Four Seasons spa. On either side of the mirror, hammered metal shelves hold plain white ceramics and clear glass bowls filled with fruits for *spremute*: lemons, limes, blood oranges. The bottles of *aperitivi*—Apero, Cynar, Campari—on the opposite wall are backlit so their red and amber liquids shine. He loves the nickel-topped square jars of espresso and cacao beans and the Japanese style trays for chocolates and *bomboloni* filled with cream or raspberry jam.

The massive gold-plated Marzocco espresso maker, which Sofia still describes as far too Rococco for her taste, is Michele's only nod to tradition. Sofia puts added emphasis on the last o—*Rococcooo*. Palma would speak like that too whenever she wanted to make a point. It was her own cruel way of reminding him of just how provincial he was. Damn her.

He holds his glass out and Michele fills it again, thinking it's the fourth not the seventh, but he raises an eyebrow as Elio's hand wobbles.

"Maybe she was right, Michele. I was never meant to be a perfumer."

"Who was right?"

"Palma!" He says it as if the answer is obvious.

"Palma? Who is Palma?"

"My teacher in Grasse when I was seventeen. The one I was sleeping with."

Michele whistles and leans across the bar. "Wait! *You* were sleeping with your teacher?"

"Well yes! Why do you find that so strange?"

"I...well, I never imagined *you* would do such a thing."

"I was quite an adventurer in my youth. I'm different now of course...I have so many responsibilities..."

"Yes, yes. I don't need your life story, Elio. But this intrigues me. How old was she?"

"Almost thirty. She wouldn't say. But she was a beauty."

"Seems beautiful women have always been a part of your life, Elio."

Elio blushes, puts his glass out for a refill. Michele slaps his hand back.

"You have to admit—" Michele starts counting on his fingers. "Your mother was a beauty from what my father told me. Then Palma and Marina. Yes, I know about Marina. All of Florence does. Sofia. And now your daughter. You are lucky man."

"Yes, I am. Wait! What are you doing with that bottle, *per la madonna!*"

"Putting it where you can't get it. A man as fortunate as you should not be drinking his brains out."

"But I am *not* fortunate, *maledetto*. Let me drink myself to sleep at least." He cradles his head on his hand.

"No."

"Okay! Then I should tell you the whole miserable story. Do you have a few minutes?"

Michele looks around. Enrico has his earbuds on. "You see it busy here today? It's like a funeral parlor. So, entertain me. Tell me what this *miseria* is all about."

So the story gushes out like wine from a broken cask, until Elio doesn't remember the point of it. He had gone to Grasse to learn how to create a great fragrance. And what was wrong with so grand a dream? Even that arrogant headmaster recognized his talent and assigned Palma, his junior associate, and the most talented young perfumer in his charge, to tutor Elio privately and to assist him in creating this fragrance he'd been dreaming about.

"It felt like an impossible dream. I had been drawn to her from the outset. I didn't even try to resist the attraction. I loved it. I embraced it. I was so young."

"With horomones raging."

"And I was in France. What do you expect?"

"What do you mean?"

"France seemed more permissive, less moralistic than here. At least I thought so back then. And Grasse was so lush, so sensual."

"Florence has its sensory beauty too, Elio."

"Yes, but it had more *rules.*" He pauses. "*Still* has more rules."

"What was this Palma's relationship with the headmaster?"

"Interesting you should ask."

"Was she sleeping with him too?"

"Bingo! How did you figure that out?"

"Just a hunch. So by sleeping with her, you were competing with him on yet another level."

"Not sure what you mean."

"Simple. You didn't like him. You felt you were in competition with him professionally. Sleeping with Palma was not just about your libido."

"But that first night. It wasn't about Jean Claude. I smelled a jasmine tree in her garden, and she kissed me, and that's what did it the first night, and then every night and every day after that. We made love at every opportunity. Jasmine is erotic, intoxicating. It's the most seductive scent in the world. She—"

"She broke your heart."

Leave it to Michele to call it as it was.

"She did." He rubs his throbbing forehead. "She broke my spirit too."

They're both glad when Enrico, headbuds still in place, leaves money on the table and steps out into the rain. Michele's eyes are fixed on Elio.

"I'd assumed, and perhaps it was through my own manipulation, that by making love to my teacher in such a forbidden way, that that passion and excitement would find its way into my fragrance. That it would not be a perfume created by a naïve, young man. I did love her...and I still want to believe she loved me... Please, Michele, no espresso now!"

"It will sober you up. What did you do after that? Leave Grasse? How did you leave it with her?"

"Well, fate intervened. The next morning I got the telegram that my father's condition had worsened. Your father wrote that I should come home right away."

Michele whistles. "That's hard."

"It was a shock. I was conflicted. But then I had an idea. I suggested Palma come back to Florence with me for a few days until I sorted things out. Then we could both go back to Grasse together. I fully intended to go back there and finish my studies."

"And?"

"Eh? What's the point! It was so many years ago."

"I'll bet she said no."

Elio kept silent, but the hand holding the glass shook.

"From what you've told me, it sounds like something she would do."

"You figured her out in a few minutes better than I did back then."

"I wasn't in the moment, Elio, as you were. And that was that? You came home for the funeral and never went back?"

"Correct. When I arrived at the station your father was there. My father had already died."

"After the funeral you should have gone right back to Grasse."

"After the way she treated me?"

"*Especially* after the way she treated you. Your time and your efforts were not just about Palma."

Michele wipes off his counter with a snap and flicks the towel over his shoulder. He looks as if he's about to grab something hard and hit Elio over the head with it.

"Maybe I was afraid. I thought about the shop and all the work my father had put into it."

"Understandable. Your father had just died and you wanted to respect his wishes."

And now the regret wells up even more.

"No. That wasn't it. My father had made it easy. He'd already found a buyer for the shop."

"What?"

"Yes. His wishes—they were that I return to Grasse. And, like your father, he planned everything out to the last detail." He glances up at Michele. "I was stupid, wasn't I?"

"What do *you* think?"

"Now you too! I come here for some male compassion after Sofia and Marina verbally castrate me and this is what I get. One more." He holds out his glass but Michele has already made a second espresso; short, dark and strong

"So! When you came into the train station, Elio, my father was there to meet you. Correct?"

Elio takes up the small cup. "It was a nice funeral arranged by your mother, may God bless her. Understated and honest, the way Gregorio would have wanted it. Not a penny wasted. But she covered his coffin with a spray of purple and white irises. His favorite flower. *Our* favorite flower."

He glances across the street at the irises inside his shop window. "I still grow that flower. Me? Imagine that? I am one of the few that still grows irises. And I once resisted everything, about Florence."

Pointing to his windows, he nearly falls off the stool. Michele grabs his elbow.

"You need to sober up before Romina gets here."

"Oh yes, she hates it when I drink. You know my father never drank?"

"Yes, I heard."

"He was probably celibate too, after my mother left. No vices. Except for cigarettes, and they killed him. You see, Michele, if he'd had other vices, they would have kept him from smoking."

The street lights go on outside. It's no longer raining. Businesses will close within the hour. Patrons will gather for *aperitivi* and *stuzzichini,* for that restorative breath that separates the workday from the family dinner, one obligation gliding into the next. They will toast friends and new acquaintances, complain about their co-workers, talk about the upcoming soccer matches, or the dismal state of the economy and the impossible mayor who limits where they can park and where they can drive, and the future of the Euro that has made all of their lives more difficult and more expensive.

Has Sofia gone home? Or did she stop for a drink at JK Place with friends from yoga. If so, he can linger longer, all night long if he wants. If only his *motorino* wasn't in the repair shop. He might just zip off to Castellina anyway. Getting to work in the morning was the tricky part. Responsibility always trumps one's urge to flee.

"My father didn't want me to go to Grasse. At first anyway. But he saw my resolve and as the years passed he became more supportive. Surprisingly so. He suddenly became my advocate, not adversary. He actually pushed me. Funny how we change roles in life. He actually had more confidence in me than I had."

"It's not too late for you."

"*Oof!* Of course it is." He stares longingly at the grappa bottle.

Michele takes it off the bar.

"The last thing you need is to slink off and do nothing. You of all people, Elio, with all that vitality and passion." He punches his chest.

"*Oof!* Vitality is for you and Romina not me. You know I have arthritis in my knees, spinal stenosis and—"

"Ya, ya, ya. So you missed an opportunity? Who hasn't? You're just scared."

"Ah! Now you and Marina agree. Neither of you understands."

"Understand what, Elio? You don't need understanding. You need what my father, whom you so admire, would call a good swift kick out the door."

"Please, Michele. I'm too tired to confront any more of life's more complicated challenges."

"Or to seize any of its opportunities."

"What opportunities at my age?"

Michele frowns and leans over the bar.

"You know what I wish, Elio?"

"What?"

"That I'd have been around when you came back here from Grasse. I would have given you a full *lavata di faccia.*" Michele chopped the air with the side of his hand. "With a talent like yours! With a business like yours? *Ma che ti lamenti!*"

27

LITTLE HAD CHANGED IN HIS PARENTS' BEDROOM. Elena's pictures still stood on the mahogany dresser beside a half-empty bottle of lavender aftershave. Family pictures spun out around them: a small Elio in a navy blue suit, white silk ribbon affixed to his sleeve for his first Communion; the three of them in wet swimsuits on the stone promontory in Forte dei Marmi. The lace doilies were freshly ironed. The mahogany surfaces of all the furniture gleamed. Not a particle of dust anywhere. Yet although Angela had scrubbed the room and put fresh white linens on the bed and smoothed out the cotton bedspread YaYa had sent them from Paros, the room still smelled of medicine and death. There were no pots of violets on the windowsills. And the chrysanthemums from Christmas had withered.

He took in the room's haunting silence and the chair beside Gregorio's bed. A lump rose in his throat. There had always been something on that chair, a book, a newspaper, Gregorio's clothes, neatly folded for the next morning. Before going to bed he'd remove the book he was reading from the chair and place it on his nightstand. In its place, he'd put a folded shirt, a clean handkerchief, socks and a rolled up belt. His trousers, with an even crease, and a tie hung over the back.

More than any other experience of that day, this one made Elio sob, almost violently, as if the raw truth of his father's passing had finally hit like a soccer ball to his chest. As if he could see his father patiently drape the trousers and curl the belt around his hand. His agenda was open on his nightstand with appointments he would never keep, marked in his familiar beautiful script.

Until then, until that moment, it had all been surreal, starting with Gregorio's absence at the train station, then continuing into the funeral. All of Florence, and many from the surrounding hilltowns, had turned out for the splendid mass inside Santa Maria Novella. They'd driven in from Fiesole, Montepulciano and Lucca, and from as far south as Rome, Bari and Palermo, even from the small island of Pantelleria. They took the *rapido* from Milan, from Geneva and from Paris. They waited one hour for the priests and their entourage to walk past the pews and up to the alter with incense misting around them. It was a service befitting a head of state.

Every friend, every business associate, every merchant, local artisans, art students. It wasn't only the Barati name, they told him, but his father's magnanimity, his professional reserve and integrity. "He never said a word he didn't mean," said one man. "He's the reason I opened my gelateria," said Vittorio. "I had very little money and he encouraged me to take a loan. He said, *The money gets spent anyway, and when you own a business you have something no one can take away if you do it right. And I can tell, Vittorio, that you will not stop until you are successful.*" Vittorio fought back tears. "He told me the story of Perche' No! The owner, who had never owned a gelateria in his life, said, *Perche' no*? Why not? And he had this very successful gelateria that all the American soldiers would go to during the war. After the war when the electricity went out, the soldiers so desperately wanted the gelato, they brought in a generator. It was one of the few places in Florence at that time with electricity."

"I had such a crush on him," said a slender, stylish woman, far older than Gregorio but missing nothing in stature. "He was just so handsome, and so devoted to you and your mother. After she left he missed her so, but he never said a bad word. And he remained loyal to her until the end. I respected that, Elio. He was such an eligible bachelor I would have snatched him up if he had been at all willing."

Angela and Luca outfitted the shop in white Casablanca lilies and his father's *iris pallida* from Elena's garden. The aestheticians made sure everything was clean and they laid out platters of *cantuccini* and tiny glasses to fill with Gregorio's favorite *aperitivo*. *Turandot* played from his makeshift sound system, one Elio would never dismantle, and even the atomizers and lipstick tubes seemed to stand in solid remembrance of a man so loved and respected. I wish you would frown at me one more time, Papa. Tell me one more time that the box is crooked, the flacon surface has smudges, that the window display is not quite right. Who will correct me now? Who will call me out when I travel down the wrong path?

In true Italian fashion, the communal outpouring was dizzing. From the throngs under Giotto's crucifix and inside the Strozzi chapel, to the clusters of friends inside the gardens of Santa Maria Novella. Even the cakes served in Angela and Luca's home afterwards had a peculiar taste, like they were not to be enjoyed because a member of their community was gone, and it was the whole that made whatever was touched, eaten, spoken all the more indicative of how we lull ourselves into false bliss. What was the momentary pleasure with Palma? What had it amounted to? Something as fleeting as his delusions of becoming a perfumer. In comparison to such juvenile flights of fancy stood all the praise for a man never valued as much as he should have been.

Back in his father's bedroom, the closet door creaked. Inside, everything looked like a miniature retail showroom, as polished and predictable as his father had been. And in the middle of it all, a metal box stood on the closet floor, radiating importance.

He had to brush dust off its surface to open the latch. The folders were lined up as straight and neat as if his father were still living in the house, each one labeled so you knew its contents without searching. One folder held his parents' marriage certificate, his own birth certificate, diplomas, reportcards. Another, all the bank and financial statements. He pulled it out and closed the box. As he tucked it under his arm, he looked down at a row of shoes, all stuffed with cedar shoe trees, polished to a sheen, some stored inside a felt bag. Many of the shoes were decades old yet still looked new. Every one of Gregorio's suits was covered in linen and zippered shut. Hats lined a polished wooden shelf; folded scarves, another. The closet walls smelled as they always had, of lavender, cedar hangers and old sachets. Even in his final days Gregorio had kept everything in order.

For some reason this made Elio angry. Why hadn't his father waited for him? If Palma hadn't insisted he stay in Grasse, he would have had one last Christmas with his father. If he, Elio, had not let his ego get the better of him, he would have sat, for one last time, at Luca and Angela's dinner table, toasting his father on Christmas Eve. But he'd chosen not to do that, and this was one decision that could not be undone. Funny, how he'd fooled himself all those months after Gregorio had spoken to him.

Angrier now, he shoved back hangers, slipped his hands inside sweaters, smelled them, felt his eyes fill. He wanted more than anything else to hear his father's familiar footsteps walk steadily up the stairs, the same footsteps he ran away from as a boy, to hide a cigarette, a magazine he was not allowed to read, a box of chocolates. He touched stiff starched collars of cotton shirts and smiled suddenly, remembering his father wielding the iron with such precision, Elena finally delegated all the household ironing to him, including the heirloom linen sheets from Prato.

The fabrics felt so good against his hands, so solid and true, he dug deeper into the closet, found a box with his first shoes, another with his baptismal gown, still another with old school notebooks and diaries and his mother's dog-eared piano music. There were letters from his mother tied with ribbons, their tops slit open. He pulled out a red sweater, thinking it was an usually bright color for his father to wear, and something hard fell onto his foot—a locked wooden box.

After limping to the bed where he settled clumsily, he jiggled the lock. The box opened easily. A rash of dust rose up with the scent of cedar. He blinked and tried to keep from sneezing. Inside was another stack of letters held together by an elastic band. He lifted it up, turned the letters over to see the address—and felt his heart stop. He tore off the elastic and flicked through the envelopes one by one with his shaking hands.

The letters, sealed and never posted, were written in his own boyish hand and addressed to his mother, almost all of them dating back to the first four years after her departure. His face felt wet from tears or sweat, he didn't care which. All he knew was that his mother had never received his letters, that she'd never known how much he grieved, how much he wanted her back. Gregorio had lied. Every time Elio asked him, he replied that he'd mailed the letters but Elena had never responded. She wanted to make a clean and final break, his father said. It would be easier that way. Easier. But it had all been deception, from his mother who'd led him to believe he had what it took to become a perfumer; from his father who hid the letters and kept silent for all those years; from Palma, who'd used him to further her own ambitions and the ambitions of a lover she could never have but would never abandon; and finally from himself about who he was and who he wanted to be.

Perhaps perfumery was to blame. It was, after all, an art founded on the antique science of alchemy. It was devised to cast spells, to seduce, to spread falsity instead of truth, to create illusions. What was a perfume anyway? It was nothing you could hold in your hand, nothing you could own or define. It was as vaporous and vapid as air. And the sense of smell, it was the most fundamental but the least illustrious in terms of art. Painters and sculptors relied on sight and touch, musicians on the ear, great chefs on taste, writers on the malleability of words. What greatness could a perfume ever achieve? A perfume was nothing more than an object of vanity, a veneer of artifice meant to delude and mislead, a promise dangled from a thread by a hypnotist, then cut away. What effect could it ever have on life itself?

Perfumery wasn't important and it wasn't real. Real was the shop that had provided the Baratis with a livelihood for centuries. Real was the food growing in the garden in Castellina, the personal relationships inside his birth city— Luca, Angela, Marina. He put the letters back in the box and slid it under the bed. Tomorrow he would destroy them, but for the moment he would pretend they didn't exist.

The rain outside fell hard and steady. He opened the window to let it brush icy cold across his face. It would turn to hail soon. So much the better. He put on a slicker, grabbed his bicycle off the front steps and took off. He pedaled along the Arno, past the swirl of lights and cars and people rushing home from restaurants and clubs. He'd meant to ride on, all night if need be, until he reached Castellina. Instead he turned into Via della Vigna Nuova and forged ahead until he arrived at Marina's front door.

28

SHE STANDS AT THE TOP OF THE STAIRS, as imperious as Catherine the Great. One hand grabs the bannister; the other presses an *Il Bisonte* agenda to her chest, stamped with the image of a bison. It's as if the artisan wants to remind us that all our refinement comes from the wild and unbridled parts of nature. Nature has no reservations about her mission. Nature is shameless, in a way. So Florence. So Marina. So out there. And, given the way she glares at him, he's not about to ask her why she's being so obstinant.

He remembers, as he stares up into her lovely face that it was just two evenings ago, at a serene new restaurant just behind the Bargello, that she'd told them all unequivocally what her plans were. It was a new therapy, cutting edge, and she had to go with her gut, travel to the clinic in Verona, and just do it. Romina had researched it too. Claudio knew someone who'd had the treatment, now available in Switzerland. It was miraculous. No, not quite. Instead, the consensus was that it was the best one could hope for, a mildly invasive treatment with minimal side effects.

The next evening over dinner in Sofia's favorite restaurant, Io Personale, in San Frediano, they all conspired around him: Sofia, Romina, Michele and Claudio. They agreed that Marina should not drive that far up north to the new Ospedale Trento di Verona and back to Florence alone. Who knew what tests they'd subject her to? And what if they wanted to do both the surgery and the treatment right away, well that was complicated too. It seemed, according to the little bit Marina told them, that the Ospedale was one of the few places in the world to offer a new breast cancer therapy and very few women were eligible for it. Since Marina's cancer was still in the early stages, and she was an older patient, she qualified. Called Intra-Operative Electron Radiation Therapy, this seemingly miraculous treatment used a state-of-the-art instrument called the Mobetron to precisely target cancer celles in only one two-minute treatment during the actual surgery. Nothing like this had ever existed. And it seemed the rate of recurrence was dramatically reduced, after just a single treatment. A made-for-Marina solution.

"I know it's somewhat experimental. What do I care? I don't lose a breast and I don't have to go back and forth for treatments I have no time for. It's a win-win for me."

Would it not be good for Elio and Sofia to accompany her, then? After all they are her oldest and closest friends, and a few days away would do them all some good. Since Marina's consultation and pre-op is on a Friday, and the surgery with Mobetron, God willing, is Saturday, they should stay the weekend, perhaps at Il Residence Hotel Castelvecchio. Yes, that would give Marina a chance to recover, with her dear friends close by. And then, after a weekend of rest, long walks, good food, and perhaps some opera, she would return to the clinic on Monday to check the stitches and determine her strength for the trip home. There was the small matter of the lumpectomy, the lump that would have to be removed and biopsied. However, given the potential of the Mobetron to kill off any renegade cells, Marina was optimistic. Elio marvels at her fortunate timing. The treatment only became available very recently.

No worries about his business. Romina and Michele will take care of the shop. Elio warned them not to tamper with any of the systems he'd put in place. I know they are antiquated, but they work. Yes, of course, promised his daughter, that familiar twinkle appearing in her eye that told him not to believe her.

Claudio, with the flair and assurance of a concierge, booked their weekend itinerary: three nights accommodations at Il Residence, breakfast (sweet or savory) included at a café just outside, passes to Museo di Castelvecchio complete with headsets and a guide, reservations to two of the hottest new restaurants, and front row seats at the Arena to see *Turandot*. Elio snapped to attention on that last promise. This Claudio might not be so bad after all.

Of course Marina will have none of it. She's perfectly capable of driving herself through the Veneto, even up the Gothard Pass into Austria if she so choses. She did so once in a Fiat Panda in the middle of a snow blizzard, so what's to stop her now? She even threatened to pack her hiking gear for one last impromptu trek through the Dolomites. "I could strap my bicycle to the roof of your car for a quick getaway, Elio. You know I pedal faster than you. Don't put it past me." She continues to stand, as defiant as his sturdiest iris stalks against a windstorm, at the top of the stairs in the form-fitting black suit that still turns men's heads.

Enter Sofia, car keys in hand.

"Downstairs! Now! Or we'll hit traffic, Marina. You know how much I hate to wait." She checks her stockings for runs and straightens her skirt. Not a hair or a thread out of place. Pearl earrings symmetrically placed. Make-up impeccable. All accomplished in a single hour after her daily bike ride along the Arno. "I never second guess myself," she once told Elio. "Self-doubt is a waste of time."

And it's that implacable resolve that makes Marina sigh and walk down the stairs, not in resignation but in something closely ressembling it. She slams the car door shut. "Your wife decides I'm going to be chauffeured and that I'll like it. So I guess I'd better like it."

She puts on her sunglasses and crosses her legs. The rose gold morning light rises over the Arno as they ride toward the Ponte alla Carraia. The light makes her all the more desireable, especially as Guerlain's Mitsouko enters the air between them.

Still, Elio's mood is dark. He thinks about the ride ahead, the *autostrada* unspooling in front, sunflower fields skimming by sturdy and golden on either side, and the verdict she will face.

What will they tell her? *How much* will they tell her? *What* will the prognosis be? Will they be direct or evasive? Will they be accurate? Have they ever misdiagnosed and overtreated or undertreated? Will she, at some point, have to make the tough choices? Long term treatment and a declining quality of life versus a shorter time living the life she wants and loves? He's read the books and seen the films and he knows how this cancer thing plays out. He's not optimistic.

Sofia drives fast. *I wish you would slow down, cara.* Once they've driven through his favorite culinary cities, Modena, Parma and Bologna, Elio will start having heart palpitations. He almost feels them start in anticipation. He places his hand on his chest. But apparently he's alone with his anxiety. Marina rolls down the window and rests her elbow on the door. Thick jade and wood bangles rattle against her strong wrists.

"So tell me about this doctor, Marina, is he as cute as they say?" Sofia checks the rearview mirror, ignores Elio's frustrated expression. And for this he gave up a weekend with his irises.

"*Maledetto!*" He's thrust forward against the front seat of the car.

"Calm down, Elio. I didn't see the policeman. He's ignoring me, thank God. I was going perhaps a little too fast."

"Listen to Elio, Sofia. Remember I'm not in *that* much of a hurry to get there." Marina laughes—and Elio senses nervousness underneath. Yet this is her. Acting as if all of life's most painful moments could be silenced or minimized by laughter. Like white paint rolled over a wall of street graffiti. It's overpowering. It's sexy.

Maledetta! Again! He feels like he's in one of those bumper cars at Luna Park.

This time a policeman does appear. Serves her right. Sofia gets out of the car to reason with him and of course he's no match for this uber-chic astrophysicist turned shop proprietor. I'm taking my friend to the clinic. It is an urgent matter. You will excuse me for driving so fast but there is no one on the road at this hour and under the circumstances... And then the policeman turns his head to see Marina get out of the car. Elio shakes his head. She is hardly a credible invalid. But from the minute her red stilettos hit the pavement, the policeman's enthralled. And because he's also confused he forgets why he stopped them. He listens, nods, kisses Marina's hand and wishes her well. He tells her his grandmother has just been treated for an advanced stage of ovarian cancer. She had a burning sensation for so many years and no one diagnosed it until she found a remarkably capable *dottoressa* in Siena. The tumor was large, mostly malignant, and pressing on her bladder. When they removed it, they found it had clean edges, and she is as spry as ever. Sofia's initial look of relief turns to compassion as she places her hand on the young man. But Sofia needn't worry; his grandmother still wakes up at four o'clock every morning to make *garganelli* and *paccheri* by hand. And then she walks with her cane to her favorite bar where she has a crush on the young owner, only recently arrived from Lebanon.

"I give her her manicures," says the policeman, admiring Sofia's pearl-tipped fingers. "I don't do it well but she likes that I hold her hand and brush a little color on. It's a little thing but it makes her feel..."

"Special," Sofia finishes his sentence. "She is lucky to have you as a grandson." By now Elio feels uncomfortable, desiring to engage but having not a clue how to do so.

Perhaps this is why our civilization has survived two thousand years, he muses as the two women get back in the car and they are once again clinic bound. He has always shrugged his shoulders at the state of Italian politics, same as his father, his grandfather and his ancestors before him. But the Italian Republic was only formed in 1946, his logical wife will say. As a republic we are still young and finding our way. It's astounding we survive at all, given our succession of ineffective goverments run by self-serving men.

29

ELIO CAN REMEMBER ONLY ONE OTHER TIME in his life when a place, a building, a structure, literally took his breath away: the Écoles des Parfumeurs in Grasse. He had been a boy then, but the sensations come back now as they stand back and take in the grand façade. Like the four enchanted actors in *The Wizard of Oz*, they walk somewhat cautiously toward one of the world's most formidable medical centers.

Today's modern clinics impress, but the Ospedale Trento di Verona dazzles. Not so much a hospital as a city of the future, an evolving and dynamic community in full dialogue with the river that runs alongside it and the romanticized city beyond.

The buildings expand and shimmer like ice sculptures at the Winter Olympics. Structures festooned with sleek and unexpected architectural details connect around a park of fountains, flowers and trees more indigenous to the tropics than the northeast corner of Italy. Nurses and interns sit on stone benches and read to patients from iPads. Orderlies push wheelchairs with a leisure stride. A slate and limestone path winds its way around a Zen rock garden toward wide marble stairs and an entrance where indoors and outdoors blend into one. It says clean. It says efficient. It says, *I am world renowned.* And it makes all the sense in the world that Marina would have chosen it.

They walk up the wide staircase to a platform seemingly walled, but isn't. Open spaces cut into white walls. Ceiling soar. Doors are of glass. They follow pearly white tiles through a rectangular opening into the most futuristic reception area Elio has ever seen. If one could imagine a place suspended in air, he was now inside it. A petite Indian woman in a turquoise sari, with a small diamond in her nose, emerges from who knows where and holds out her hand. She smells of marzipan.

"Good afternoon and welcome to the Ospedale. I am Sarina, your medical concierge." She shakes their hands and speaks slowly in a cultivated English accent. "Marina, Mr. and Mrs. Barati, please follow me."

She lowers her head, turns and leads them through another set of glass doors, into a sunny room whose glass walls look out over a Japanese garden. The white canvas sofa and sculpted plastic chairs would not have been out of place in a gallery. Botanical prints on walls. A pitcher of water with lemons and herbs. Soft music plays from somewhere unseen. Although he can't detect them, he feels the soothing effects of lavender and sage. On a round mirrored table by the entrance is a bowl of white ostrich eggs. Her computer screen flashes pictures of the Serengeti. There is nothing superfluous, not even an extra sheet of paper on the her desk, which is a lovely dark wood, like her chair. She invites them to sit down and does so herself. Her eyes are lovely—the most talkative part of her, he decides—and sits erect in his chair.

This room could be in an entirely different place. In the tropics, in Manila. In Africa. It's distinctively un-Italian. Marina, you have done it again. He fights back the impulse to relax, and just as he's about to ask a question, a wiry Indian gentleman pushes through the glass door, wearing a flowing white linen tunic and mint green trousers that pool around his ankles. He holds out a small wood tray with three damp rolled up white towels. They smell heavenly. Lemon grass.

"This is Solly," says Sarina with a gracious sweep of her hand.

Using a small utensil Solly unfurls and hands a towel to each of them. They wipe their hands and place the towels back on the tray. Elio holds his fingertips to his nose and breathes deep. He's no longer anxious. He never wants to leave.

"Would you all like some tea?" ask Sarina.

So mellow now, they nod. They would say yes to anything.

"Earl Gray or Darjeeling?"

Oof. A decision to make. Elio and Marina shrug.

"We'll all have Darjeeling," says Sofia, taking control, leading them. Elio and Marina know nothing about teas. Black, white, green—they are all the same, boiling water with a pleasant scent but something to drink only when one is sick.

"It's my choice as well. Solly will bring us some." She nods at the young man, whose teeth gleam whiter than the walls, before he exits through the glass doors and enters the stream of medical personnel in crisp white coats and fashionable shoes. They all seem so alert and so terribly young. Arms hold iPads as they swing past.

Sofia and Marina are otherwise engaged as they gush over the scent of lemongrass, the contemporary fabrics, the minimalist décor. Elio swivels his head back to see Sarina type very fast. She asks for Marina's full name and birth date. Marina's too distracted by a malachite elephant sculpture to hear the question, so Elio answers for her. Sarina frowns and then at the screen. What is she typing? Far too many letters for a mere name and a birthdate. She looks up at Marina, types furiously. What has she witnessed in Marina's gait, in her eyes, in the tone of her skin? Does she look healthy? Or does she radiate something which provokes alarm? If only he could lean over and read the screen.

"Address?"

Marina, still holding the malachite elephant, gives her the addresses of both her flat and her business. Sarina's fingers fly again, inspired, as if she's composing a short story out of Marina's abrupt responses. And it is at this point that the glass door swings open again. A tall man in a white labcoat enters. His very presence gives him away, and Marina immediately snaps to attention.

Elio has stood up. So has everyone else. Widely spaced, pale gray eyes behind silver-rimmed spectacles. Warm, gold toned skin. A calm voice. Hands grasp other hands. Does Marina have to stare up so adoringly? But Elio does so too.

"Marina, what a pleasure to see you. You look lovely as always. Hello, Mr. Barati, Mrs. Barati. It's kind of you both to accompany Marina." A slight accent but Elio can't place it. From his appearance, maybe somewhere in the French West Indies.

Doctor Charlot Duplessis waves them into their seats. Sofia obliges, but leans forward. All right, Sofia, do you also have to stare at him like he's some sort of deity? "We wouldn't have dreamed of having her make this difficult trip on her own."

"Yes, that's always a good idea. The support of family and friends is so critical at a juncture such as this one."

Elio's shoulders jerk.

The doctor pauses; he's just realized his mistake.

"I'm sorry. I didn't mean to alarm you, Mr. Barati. By juncture I mean at this point—when after considering all the variables, the possibilities and the risks, we are even more confident that we have chosen the right course of treatment for Marina. For both her health and the way she wants to live. We consider the whole person, not only the illness."

He pauses. They adjust in their seats without saying a word. He adds calmly, "I ran into Solly and ordered up some of our almond cakes, just baked this morning in our bakery."

Elio shoots a disapproving look at Sofia, who ignores him and smiles at the doctor. "That sounds absolutely delicious. Thank you."

Sarina fixes her sari, reaches for the paper that slides noiselessly out of the printer. She hands it to the doctor just as Solly pushes a silver tray through the door. On it is a teapot, blue and white English china cups, one silver bowl with cubes of sugar and another with slices of lemon.

"Thank you, Solly."

Solly places the tray on the glass table, carefully lifts each cup and pours the tea.

"I promise we will make this as painless as possible, Mr. Barati. Please put your worries aside. You're here for a number of days and we don't want to make your stay unpleasant."

"Milk or lemon?" asks Solly.

"We all take lemon and one sugar. And if he wants an unpleasant stay, he will have one. It's his nature."

"Marina, please."

She smirks. Funny how she takes the teacup from Solly's hand and stirs her tea as if she's accustomed to doing this.

Using small tongs, Solly drops a slice of lemon and a cube of sugar into a second cup and hands it to the doctor, who gives it to Sofia.

"That is our philosophy here. Every patient is an individual. No two cases are like. When we study medicine we learn that every organism is unique. The basic physiology of the human body is what it is. But within that there are nuances and quirks in all of us."

He passes the next two cups to Elio and Sarina, then accepts one from Solly for himself. He stirs thoughtfully. "We do all we can."

His cool demeanor is starting to annoy Elio. "And what if all you can is not enough?"

Sofia rubs a hand over her eyes.

"That's a fair question, Mr. Barati. Do not for a minute be concerned about raising it. May I?"

Marina nods and slides over a bit so he can sit next to her. He cradles his tea cup in his hand, looks down and then around at all of them.

"Here is where we are. Marina received her initial prognosis in Florence only a few months ago. Her doctor is a highly competent oncologist, and his prognoses are almost always on the mark. I say that with some caution, because medicine is an art as much as it is a science. Part of the appeal of the profession, I would say. Anyway, the initial biopsy revealed malignant cells."

"When was this biopsy, Marina? I was never told."

"Shut up, Elio. I didn't tell anyone. There was no need."

Sofia kicks her leg back and forth like she always does when she's upset. "It's just that we would have been there for you, Marina, we never knew..."

"And you didn't need to know, Sofia. It was a biopsy. That's all. An outpatient procedure. I went to a Sting concert on the same night, for God's sakes."

Sofia stifles a laugh; the doctor seems relieved.

Are they all mad? Still, it's re-assuring that the surgeon can smile. And the smiles grow wider as the almond cakes arrive, moist and delicious and reminiscent of his grandmother's fresh baked *amaretti* with a touch of Amaretto di Saronno liqueur. They all bite in, dipping the cakes into their tea, and the conversation turns to Verona and the architectural wonder of the hospital. It draws experts from every corner of the globe—a European cancer center of excellence.

"To re-assure you both, Mr. and Mrs. Barati—I know Marina needs no re-assurance—but this hospital recently published a study of 226 women with early stage breast cancer who received but a single dose of IORT during surgery. And after a mean follow-up of just four years there was just one local recurrence."

Sofia gives a cautionary glance at Elio, but Marina winks at her beloved physician. "And that is why I came here. Thank you for re-assuring them. You can't imagine what it's been like. I feel like I have two mothers on my case."

"As well they should be. We are physicians not gods. We are imperfect too, but we are here to serve our patients and we invite you to question us as you feel you need and to challenge us to do our best. And—in the end, it's the support network you have at home that will save your life, Marina."

They all nod. What is one to say?

The doctor puts his hand out for Marina's teacup, which she relinquishes, reluctantly. "Well, listen, we need to get you into a hospital robe and send you down for a few tests."

"You mean I can't hang out here all day?"

That not so subtle flirtation she gets away with so seamlessly.

"Absolutely not. We were actually thinking you should spend the night."

He ignores their questioning eyes.

"It's just that your surgery is very early in the morning and it's best you settle in here, into the Zen of the moment, so to speak. There's less background noise here. Less stress, less anxiety. The more you clear your head of all of that, the more successful your surgery and your treatment will be."

Nonsense.

"Trust me, you will not regret it. Our beds are as comfortable as they are at *Il Residence,* your room overlooks the garden, the staff is exceptional, and we serve a five-star cuisine that rivals some of Verona's best restaurants."

"If you say so."

"I do. We want to monitor you carefully, check your vital signs throughout the day and night, have you get your head into it all. We do a bit of yoga and meditation both at night and in the morning."

"Yoga? Me?"

"You're flexible enough and we believe it's best for our clients to be centered and relaxed. From the minute you walked through the doors of the Ospedale, you entered your journey of healing. We don't want to break that momentum. You're here. Your mind is made up. And the healing is about to begin. Do we all agree?"

And with those cool gray eyes scanning the room, then resting on each one of them, all they can do is nod. Yes, the healing has begun. There is no denying it. But they are not too resigned to accept another tray of almond cakes that Solly passes around.

THEY SAY LAUGHTER IS THERAPY. They say it helps heal both souls and tumors and all sorts of things that turn our lives inside out. If that is true, then this moment is doing its share in curing Maria of her cancer. She's laughing like he's never seen her laugh before. Tears stream down her cheeks.

"I can do this. Watch."

Elio twists his rigid torso around on the yoga mat while Sofia and Marina on either side slide effortlessly into positions that make it seem they have no bones, no joints, and no capacity for pain. He, on the other hand, has plenty of capacity. It's pain tolerance he doesn't have. He winces as he stretches his arms and legs out and lays his back on a plastic mat that smells invitingly of lavender. He fumbles again with the Mexican style blanket under his feet, which he was supposed to have folded in fours and it's now unfolding in all sorts of strange ways and he can't manage to make it look right. He has two styrofoam blocks that he's to stack on either side of him. But somehow his set looks nothing like everyone else's. Are they to go vertical or horizontal? All he hears around him is soft music and deep breathing. He's the only one who seems to be out of sync. Marina stretches out her limbs blissfully but he sees her chest shake up and down as she stifles more laughter.

"I would never in a million years have imagined this, Elio."

"Neither would I," adds Marina's co-conspirator, his wife.

"Listen to your breath," says Tanya, the instructor who is half Elio's age and half his weight and who has now decided it's unacceptable that he hasn't pressed his entire body from shoulders to toes up along the wall. The only part of his body to rest on the mat would be his head. Thank God. He could never do a head stand.

Yet, everyone else in the room is now pressed against the brick wall from shoulders to toes. Some actually do stand on their heads and balance on their hands. Sofia and Marina have opted for the head on the mat position. He can't even do that. He's flat on his back, legs up at a right angle with his feet against the wall. He feels fine. He wants to, and can, take a nap. But Tanya will have none of it. She moves in closer, her apricot painted toes touch his mat. He feels a light breeze as her hands reach out. If he keeps his eyes closed, he won't know what's happening.

"Just relax, Elio," she says, and lifts his feet from the wall.

"Okay, okay." *What does she think she's doing?* He stiffens, makes her job harder.

"Yoga breath."

"All right, all right, but it's not so easy."

He still hasn't figured out how it works, but he lets his diaphragm expand and then releases the air out, softly but with force. And he does it again and again until his shoulders seem to melt into the mat. He takes deeper breaths. It all seems so backwards but he does feel himself loosening up. The tension around his neck is no more. He hears his own breath, and for some reason, its sound comforts him.

Around him all is dark except for white scented candles on a window ledge. The scent of lemongrass fills the room. He adores it. There is a soft chanting in the background, a melody he can't place. He senses shadows of people around him, stretching and breathing on mats. It matters little who they are, what they look like, what they do, and what they think of him, or of anything in particular.

Marina and Sofia dream away, bodies pressed to the brick wall. Eyes closed. Their heads on their mats, cleared of thoughts and of worries. Their breaths soft as a whisper. All is suspended even though it continues to exist, who knows where. He dreams of water and wind, and stone, and rolling seas and of the light in Greece. He thinks of Sofia's celadon eyes, and Romina's quirky sense of style, and the calla lilies like white trumpets outside YaYa's house. He wonders if the shop is something to hold on to or if it's time to let it go. What if the shop itself was whipped away inside a tornado like in *The Wizard of Oz?* Maybe then he would be free to take that trip to Morocco Sofia has always talked about. He's always wanted to roam at dusk through the narrow streets of a medina in Fez while an imam sings the evening prayer from a mosque whose minarets are suffused with a soft golden light. He wants to run his hand along blue and white Iznik tiles and pick out the smallest imperfections, the irregularities in their colors. Their illusion of symmetry against glossy white. Swirls, lots of them. But maybe I could stay here a little longer, a few more hours, a few more days.

And he is sliding, his legs are pulled and lifted effortlessly. They are now guided up up along the wall. He knows Tanya is holding his feet but he barely senses her hands. And like a rag doll he moves. Until he is against the wall, all of him but his head on the lavender-scented mat. As she lets go he stays there and he breathes again, out and in, the reverse of what he'd always done, the opposite of what has always made sense until now.

30

"It's easy to say there was only one recurrence. That's like saying it has a ninety-five percent success rate, which means nothing if you're part of the five percent." He saws away at his *vitello tonnato* and pops a piece in his mouth. It's not bad but it could be better.

"Enough, Elio. You are making me crazy with your paranoia."

"I simply don't see how you can be so calm."

"*You* were calm. At the hospital. You were calm the whole time once Marina went into surgery. Now we're having lunch and you're bringing up every possible thing that could go wrong. *What* is your problem!"

And she does something she's never done before, crumples up her napkin and throws it at him.

Of course it doesn't travel far and lands next to his wine glass, which is begging for a refill. But she's not finished.

"What really troubles me about this, Elio, isn't even that you're being so hopeless and so negative when Marina needs us to be strong for her, it's..."

She turns her head abruptly, refuses to look at him. "It's just that I wonder, if it were me that had this cancer, would you care as much, be this obsessive, this crazy?"

He puts down his knife and fork. This is so unlike Sofia. She had been unusually quiet when they strolled over here. It was unlike her not to want to stop inside the Arena and walk up to the top tier to see the entire city radiating from its historic core. It was unlike her not to want to linger along Via Mazzini and scout the newest fashion finds. Just yesterday she'd remarked she had her eye on a studded handbag from

Valentino. And she's on a quest for curtain fabric, an endeavor that's likely to set them back a few thousand euros. But now her lovely eyes look wet. He's undoubtedly done something very wrong.

"Sofia *cara*, what are you saying? I would be devastated if that were you in the operating room right now."

She wipes her eyes awkwardly and shakes her head.

"Would you? Would you have grilled the doctor the same way? Would you have come up with so many repetitious and lame questions? Would you have panicked at the very thought that the treatment *might* not be successful, a year from now, five years from now, *ten* years from now?" She clenches her fist. "I'm sorry. I'm being foolish."

But the tears spill and he hasn't a clue what to do. Outbursts of emotion are his thing, not Sofia's. He was always the one to feel envious, especially around some of her younger astrophysicist colleagues who'd occasionally come by the shop and invite them to dine on the stone terrazza at Il Salviatino, a restored fourteenth-century palazzo in Fiesole, from which they could all stare up at the night sky and make predictions about the next asteroid to hit earth or an imminent galaxy siting.

Elio would sink back into his chair, *aperitivo* in hand, as the pianist Carlo let his fingers succumb to the melody of the moment. Meanwhile the star scientists dissected the universe with theories, new data, and the occasional flippant remark. According to Sofia, the mouse galaxies were more fascinating than other galaxies because of their peculiar colors. Their tails started out blue and terminated in a yellowish color while every other spiral galaxy started out yellow and terminated in a bluish color. Why this made a smidgeon of difference, Elio didn't know, but he found himself tuning into every word and hand flourish when she explained the phenomena of these mouse galaxies that were constantly colliding against each other for over 290 million years. "Not unlike life, relationships, marriages," she'd remarked. "The universe is our road map. It just stretches out over millions of years instead of our meager string of centuries. Compared to the universe it's as if we barely exist at all, barely a pinprick in the dark sky."

Even though she abandoned both astronomy and astrophysics so many years ago, Sofia remains enthralled by the mysteries of the night dome. That infernal telescope on their terrace in Castellina is her most prized possession. Once when a tornado-like windstorm hit Castellina, she refused to come inside without the telescope. He's convinced that if the house were to catch fire, she'd rush to salvage the telescope and let everything else burn: jewelry, clothing or even their family photo albums.

When the fiery Chelyabinsk meteor hit Russia she immediately invited Marcello and Silvia, two of her astronomer friends, over to the house so they could talk well into the morning hours about the probabilities of future asteroid strikes. While they were appalled by the casualties, frisson ignited in their voices. Space had at once become real and palpable even beyond their rarified astro-circle. It was no longer in the abstract, no longer a block buster film fiction fantasy. This gave heft to their field of study and their passionate commitment to its evolution. Elio had to admit, while the terminology confused him, the overall conversation did not. He listened with the guileless curiosity of a schoolboy. The small asteroid had apparently entered Earth's atmosphere over Russia at an estimated speed of around 41,000 miles per hour, approximately fifty times the speed of sound, and in an instant, morphed into a sizzling superbolide meteor. That alone made Elio experience a level of wonder he hadn't experienced since he was a boy. Imagine the dazzling light of that meteor, a fireball brighter than the sun, radiating intense heat, casting immense moving shadows over Chelyabinsk. Because it moved so fast, Sofia told him, and entered at a shallow atmospheric angle, it exploded. Just one bright flash, spewing out small fragmentary meteorites like so many fireworks and sending a powerful shock wave through the atmosphere. Over fifteen hundred people were hit by shards of broken glass from windows blown out by the shockwave.

But it was always in those moments that he questioned himself, and her. Was he interesting enough? How could he be, without the education or the intellectual mooring that made her so engaging in every social situation? There was barely a topic Sofia was not well versed in, and she had an infinite capacity to impress new acquaintances and even old friends with information she would gather, from an article, a simple conversation, or an observation set inside a context that suddenly had a relevance it didn't have before. How does she do it? Is she really that much more brilliant than he could ever become? Or is it simply that her passion to know was more substantive than his own?

She looks away from him now, blinks back a renegade tear, her hand rubs the stem of her wine glass. She's not had too much to drink, very little in fact.

"I'm sorry, Elio. It's just that your reactions today. And yesterday. They bother me." She wipes her eyes. "When it comes to Marina you are always so passionate, so alive! I can't explain it. And, darling, I'm glad you are because she's my friend too, and I want more than anything for her to be well and lead a long life. But I see a passion for her you don't show to me."

Had a bomb exploded in Piazza Bra he could not have been more shaken. He almost wished it had. But leave it to Sofia, even in her distress, to put it out there so clearly and precisely.

All he can do is look down on at the table at the remnants of a pleasant but light meal. Some melon and prosciutto, the mediocre *vitello tonnato*, an exceptional tomato and basil bruschetta, olives, crusty bread. But Sofia has barely eaten.

He reaches for her hand but she yanks it away.

"Stop. Maybe you do, Elio. I'm not being fair. It's just that..."

"Ha! I told you that yoga stuff is bad for people."

"Elio, stop. Now you're making me laugh."

"Well, you should, because the very notion that I have lost my passion for you is so ridiculous it deserves a laugh."

She sighs. "Sometimes when I see you look at her, you get this expression, like you're still in love with her. Your eyes go all soft, and I see your mouth compress as if you're trying to hold something back. Or, it's as if, from a distance, you love her more than ever."

"You are the love of my life, Sofia."

"But she was the first."

"The second actually, and that was a long time ago, when I was still very young and very stupid."

"Not stupid. Uncontrollably and passionately in love with a very sexy, older married woman. I don't think that's so stupid, Elio. And I don't think your illicit and naïve affair with your teacher was stupid either. Intellectually I quite agree with it all. I would think it absolutely appropriate and marvelous had that adventurous young man not ended up as my husband today. Oh, I am such a hypocrite."

"Precisely. I'm going to order another bottle of wine."

"I'm fine, thank you."

"No, you're not or we wouldn't be having this conversation."

"Elio!" She flirts with him now, though she'll never acknowledge it.

"Really. But I'm quite enjoying being the object of jealousy. A love triangle with me in the center. That *is* reason to celebrate. I'm going to order the Amarone." He points to the name on the wine list with the heftiest price tag and holds it up for the waiter.

"You're mad. That's far too expensive and we'll never finish it."

"Speak for yourself. The evening has barely begun. We've left our only child at home to work in our shop while we indulge ourselves. Our dear friend is in a deep sleep in a clinic where she has a butler and a bed with 600-thread count Frette sheets. And we have a night entirely to ourselves."

"We have most nights entirely to ourselves. Our daughter is grown up."

"Yes, but tonight is a special night because we are away, and because my wife is jealous, and I intend to celebrate from now until who knows what time. Perhaps all night long. Maybe we should go out dancing."

"I repeat. You're mad. And you're a terrible dancer so I think I'll pass."

"I'm more sober than you because my alcohol tolerance is better. Look. Marina will be groggy all day tomorrow. Who wants to be around a groggy person after surgery? And she will be all gooey-eyed over Doctor Heartthrob. We can go see her at night. She doesn't need our company. In the daytime we should go on a *gita* into the country. We can get up early and drive out. Maybe rent vespas."

"How are you going to get up early if we go dancing tonight?"

"I thought you didn't want to go dancing."

She steeples her fingers, challenges him with those eyes. He loves that she doesn't protest as the sommelier fills her glass. Ah, the power of scent. The wine's bouquet is all too intoxicating, even for a empirical-minded scientist like his wife.

"*Oof!* I'll sleep it off. I only need four hours. You know that."

She narrows her eyes in that very sexy way she has.

"*Va bene.* I'm game. Do you want to go by Lago di Garda, or way up to Cortina D'Ampezzo and stare into some of those amazing alpine lakes where the reflection of the mountains in the water is as sharp and clear as the mountain itself?"

"Well, I guess I know where your preferences lie."

"You have to admit they are amazing. You look at the mountain above and its reflection below and inside the water you can see every crevice, every geological demarcation of color and shape. It's as if a master illustrator had sketched it below the surface of the earth."

He reaches into his back pocket and pulls out a brochure he'd picked up earlier.

"Here we are. *Villa Felice.* Love the name and it's surrounded by iris and lavender fields. Such a magnificent garden. Why don't we drive out now and stay the night?"

"Instead of dancing?"

"Enough with the dancing. Well—look, we can do anything we want so I'm throwing out all the ideas as they come."

"But sooner or later we have to decide. We have to make a rational choice."

"Or an irrational one."

"I'm not good at those. That's why I married you."

There is a reason Amarone is the jewel in the crown of the Veneto's wine-making empire. It loosens the tongue so one starts to think and speak like a poet. And, more than any other wine, even more than his cherished Brunello, it makes one brave and truthful.

"Besides, Elio, it's too late to check out of the Residenza. We'll have to pay for the night. And we don't even know if your Villa Felice has a room available. We're entering the high season. By the way, that's your third glass of wine."

"Really? I've lost count. My question is—why haven't you?"

She smiles, clinks her glass with his, and puts it down.

"Because I know I'm to be the one to drive us to your villa tonight. Too bad. I was hoping to help you finish this bottle."

31

"YOU DID *WHAT?*"

"Stop laughing, Romina. Or at least do you have to laugh so hard? I hear Claudio laughing too in the background. This will be all over Florence. I actually almost stood on my head. Sofia, tell her."

"I can't. I'm driving. And you didn't stand on your head."

"We have this bluetooth thing. Your hands are free. "

"But my mind is not. When I drive, I drive. Romina, your father did go the distance, or his interpretation of going the distance, in the yoga class until he fell asleep and had to be shaken awake by the instructor. She was pretty so he didn't mind so much."

In the background, Claudio says, "I wouldn't either." And then he lets out a yell because Romina probably jabbed him. How relaxed they seem. He wonders about the day's numbers. They're heading into peak tourist season and can't afford to be behind last year.

But he doesn't ask. There is little he can do from here, so he stares out the window into the not-so-quiet darkness. Sports cars zip by, their tail lights swirling like fireflies on speed. The occasional vespa leans in, light and fluid in its even glide. No cypress or sunflower sightings, no rolling velvet hills. No vineyards or manicured nature of any kind. Muted whiffs of flowers and greens mediate the assault of deisel fumes from rumbling trucks that cut them off yet again. Sofia presses down hard on her horn. "*Deficiente!*"

So what if he doesn't feel compelled to name the smells? They are what they are. They will make themselves known in due time.

Scent is more intuitive than intrusive. It alerts us to danger, to possibility, to uncontrollable urges, to that primal part of ourselves we try, with modest gains, to suppress. Perhaps it doesn't always need a name. Perhaps it never does.

He could easily fall asleep. But he's jolted back and forth by Sofia's jerky driving and the undulating road. She turns up the radio because she doesn't like him to talk when she drives, and she keeps a paper bag filled with chocolate truffles from Vestri so she can pop one in her mouth whenever she starts to feel sleepy. He hopes she'll leave at least one of the *gianduia* pieces for him. If not, so be it. He enjoys being alone with his thoughts as a spring wind blows in from his open window, annoying Sofia who tries unsuccessfully to tuck a renegade hair back into her chignon.

Tell me again why we are going to this place? she will want to know, and he'll indulge her with an answer, even though he knows she's enjoying the drive as much as he is. Truth is he doesn't know. He found the brochure about Villa Felice among others at the Ospedale's hospitality desk. It struck him as strange to find a hospitality concierge at a hospital, but it made sense given the number of friends and family members accompanying loved ones. They need the comfort such distractions provide, and the Veneto offered so many, from the limpid Lago di Garda with its lakeside towns and castle fortresses to the sculpted majesty of the Dolomites, its romantic Shakesperean cities and grand Palladian villas.

But for him, right now, and perhaps for Sofia too, a simpler countryside beckons. Countryside in the form of quiet roads and open fields that melt seamlessly into the volcanic Eugean hills, in vibrant gardens and old Venetian farmhouses and the scent of firewood from the dining hall inside the main villa as its owner opens the car door and welcomes them to his home, making it their home for two nights. And perhaps for Elio and Sofia, the car ride and the nights ahead were necessary. He had never considered before today that his marriage might not be on solid ground. But for some reason, as the lights of cars leaving the villa slide past like beads from a broken necklace, he thinks it might be. There had been a divide between them for quite some time now, not unlike the river Adige that ran through Verona, or the Arno back home that divided the commercial historic center from the grass-roots artisan district of San Frediano. Unspoken, distancing, subtle but profound.

When they spoke it was about the big questions: politics, climate change, the immorality of war. He watches the political billboards charge past and they both shout out their own commentary. They are both proponents of social justice. Well, that was very Florentine in the end. One could credit the Medici for the Renaissance but Elio prefers the other argument. That the Florentines, artisans and masters of critical thinking, have always been on the right side of history. It was fitting, then, that the dark ages would be extinguished by the bright light of this superior and art-inspired intellect.

We Florentines are and will always be progressives, unlike the Northern League in Lombardia. We welcome our immigrants, not as wholeheartedly as we should since we don't understand them, but we are better than most. Nor are we as irresponsible as the *meridionali* of Lazio. We pay our taxes, stop at traffic lights, give up our seats to the elderly. We are a trustworthy lot. We don't cheat one another and we believe in an honest day's work whatever ones circumstances. So there is so much to discuss, and one could pour glass after glass of Brunello, and clear away the dinner dishes and retreat later into two separate rooms, he to his stylish recliner—Sofia would have it no other way—in the living room with the television and a *partita*. She, with a novel by Czeslaw Milosz in the music room of their Florence flat or at her telescope on the terrazza in Castellina. She would, halfheartedly, offer to make him a cup of chamomile to help him sleep, and he would say, yes, and never touch it but leave the cup on the table for her to clear away afterwards. She hated doing that. She preferred instead to spend hours on the terrazza, going from the telescope to her chair beside the potted geraniums and the lilacs that smelled magical on spring nights. What did she think of then, while the stars gathered, like eyewitnesses, in the night sky?

32

FOR ELIO THE IRIS ROOT WOULD ALWAYS remind him of his childhood, not unlike Proust's madeline, or the lemons of Sicily for his mother, who kept a bowl of them on the center of their dining table. The bracing scent of lavender aftershave gave his cautious father the emotional prowess to face each day's confrontations. But the iris root had always been Elio's alone to understand and define.

Until now. Sofia has her own interpretation, insisting as always it's the right one. "I pick up more in the root, Elio. Chestnuts, pine, thyme. Take a deeper breath. Maybe you're not picking this up because I'm younger than you."

"Ouch."

They are in the sprawling iris gardens outside the villa, whose warm stucco walls are just now reflecting the light of the rising sun. Since it sits high in one of the hills, it catches the sun first while a pleasant morning chill lingers over the bountiful English gardens. He likes that they're alone. With so many conflicting thoughts moving about in his head, he's not in the mood for light conversation.

"Just offering up some answers. Our sense of smell diminishes with age. Fact of life. What can we do? Smell it again."

Now, that she mentions it, yes, he detects a hint of chestnut, even of mint and basil in the iris root he holds in his hand. It recalls the ever-pervasive vapors of his mother's linen chest, his iris gardens in the earliest days of spring, and later when they bloom en masse.

"I wonder why anyone cultivates the orris root for commerce anymore, Elio. It's lovely but—if it's so expensive to grow and it doesn't make much money…" She squints up at the sun and puts on her wide-brimmed straw hat.

"Still, the iris is precious and if we let it die, we die with it in a way."

"That is a bit melodramatic." But even so, she kneels down to sniff a pale blue iris pallida with her eyes closed. "I can't decide which floral smell I most prefer. I always thought the lilac or the peony. Both, opulent and heady. But there is something both distinctive and understated about the iris."

"It ressembles the violet in a way."

"Not at all. The violet is a bit of a tease. The iris…hmm."

"*Hmm* what? What are you thinking?"

"The iris is equally sexy but more thoughtful. This is an intelligent flower, one with a purpose beyond its romantic appeal."

"The romantic appeal is quite important."

"I'm not dismissing that. Intelligence and romance are compatible bedfellows. This one smells glorious. It has that earthy vineyard smell that one associates with the hardiest strain of irises."

"Some of ours smell just as good. Better."

"You only say that because you think we have a claim to the flower other provinces don't. But nature doesn't work in provinces, or for the Commune in Palazzo Vecchio. Nature doesn't care that we commandeered the iris as our national emblem, plastered it all over our flags, reversed its colors because of a stupid civil war, and stamp it on every tourist knick-knack made in China. Nature does what nature does. As far as nature is concerned, your Tuscan irises are no different from the irises grown here. And if nature wants to grow irises in Morocco or India, nature will do so."

"What about Tommaso?" Elio asks, thinking about their friend down the road from their country house. "He works like a demon in his fields and he still cultivates the old-fashioned way. He should think about retiring soon. So much work for so little return. At least that's what it looks like to me."

"Good old Tommaso. His work ethic is like no one else's. We should pay a visit. It's been so many years. We go on about our work, we merchants, while the creators like Tommaso keep us grounded. And don't talk about his retiring. You refuse to retire, why should he?"

He almost responds, but he's caught on something else. He's not a creator in her mind and, sadly, not even in his own. He stopped creating years ago.

When did it happen? When was that part of himself so willfully discarded? Was it after he left Grasse? Was it on the day he refused to sign the agreement that would have sold Profumeria Barati once and for all? Was it much later? After Romina was born? When his competitive nature took over, when he had to outperform all the other perfumery owners in the commercial sector? When he began to evaluate every year of his life according to revenue made and debts paid?

In his younger years the thoughts ran wild in his head, fresh ideas popping like champagne corks on New Year's Eve. The ideas never stopped. Over time he just got better at editing them or setting them aside. When responsibilities filled his day from the first brush of sunlight across the Arno to the amber light of dusk. It was only after admiring yet another marvelous sunset from Ponte Santa Trinita' that he would rest. Sometimes over a glass of grappa in the Fusion Bar at the Gallery Hotel Art, recognizing himself the oldest patron by a good forty years, he would consider the composition scribbled in a notebook inside a credenza in his bedroom, along with several old amber vials held together with elastic bands, their contents rancid by now. Missed opportunities in liquid form. An idea rendered lifeless. This is the way a writer lives, manuscripts buried under folded white business shirts or tucked behind cannisters of flour and sugar on a kitchen shelf. Objects never discarded but moved from place to place until they're forgotten.

What would he think of his perfume today? Would it speak to him at all? Would he be able to tease out the nuances the way he did back then? Would he defend it with the same resolve? But most important, would it smell like the Grasse jasmine engraved forever in his memory ?

The morning light moves over the flowers in a silvery gold wash. The roses smell heavenly, and the hyacinths and peonies pop with color across the velvet green field. Some stir in the breeze. But the iris stands tall, impervious to what's around her. The Grand Dame of the fields. The other grand dame, Sofia, studies each flower as if she were researching a dissertation. All she's missing is a microscope, even though her eyes are as keen as the sharpest and most modern lenses. This is a garden not a laboratory, he wants to say, as she rubs an iris root between her fingers.

But these fields are a triumph of both science and art, she will respond, a necessary collaboration. Art alone could not produce, much less sustain, such a garden. Regardless of color, produce or floral preferences, you still have to plant according to the seasons and the whims of weather patterns that today shift as easily as an adolescent's moods. Horticulture is an art intimately connected to science at every turn, and equally connected to business. It has given us modern methods and machinery and sharper insights into the way flowers and all plants grow and thrive. You have used science to your benefit, Elio, in more ways than you recognize.

This conversation playing out inside his head becomes real when Sophia introduces him to Alba, a white-haired woman in her seventies wearing chic square-rimmed black glasses and a floaty black dress that drapes over a slim girlish figure. Alba manages La Felice. She is a gardener, a horticulturalist, a chef, and a musician.

"Can you add more talents to the mix?" Sofia asks gleefully.

"They are all related in a way. *Cara*, I did the same thing for so many years. Advertising. Marketing. Offices in Milan and New York. Unfaithful husbands. Tyrannical children. BlackBerries. Cellphones. You name it. But I ended up here. My latest and perhaps my last venture. It was a roundabout course."

"What prompted you to leave advertising?"

"Oh, nothing prompted me. I was fired."

"Oh."

"Funny how that always makes people uncomfortable. I saw it as a sign."

"A sign."

"Yes. A sign to chuck it all and move on. But I always found solace in my kitchen and in my garden. And then I met Sergio and a sort of magic happened. Not the sexual kind. But the culinary and the gardening kind."

This is said with the aplomb of a much younger woman, and the grace of a much older one. And even though her moderately tanned face wears a criss-cross of lines and freckles, Elio finds himself drawn to her. Someone else for Sofia to be envious of.

"Sergio and I decided to open a cooking school in a fifteenth-century villa in Vicenza. It had marvelous, frescoed ceilings, a number of sleeping rooms, a garden that needed tending, three wood-fired ovens, olive trees, a vineyard, and a bocce court. That was our first foray into the world of tourism. We still have the school, in addition to the villa. In both places, I let Sergio handle the kitchen and I took on the garden. Something happens when I put my gloves on and dig into the earth. I feel absolutely invincible."

She invites them to breakfast in a loggia overlooking the garden and the swimming pool. Its elegant simplicity, stucco walls, beamed wood ceiling, white linen tablecloths, the perfect setting for the meal they're about to share: *caffè latte, cornetti* filled with honey, and a basket of peaches and grapes. The air is wonderfully transparent. Prickles of scent from an herb garden—sage, rosemary, basil, oregano—make Elio imagine crushing and sprinkling some into his soft boiled egg. And Alba will not stop talking.

"We made a decision at one point about Villa Felice— because that's what it is for me, a place where I am always felice, *joyful.* I have only the things that promote felicita: my piano, my books, my plants and my kitchen. I don't know what else one needs. Do you?"

"My wife would say a telescope."

"But only if you truly understand the stars. You would get bored with it."

"Are you an astronomer?"

"Yes, but also astrophysicist. But only on an amateur level. It was my field of study at the university. Elio and I own a perfumery in Florence."

"Ahhh. An old-fashioned one, I hope, with all those lovely atomizers and irises in the window."

"It's a blend of the old and the new. Elio will not have it any other way. He knows fragrance like no one else. He even has a perfumer's organ in the back."

"Really? A real perfumer's organ with oils and vials and scent strips?"

"The entire operation, in mahogany."

"How interesting. Did you ever—?"

"Yes."

"Yes, what?"

"Yes! I did once entertain the notion of being a perfumer, an actual creator of scent." He hears irritation in his voice.

She seems amused. "That was not my question."

"What was it then?"

"Were you at one time an actual perfumer?" She smiled. "You see, your wife studied to be an astrophysicist but became a merchant instead. A merchant who still loves her *métier*, so she engages in it as a hobby, staring into her telescope at night. You have an actual perfumer's organ in your shop, you smell different oils and put them together, so I naturally assumed your life had followed the same pattern."

"Well, I did study for awhile but then..." He turns his attention back to the irises.

"Life takes over. I know. It did with me too. For me it was all about greed. Would love to say it was only about obligation. That was part of it. But my three children would have been better off had I run a cooking school or studied horticulture. I spent so much time away from them, on business trips to luxurious places with an expense account that would make your hair stand on end. I wasn't happy but I liked the salary. I would fly to Milan and shop the showrooms, and we would vacation in five-star properties. *Bella vita*, as my mother would say. No wonder my husbands were all philanderers. They were by nature, likely, but my perpetual absence helped them along."

She nods at a waiter who fills their crystal goblets with blood orange juice from a ceramic pitcher the color of sunflowers. It's amazing how soft the voices around them are. No one speaks above any one else. Of course there are no other guests. It's only Sofia, him, and the staff. One can hear the flutter of birds' wings and the familiar kitchen sounds of china and cutlery being stacked and stored. There's a faint scent of baking, a crostada perhaps. Given the presence of so many fruit trees it would not surprise him.

"So, Alba, you were saying you'd made a decision about Villa Felice."

"Yes, Sofia. We decided to turn it into an organic farm. We've been so profitable I thought it was time to give back to the earth that has been so generous to us. And I want to do my part to help our planet while I still can. Sergio and I were going over our numbers one day, which weren't as strong as the prior year, and decided to throw ourselves on those hammocks out there and think creatively about what we might do."

"I think better in a hammock too." Elio takes a deep breath and a whiff of lilac tickles his nose.

"And on that hammock, Sergio reminded me that we had a legacy to protect and an opportunity to do something meaningful. We want this nature to be here for them."

Alba smiles at two small children who catapult into the pool, splashing water around. The light spray feels good. Alba has such lovely blue-green eyes. So do they. They must be her grandchildren.

"We were lucky. The villa was initially restored according to the highest standards of biological architecture. The owners were ahead of the trend. Our agricultural production has always been organic but now, as Sergio and I decided that afternoon, we're going to make it a full-circle organic farm. We have fruit trees, vegetable gardens, cattle. It's a new phase for us. But an important one. As one grows older, one wants to continue to work, but one works for different reasons."

"And it's good to take stock of those reasons from time to time," says Sofia, her focus taking in the hazelnut trees and nineteenth-century garden, which becomes more romantic the longer they are outside. "Sometimes those reasons reveal themselves gradually, the way the magic of this place reveals itself. It's quietly taking hold. Don't you think so, Elio?"

Of course he's stopped listening. He walks over by the pool edge and looks in. He wonders if it's too early and too cold to take a swim. It's not quite summer yet. He dips his toe in. It's cold. But the sun glitters on the water's surface, brilliant turquoise ripples. The children do somersaults, loping about like salamanders below the water's surface. They splash him and shout out that they're sorry. All he can do is slip out of his clothes as he'd put on his bathing trunks without Sofia knowing, and walk down the ladder.

He feels cold shock waves all over his skin as he descends, very slowly. He has only the option of diving in, start swimming fast, before his lips turn blue.

So he does.

33

ALBA AND SERGIO SEND THEM OFF with lunch baskets, a bottle of Prosecco di Valdobiaddene, and bunches of blue and white irises tucked inside, the latter of which Elio assumes they will have to leave at the Ospedale since they won't survive the trip back to Florence. But Alba insists because they're her favorite flower too, and giving irises is a gesture of friendship. It means the recipient is bound to return to Villa Felice at some point in time—a tradition Alba herself has created. "Because they are becoming as precious here as they are in Tuscany, and as precious as friendship. So we should enjoy them while we can. *Arrivederci.*"

On the road all Elio can think about is the irises. A sudden phone call from Marina disrupts his reverie—Sofia picks up—she's recovering quite nicely. She's had a full breakfast and is doing some killer stretching exercises. Dr. Charlot Duplessis will not let her rest, apparently. He's glad, but did she have to choose just this moment to tell them so?

"He knows how irritable I get when I can't be busy," Marina says over the static, "so I've signed up for a Tae Kwon Do class. Come here before it starts so I have an excuse to cancel."

"Not a chance. Elio is driving."

"Now, that's not fair, I don't drive as slow as she says."

"No. Slower. Anyway. You know how he is. He wants to drive past the Palladian villas and take in the scenery. It will take longer than our drive to Florence tomorrow."

"Well, I will not be coming home with you tomorrow. I'm doing very well but I need to rest up here for a week. Give the incision the time to heal."

"Are you sure there isn't another reason?"

"I'm not about to have an affair with my doctor, Sofia. Don't think it hasn't crossed my mind. Look at it this way. You and Elio can have a leisurely ride home. Maybe stop for a romantic night somewhere."

"We've already done that."

"Really? So do it again. Mid-afternoon is best. I want details. Elio, are you listening?"

"I'm driving."

"Better keep your eyes on the road then. Take your time. I'm fine here."

"What about the Tae Kwon Do class you want to miss?"

"I'm warming up to it."

MARINA'S GLOWING FACE makes him smile like a five-year-old at a carnival. She sits up against puffed feather pillows, surrounded by some of the most luxurious bed linens he's ever seen. No doubt she grilled the attendants on thread count, country of origin, fair trade practices, and anything else that enters her ever-energetic mind. She's perfectly coiffed, wears a white satin nightgown and a brilliant tangerine lipstick. No boring hospital gowns for Marina. Her silver breakfast tray sits on the windowsill beside multiple bouquets of flowers, the entirety of Florence's commercial sector represented in tiny cards tied with colorful grosgrain to the stems of lilies, irises, roses and their sturdier prerequisite, sunflowers. But the pervasive scent in the room is a mixture of soap and fresh linen.

"You look wonderful, Marina," Elio says, voice breaking in a way he hopes is noticeable only to him. He slides his hand into his pocket for his handkerchief just in case. It's all behind her now. It has to be. He feels his eyes well up.

Confirmation enters the room with the click of high heels, the smell of marzipan and the intrusion of a crisp citrus aftershave. Enter the victors, iPads in hand, Sarina and Doctor

Charlot, their smiles as sparkling white as their lab coats. And Elio notes yet again how very attractive they both are.

"A success?" Elio blurts out before he can stop himself, hand clutching handkerchief.

The doctor is taken aback only for a second. And then the smile returns. "Yes! The surgery was a success. We are very very happy with the outcome."

Elio sighs, closes his eyes, and feels the doctor pat his arm before attention shifts to his patient. He circles around them, takes Marina's hand and kisses it.

"Courageous from beginning to end."

"We had no doubt about that," says Sofia. "But what *was* the outcome? Were there any complications? We are both anxious to hear."

"It went very well, better than I'd imagined. And I went in feeling optimistic. Most important, when we removed the tumor the edges were clean. So we were all encouraged, elated actually, especially the oncology students brought in to observe."

"I never knew I would be an object of study," says Marina, sitting up even straighter. "All these good-looking young doctors around me as I went under. For a second I imagined I'd died and had arrived in Dante's Paradiso. I was delirious with joy."

"Probably from all the anesthesia," said Elio. *Why hasn't the doctor let go of her hand?* Charlot catches his eye and places her hand gently on the bed.

"Marina's was a special case. That's why I wanted my students there. The cancer was so contained, unusual after so much time has passed. The tumor hadn't grown much. And for awhile, if you recall even after the biopsy, the chief of oncology wasn't sure whether or not to call it a cancer."

"So, if the edges are clean, it definitely means the cancer hasn't spread." Elio wants to get back to the central point.

"All evidence is that the cancer hadn't metasticized. We thought that the case based on the biopsy, but no one really knows until surgery. The edges were clean, as I said, and I detected no renegade cells around it. Be sure, I searched for them with a vengeance. I went everywhere the needle biopsy went. I removed any sentinal lymph nodes that could have been affected." He raises Marina's arm to show them a small surgical scar. She flutters her eyelashes at him playfully.

Sofia needs to know more. "If you've taken out lymph nodes, will her immune system be compromised?"

"Given the risks and the choices I had to remove them. I'm not concerned about Marina's immune system. It's as hardy as the rest of her. She's a survivor. She takes good care of herself with her diet and exercise. She's a positive thinker, has high energy, and self-advocates like no one I know. That makes a difference. It may even have been a key reason the cancer didn't spread. I don't have an answer. But I do know that a lot of healing starts here." He points to his head.

"That's for sure," Sofia concurs. Elio is silent. *What if the mind wants to heal but the body can't?*

"And then, right after the surgery, we were able to deliver just that concentrated and precise dose of radiation with the Mobetron and kill any residual cancer cells before they had a chance to multiply," said the doctor as if he has just read Elio's mind. "Today we can do in two minutes what we used to do with weeks upon weeks of continued radiation treatments. And we don't attack healthy tissue in the process." He draws his fingertips together. He can't contain his own joy. "Mr. Barati, this technology is our answer to what was once an imperfect and, I believe, an inhumane solution."

"The imperfect solution being External Post Operative Radiation therapy," Sofia says.

"I can't tell you how happy it makes me to see a patient get the right treatment and in a hospital such as this one." His eyes rest on Marina again. "My sister did not survive her cancer. She had to make that very painful choice. Agree to a treatment that *might* cure her illness, while giving her an awful quality of life—or to just let nature take its course. Choosing to die, in effect."

"*Per la madonna*, if had it been the old way I would not have had treatment!" Marina is almost shouting, from euphoria or residual anxiety, who could tell? "Those treatments will kill you faster than the damn cancer. I would have gone on to enjoy my life with what little time I had." She smiles at Sarina and the doctor. "I'm over seventy. Anything more is a gift. So, I'm thinking I will still go to India. Better late than never."

A chilling look from Sofia keeps him from opening his mouth.

"I'm still impressed by the science, and the new technologies," she says, turning back to the medical staff. "That you were able to deliver such targeted radiation so quickly after surgery and with such precision."

"We used electron beams not x-rays," the doctor explains. "The electron beams improve dose distribution, limit penetration beyond the tumor bed, and deliver the required dose much more rapidly. The patient gets only what she needs, where and when she needs it. One treatment. That's it. Finished."

"Even medical science has to work at becoming more precise," says Sofia.

"And why wouldn't it? Medicine, like life, is both an art and a science, and a tireless and an often frustrating work in progress," Charlot says, his hand once again reaching for Marina's.

34

ELIO BARELY REMEMBERS LEAVING the Ospedale and turning on to the autostrada for the ride back to Florence. He remembers turning the steering wheel and the car into the direction of the wind. He remembers that Sofia's perfume took on a distancing but honeyed quality as she waxed on yet again about the miracles of science. He remembers the teasing vapors of Alba's irises bundled on the back seat. And he remembers the quality of Marina's voice. It had the tenor of nostalgia that set uneasily with him.

A stopover in Bologna for a a hearty *tagliatelle al ragu* and prosciutto sliced to just the right thickness makes him stand and stretch with sheer joy, even though Sofia decides he's not to drive any longer given the effect of the revered Sangiovese wine of Romagna. At that point he doesn't care what she or anyone says. Others' opinions of him matter nothing. He's inebriated for sure, but not only from the wine.

He vaguely recollects walking under the scholarly arches, stopping for a *macchiato* and a political discussion with a disgruntled local. Yes, Italy should stay the course. After the Berlusconi years, one had to rethink many things. We are in a time of transition, said the local, and who can you trust? Not the right. Not the left. And then there is Germany and the European Union and the masses of Chinese tourists one can't figure out. And the brutality in Syria with no one knowing what to do. And who knows what position our new Prime Minister, your mayor in Florence, will take, Elio? And life has become far too expensive. Think, that so many Italians are selling jewelry to pay their bills. Family gold in the form of communion crucifixes and dainty bracelets for newborns, and all those thick gold wedding bands that men slip off from time to time. Now they will not own them anymore so there's a problem solved. So do you think infidelity will become more prevalent? asks Elio of Sofia as he eyes an after-dinner glass of Amaro. Sofia shakes her head no and he negotiates for a gelato instead. She sighs as if she's just made a concession to a moody child.

He thinks he drank down the Amaro, slipped a chocolate bar into his backpack, which he then threw it into the backseat. Sofia scolded him for flirting with a college girl.

But the most vivid memory, one he will never shake, even inside the fog of his brain, is of Marina's reaction when the doctor touched her hand, of the doctor's face, flushed and rejuvenated, as if he were suddenly twenty not forty, of a slow erotic tension he could not define, and of the way she said good bye to Sofia and to Elio, as if it were for the last time.

He and Sofia get into the car. She lets him drive. She says nothing. He wants her to remark on what they've both just seen. The fact that she doesn't means his suspicions are true. So he turns his head away as he releases the clutch. Warm tears cloud his vision and he successfully blinks them away.

Sofia leans her head against the window and stares serenely at the passing scenery. He knows not to disturb her when she's lost in thought, instead driving at a faster speed than normal past more fields and rolling hills and exits for towns he's never heard of, past the AutoGrills and gas stations, and gradually the thick knot inside him starts to loosen and unravel as the road unfurls mile by mile. His suspicions shake loose. No point in holding on to them. They are what they are. What's going to happen is going to happen, Romina says. Elena said the same thing when she was Romina's age and a young mother in a claustrophobic marriage. Marina's life is hers. The treatment and the passions it rebirths have put her in a place where he, Elio, cannot follow. She is beyond his grasp. She has left him, pure and simple.

And still, even inside the cloud of confusion about Marina, about life, and mostly about himself, Elio remembers the gardens at Villa Felice, Alba's irises in the back, the cold water in the pool when he threw himself in, the gardens they drove past and the gardens they visited on a whim. It was, all of a sudden, all about the flowers, their histories, who cultivated them and why, their potential for their survival. How would climate change affect the fields over time? Did it make sense to cultivate for profit, or should one grow them for the simple joy of it all or perhaps simply to keep them alive? But what was the sense in that? Will there be a time when the Tuscan hills will no longer be carpeted with flowers, no yellow broom, no bursts of peonies or towering sunflowers. Precious, they are. More so than gemstones or oil because people didn't miss them as much. Not yet. People won't miss the flowers until it's too late. That's why his mother took such care. That's why his father, stiff old man that he was, said his most peaceful moments were in the gardens of Castellina. That's why Elio tends the beds as if they were his children, not always succeeding because he too has capitulated to a culture where one consumes and discards. His modest iris fields are precious too. More than he'd even realized. As precious as life itself must feel to Marina in this moment. Why hasn't he paid attention? There was no shaking off what he now knows. Like Marina, there will be no turning back.

A LITTLE LEARNING can be a dangerous thing, his father once said, probably in response to Elio's restless nature and need to explore everything about everything. But it was too late for ignorance. And, for some reason this morning, he does not have the patience for it. He pushes the bedroom shutters wide open before leaving the bedroom and walking downstairs into the kitchen. Sofia has placed a pitcher of sunflowers at the center of the table. She's sliced open one of her freshly made croissants and filled it with Nutella. A cluster of juicy red *frutti di bosco* nestle alongside. She looks delightful in a white linen dress and red sandals. Her hair is loose. Summer is arriving in Tuscany.

He picks up his mobile and thinks he should call Marina. Thank her for waking him up. Sofia rinses out her espresso cup and reaches for lipstick inside her handbag, pulling his attention in another direction.

"I've decided we should make a weekend trip," he says out of the blue.

"We just had a weekend away." She pulls out the lipstick.

"Not really."

"What do you mean, not really?" She swirls up the color, apricot, a good shade for her, and goes to the mirror. He hopes she won't pin her hair up today.

"Well. We only went to Verona."

"For you that's major."

"Good point but don't dwell on it. We should do something new."

She raises her eyebrow, applies her lipstick meticulously as always.

"We should go outside Italy. Another country."

"*You* go to another country?" She blots, checks herself out approvingly in the mirror.

"Yes, well not far. To France."

"Oh! Don't tempt me." She dreamily sits, rests her chin in her hand. "A Paris weekend?"

"I'm thinking Grasse. It's been so many years."

If she's disappointed, it doesn't show. "The south of France?" She gives a small sigh of pleasure. "Nice, Saint-Jean-Cap-Ferrat, Antibes."

"Villefranche-sur-Mer."

"Those pastel buildings set against that brilliant blue sea. *Une rêve!* I would somehow still like to end up in Paris, though, and do some shopping. Grasse won't be the way you remember it."

"Nothing is." It hits him. Will he regret being so impulsive? "But that's a good reason to go."

"If Romina and Claudio agree to mind the shop, I'll gladly go. But I want to take a couple of days and go down by the sea along the Côte d'Azur now that the weather is warming. I love the smell of jasmine in Provence."

She kicks her leg out flirtatiously, then rubs his knee. Those eyes. They're the reason he can never say no to her.

"Let's plan on it then!" she says abruptly and stands up. "Romina and Claudio will mind the shop. They have the stamina, if not the patience. I never thought I'd see the day you would do this."

"Do what?"

"Leave the business in Romina's care, on a whim. She's responsible. No worries there. But this is so unlike you."

"I like being unlike me."

"And it suits you."

She wraps her arms around his neck. Work can wait. A few minutes later they're making love with the bedroom shutters wide open. When was the last time they did this?

35

HE EXPECTED TO BE OVERWHELMED as he had been over forty years ago. He expected an embrace, the lush smells of summer hanging in the air like ripening figs. He expected to feel the mythic town's sensuality and sexuality, its aura of naughtiness and provocation. He wanted to see children do somersaults in front of flower merchants inside the Place aux Aires. They would have dirty clothes and scraped knees and maybe one of them would be Nathalie's grandchild. He wanted to be tempted by pretty women with swinging ponytails, wearing linen sun dresses that looked likes slips and carrying totes filled with flowers or baguettes on their shoulders. He expected to settle in with a croissant and a dab of raspberry jam and watch the doctors from the clinic stroll past. He expected the wrought iron gates of his old alma mater to open up on either side of the stone path. He expected the sculptured gardens and the spark of color from windowboxes to send a frisson of erotic memories through his brain.

It doesn't happen.

Where is the carpet of filmy white jasmine glowing in the sun? The nectar-like scent of mimosa? The unanticipated sensations that crept intrusively under his skin at night's first grazing upon his flesh? It's August, that voluptuous summer month when the scent of jasmine should dominate all others. Romina couldn't take over the shop as they'd hoped, so Elio and Sofia waited for the summer holiday when the flowers would be their most extravagant. When one's eyes should take in a prolific explosion of vibrant blossoms and scents: lavender, hibiscus, mimosa, orange flower, jasmine. But instead of fields, he and Sofia scan row after row of vacation homes and condominiums. The uniformity makes their intrusion all the more barbaric. At least if one must build, construct something inspiring. Like the American Shakers who believed a functional object should be made beautiful. Like the Florentines too. Make anything you need—a cheese grater, a television, a shawl—beautiful.

"It's an insult to nature, to beauty," he rants to Sofia as they dodge a gaggle of tourists inside an intolerably crowded Place aux Aires. "It is the way I feel sometimes when you wear too much makeup."

"I don't do that often."

"True. But when you do it makes me mad."

She stops, looks at him quizzically, keeps walking. She has her new camera around her neck and everything is a photo opportunity.

"I understand change, Sofia, but there must be respect for nature, for heritage, and for the authenticity one can never replicate."

He looks with disgust at a new vacation home, which is the exact duplicate of its neighbor.

"We have the same *villette a schiera* in Tuscany, Elio. I would just as soon leave the province before I would live in one."

She stops to snap a photo of a vase of geraniums on a pile of stones. "Still, I do love how everything here is so round and sensual, more feminine. Florence is in most respects a more masculine city. And I love the smells from all the bakeries."

For her this is all new. For Elio, it isn't. "It was magical here once."

"You were younger."

"Not the only reason."

"It is a bit overdone. Like it's either trying to force an image or hold on to its past unsuccessfully."

They stand outside a perfumery, one of many lining the street. The synthetic rose smell pumped out into the air unsettles Elio, as do the prerequisite bundles of lavender and the ubiquitous signs for specials and discounts. It's all so contrived. So Grasse-ish, of the same ilk as those paintings of Tuscany with overly manicured vineyards and evenly spaced cypresses. While his province does have its symmetry and order, there are irregularities, necessary and beautiful. Grasse always had its own. Were any preserved?

They find refuge in Nathalie's café, now run by a Turkish family, but the old structure is still there, as are the freshly pressed blue tablecloths and white vases filled with flowers. The wooden beams and window ledges have been painstakingly restored. There is new artwork on the walls, some of it as whimsical as the metal sculptures positioned outside. It reminds him of Michele's. The owner brings their croissants and café au lait, which they enjoy pouring into the large cups that settle cozily inside their palms. And for a moment he has returned and it all comes back to him. The twins and Paola and Jean Claude and beautiful Palma and all those seductive nights, and the most provocative memory of all, that of promise and possibility, a future opening up like a jasmine blossom before sunlight will cause it to whither. Like a flash, the memory comes. Like Romina's watercolors. What had she said? That one had to work fast with the brush, take up just the right amount of color and stroke with eyes moving up and down from the sky to page, to capture the light as it enters the frame of one's vision.

After the café, he sits down on a stone bench, waves Sofia on into a shop where she'd been eyeing a pair of shoes. It comes over him. He really does want to get on a train and go back. If someone had told him that Florence would seem fresher and more contemporary than Grasse, he would have laughed. Give me the lobby of the JK Place right now. Or the aisles of La Strozzina, or.... What was it that Michele was raving about? Ristorante Ora d'Aria. You walk down that narrow street behind the Uffizi, a tiny treasure of a *hood*, as Romina calls it, and you come upon an olive tree. And why is it there? Well, it commemorates those who died there from a terrorist bomb. It's a symbol of peace and unity. And inside Ora D'Aria with its clean lines and white spaces is this overarching sensation that tells you you are about to spend a fortune and you won't mind at all.

An elderly Frenchman sits down on the bench. They begin to talk; complaints bridge the divide of language. You need to go outside Grasse, the man tells Elio. Wander a bit. Go to Gourdon in the Alpes-Maritimes. Go to Pegomas, where you will still see pickers in the jasmine fields before dawn. They all come from Eastern Europe now, but the rituals haven't changed.

"One ounce of the perfume contains 1,000 jasmine flowers," interjects Elio. The man seems notably impressed. "I fell in love here once too, but that is another story."

"Ah! With the lady over there." The man stares admiringly at Sofia through the shop windows. Bare legs crossed, she's buckling a pink t-strap around her ankle.

"Well. Not exactly. A Frenchwoman."

"Eh! Good you did not end up with her. They are vipers. All of them."

Elio spots a wedding band. "Your wife is French?"

"Yes, from Bretagne. A tiny blonde with blue eyes. She was a doctor there at the clinic."

"I'm so sorry," Elio says.

"Oh she is still alive. But she had a small accident. Fell off her bicycle. No helmet. We don't like them in France. A brain injury. She is all right but she can no longer practice medicine." The old man shrugs as if this is all a matter of course. "*C'est normal.*"

"What type of medicine did she practice?"

"Endocrinology. She was one of the hospital's best. Still, she found a new love, aromatherapy. Or aromatherapy of sorts. When a doctor, she discovered that so many people had thyroid and endocrine issues and she believed all was related to the way we live, our unrealistic expectations, the superficial pressures we take on. All the things that weigh us down."

"Like?"

"Like everything. Our antiquated thoughts. Our possessions, so many of them unnecessary; the way we think our work defines us. She said to me one day, *Richard, yes, I was a doctor and for awhile I didn't want to let go of the prestige. But once I did, it was as if I had wings.* She felt free."

"So what does define us?" Elio asks, more of himself than this man who seems to have it all figured out.

"The stars define us." Sofia approaches them carrying a shopping bag, but casts her eyes at yet another boutique close by. "Ah, *les dentelles de Grasse.*"

The lace shop, which he remembers, has not changed. Intricate lace dresses hang on satin hangers. Christening robes spill out of straw baskets.

"Those are children's clothes for the most part," the man from Grasse informs them.

"And I'm preparing for grandchildren," Sofia responds. "When the first comes, I will have a gift, something I bought in Grasse years before she was even born."

"And how do you know she will have a girl?" Elio asks. "Or have anything. Things with Claudio are not..."

"Oh hush, Elio. Don't spoil the moment. I'm going in to buy that tiny lace dress with the embroidered lilies of the valley on the collar and the sweet blue ribbon around the waist. *Prezioso!*"

Lily of the valley. Makes something smart inside him. A glass of wine would be perfect just now. Maybe two.

The man pats his knee.

"Like my wife. She dusts off the past and keeps going. The past educates us. But that's all." He nudges Elio's arm. "My Fabienne, at age seventy-five, has a point. She wants to teach people to heal without conventional medicine. Encourage the body to heal itself. So she became a masseuse and now she helps everyone who just needs a bit of respite from life or anyone who doesn't want to become dependant on medicines. She works with her hands and her sense of smell, which is still exceptional, even after her fall."

Elio is envious of this former endocrinologist from Brittany. What types of scents does she create? Do they include lavender, eucalyptus, lilac?

The old man slaps Elio's knee again.

"But! But, *mon dieu!* Consider us fortunate. She survived the fall. She still loves to garden and we hike in our sprawling national park four seasons of the year. I am older than you, but not so old that I still can't live life fully. I have a bit of arthritis. But who doesn't?"

Elio nods; his joints can ache too. "What I lament most is that I can't smell things the way I used to, especially when I was a perfumery student."

"None of us can do anything of what we did at seventeen. Studying perfumery does require a very acute sense of smell. Beyond the perception of most people. But you do smell the jasmine here. Don't you?"

"Not at all. I was remarking to Sofia that it was so much stronger years ago."

"Seriously?" The man is taken aback. "Maybe your memory is a bit rusty. Every time the wind stirs, the jasmine enters our field of scent. Are you listening hard enough?"

"Listening?"

"Yes, listen with your heart and your nose will follow. Stop putting too much pressure on it. Stop making it about failure and success."

"Not sure I understand."

"Just sit back, close your eyes. Watch me."

Elio smirks. Someone told me to do this once many years ago and I listened, but she was a lot prettier than you.

"Do the same," the old man prods. "You are hesitating. When we hesitate, we lose."

Elio closes his eyes. "But I can't do it well. Besides, what's the point—it's all dying anyway. Synthetics are the way of the future."

The man sits up stiffly. "Well, I suppose if that is your attitude... But I am taking in the jasmine and it's as glorious as the skin of a beautiful naked woman."

Elio's eyes shoot open, mostly to ensure Sofia hasn't heard. No, she has left the lace shop with yet another package and is now in another boutique, checking out the most expensive handbags in the place. Better close his eyes before his blood pressure rises.

"I know what you are saying but it's frustrating. I tried to smell a perfume oil and I couldn't name the scent."

Old man shrugs. "So?"

"So! It was cypress. The scent every Tuscan knows from birth."

"When did this happen?"

"I don't remember, a few months ago."

"Hm. *That's* your problem! You look behind you all the time."

"I know but the past is relevant."

"Yes, but it is past." He closes his eyes and breathes in deep. Peeking through one eye, he nudges Elio and winks. "*Bon! Écoutez.*"

Quiet. The rustle of a slow summer breeze. A hummingbird. Sofia's perfume Calèche is not too far away. And now something intrudes. A flower. Like a spirited child who slips under a dinner table and tugs at the tablecloth. It suggests mischief, and it makes him smile.

"You have it now?"

"Yes, yes I do."

"It's dusk. That's the best time."

Elio nods, sits for a moment, lets the scent take him by the hand and play. But all too quickly the game leads him to a jasmine cluster at the back of a garden he knew too well. Melancholy descends. "Can I open my eyes now?"

"Whenever you like. As long as you are not too distracted by everyone leaving work and going for a Pernod across the street."

Elio's desire for one of those Pernods is interrupted by Richard taking out his mobile and typing.

"This is not the time to use that infernal thing. I'm still smelling the jasmine. Don't ruin the moment."

"*Calmez-vous.* Look at this."

On the screen is a photograph of an open field. Mounds of just-turned earth stretch out in long evenly spaced mounds. Behind it roll the hills of Grasse. A young woman and a young man kneel on the ground. She holds a handful of soil. He stretches a long yardstick along one of the rows. They both look up at an older man standing beside them. He holds a walking stick in one hand and a handful of seeds in the palm of the other hand. He seems to be giving instruction.

"*Les Fleurs d'Exception du Pays de Grasse.*"

"Who are they?" Elio asks.

"An association formed by the young people of Grasse. Their motto is: *The sense of the land, the land of the senses.*"

"And they grow jasmine?'

"Yes. And iris, rose, tuberose, mimosa, and other flowers for perfumery. They are working to preserve what we have. And they have, of their own accord, instituted sustainable growing practices that respect the environment and the landscape that make Grasse unique in the world."

Elio turns this new information over in his mind. "But how much of an impact can they have? Market forces are against them. A landowner in Grasse makes more profit selling to developers than by growing jasmine when ten thousand blossoms get you all of sixty-five Euros."

"You are looking back again, Elio."

"What looking back? This is happening now and the trend isn't about to change anytime soon."

"History tells a different story. After the Dark Ages we had the Renaissance. You of all people should hold on to that perspective. Remember the present trends will one day be past. And given the speed at which young people with their technological prowess and their global exposure travel, the trends will change even more quickly. "

"I honestly wish you were right."

"Go to the fields, Elio, and talk with these young people. You will be astonished."

"I hope so. I'm curious to see what arrow they have in their quivers."

"It's simple. They have hope."

36

THEY SAY THE SCENT OF JASMINE as it shakes loose from the filmy white blossoms is like falling in love. And this morning at dawn he revisits his first love and all the loves that have followed. It's the moment when he first saw Sofia on the train, when Palma's lab coat brushes past his desk, when Romina opens up Diorissimmo on her sixteenth birthday and L'Heure Bleue on her twenty-third. When Michele gives him a fist bump for Profumeria Barati's prosperity. And when Marina says goodbye at the hospital with an expression so full of love he can't speak.

"Listen to Jacques, Elio. Your head is in the clouds."

It's too surreal. Admittedly Elio is envious of this tall, lean man with his thick silver hair and a face wrinkled from working under the sun in jasmine fields only a few miles outside of Grasse. He wears a checked blue and white shirt with jeans and moves around with the same vitality as Michele. As he walks ahead, sometimes backwards, he recounts the history of his *terroir*. Elio wonders what drives this man. This field could no more hold the millions of flowers required to make Jacques profitable than his own modest garden in Castellina. But Jacques talks as if such realities were meaningless. As he passes between the rows, his hands graze the flowers as if stroking the cheek of his newborn child. He stops every few steps to close his eyes and smell more deeply.

"Try it," he says, with the reverance of someone staring up at a stained glass Madonna in Santa Croce.

So with equal reverance, because he will do whatever this gentle man asks, Elio closes his eyes. Three deep breaths and the delicate unmistakable bite of jasmine flower takes him everyplace that's brought him happiness. He'd once read that the scent of jasmine "is like the room your lover walked hrough a half-hour ago." Now Elio can choose to follow, or not.

"I notice that the women in the field pick the flowers one by one and in exactly the same way," asks Sofia, making a twisting gesture with her thumb and forefinger. "What's with that specific movement?"

"Keen observation," says Jacques. "The flower is so fragile. You see?" He hands her a blossom he's snapped off in exactly the same fashion. "The leaf is practically transparent. That precise twist of the wrist with just the right force prevents any damage to the blossom." He does it again, hands her another. "And it's an artful gesture unto itself. A ritual. Not unlike celebrated rituals around the world. The ritual of serving tea in China and Japan, our rituals when we decant our wine and pour our champagne. We even teach our children at a young age how to present and serve a wine to our dinner guests. You Italians have certain rituals when you prepare and present an espresso. That motion, that twist of the wrist is a ritual deserving of the flower."

Sofia brings the blossom to her nose. "This is a treasure."

He looks out across his land. "One day this field may be gone. I will fight to keep it, though, and the best way is to cultivate superior absolute. I will not become rich but profitable enough, I think, to keep this field alive and to pass it on."

"I have a shop in Florence, passed down through the generations. A family business. I wanted to pass on to my daughter. She's not interested. I'm not sure future generations are wired the way we were."

Jacques's calm blue eyes study Elio in a way that makes him wish he'd kept quiet, and he adds quietly, "I suppose a shop is different from a flower field."

"No, Elio, not necessarily. Your father taught you your *métier*, as we say. It's not much different."

Elio finds that a kindness. "But my daughter—

"You daughter will craft her own life. And I'm not worried about Grasse. We are small, which is a good thing. We only need a few dedicated growers, and we have quite a few, mostly young. Jasmine is more than a treasure. It's *le grand amour*, the love of my life. In France we talk about the *coup de foudre*—love at first sight. It's the way you feel when you see your first born or when you meet the man or the woman of your dreams, or a house you walk into and want to stay in forever. It was that for me the first time I came to Grasse as a very young man. And it has kept me here since."

"How many years?"

"Forty-five." He shrugs, eyes turn to the field. "One does not neglect, much less abandon, the love of one's life."

"And it's not such a bad place to be trapped in forever," says Elio without guile but without any awareness of why he's saying it either.

"We are as blessed as the flowers, we are here between the mountains and the sea, under Mediterranean sun and surrounded by the Parc Naturel Régional des Préalpes d'Azur. This is why the exceptional olfactory properties of our flowers are unequalled anywhere in the world."

Jacques face breaks out into a smile. "I like to think I make love to my fields. It satisfies us both."

SO EVERY GROWER HAS A STORY. There is Elise at Le Domaine des Collines. She is younger than Jacques, Romina's age. She tells Elio and Sofia that when she was a student at the lycée she hated mathematics.

"If you don't do well in school, my mother said, you will spend the rest of your life picking jasmine. Because of the way she said it, I thought it would be a bad thing. So I studied as hard as I could, graduated, became a *comptable* and moved to Rennes. I was miserable. Rennes is an artist's city but it rains all the time there. I missed the sun of Provence, and the hills, the flowers, working in the fields with my mother and father and brother. And the food. So after two years I came back."

"And your parents?" Sofia asks, likely thinking of her surprise if Romina did the same.

"The hardest part was the new business relationship, so we focused on areas they couldn't do as well. I built our website and set up billing so we could accept credit cards. I developed a more precise cost benefit analysis so they could actually see where the money was going and the targets we had to reach to offset expenses. I did some events in the piazza here and in Paris to give our flowers visiblility. Would you both like some more tea?"

Elio nods happily. "These shortbread biscuits are delicious."

She blushes in a way that makes her seem so much younger than her thirty years. "My grandmother's and my mother's recipe. Something else I want to keep alive and pass on to my children."

"Are your parents retired now?"

"They are. But they come down to the fields from time to time to help out and to talk to the pickers. Our pickers are like family too. They have been with us for years. My mother makes them breakfast up at our house and then they come back there for lunch every day. My mother is from Bretagne and they love her crêpes. She fills them with *confiture* in the morning, *jambon* and *frômage* at lunch, and spinach with veal in the evenings. And she always folds up a few in triangles and dusts sugar over them as a treat. They don't mind the repetition. It's re-assuring. Since our *métier* is subject to the whims of nature, we need some things in our lives to be consistent and predictable."

ADELE FROM LES FLEURS DE MANON tells them she's always wanted to be an *agriculturice*, continuing the work of three generations. "There's nothing more gratifying than working with nature to draw out its gifts to us. As an *agriculturice* I get to respect and understand nature with an intimacy others cannot even imagine. And I am Grassoise, it's my responsibility to protect our patrimony."

She doesn't offer tea and biscuits, only tall frosted glasses of freshly made lemonade with mint leaves. It makes Elio think of bergamot. Lemon gives zing to things, but the mint mediates and rounds it all out so one doesn't need to pucker ones lips too much.

"WHY WOULD I DO ANYTHING ELSE?" asks Yann. "As a child I worked alongside my parents and my grandparents. I never tire of cultivating the rose, the jasmine, the iris, mimosa, the tuberose. Each has its quirks. Each is as unpredictable as nature herself. She is our master in the end. The natural materials we grow for the perfume industry are never the same because no day and no season is the same. All is dependant on the *terroir,* the rainfall, the direction of the winds. We have to do a lot of adjusting all along the production chain."

His hands are calloused, though the cuticles remain soft and clean. It speaks of care. Cautiously Elio ventures, "But Grasse, it will never return to what it once was."

"*C'est la vie.*" Yann gives a Gaullic shrug. "We Grassoise are not mourning that change. We were born into it so we are not bound by the past. Our frame of reference is the present. We are preserving what we have and perhaps moving into the headwinds of something new. Don't quite know what that is yet."

"This new market is still evolving. Who knows where it will lead?" Sofia says. "The real tragedy will be if the fields disappear just as the demand rises."

"The headwinds are in our favor. Our *terroir* will still yield flowers with properties valued around the world. In the meantime we must stay fit and healthy for the work ahead. My brother is preparing a light repast inside—some bread, cheese and *charcuterie.* Are you hungry?"

"Does the repast include wine?" asks Elio.

Yann smiles cherub-like. "Of course. This is France. We do with wine what the world does with perfume. Stick your nose in the glass and smell what's to come."

37

SOFIA SEES HER FIRST. When was the exact moment? When she looked down to put the small can of *foie gras* into their food basket but happened to spot the black patent pumps and sheer black stockings? Or perhaps it was the sight of a filmy black and white scarf knotted in just the right way at the collar of a cream, black, and silver Chanel knit jacket. The long pearls were knotted too, just below the scarf and they loop down almost to the woman's waist. The slender figure implies a youthfulness one finds only in chic French women d'*une certaine âge*. Her slim black leather skirt stops right above her knees over shapely legs. Lots of chains and beads around her waist. In her ears multiple piercings sport tiny hoops and pearl studs against the short, white boyish hair. She holds her cellphone up to pay for her purchases: pâté, bitter greens, a small bottle of champagne, olives, cigarettes, and packs them herself into a canvas bag. She carries the small purse Sofia has always coveted. A quilted Chanel bag with gold chain shoulder strap. She knows how to select, prune, discard. She separates easily, from things and from people. She is never a slave to her past. She moves on. She regrets nothing and forgets everything. Those ankles. Sexy, for a woman so old.

He lets Sofia admire the ensemble as he sniffs a warm baguette just pulled out of the oven. Tan crust crackles under the press of his hand. Smells as delicious as it feels. It will go well with the sharp and creamy Roquefort Sofia drops in the basket while her eyes still follow *la française*. Their basket, unlike hers, is crammed with small boxes of berries, apricots, a bottle of Evian, a chunk of Camembert, the Roquefort, fig jam, dark chocolate. He reaches for a bottle of Côtes du Rhône, and *la française*, now roaming the aisles, rubs against his elbow by mistake.

"*Ah, pardon*," she says in a silky voice that sends an odd shiver up his spine. Then something he's not yet aware of provokes a second glance, at her ankles, the fleur de lis tattoo pressing against the flesh of her neck, the way her jacket molds to her torso. The unmistakable scent trails her like an undercurrent. *Muguet.*

"Elio, be careful!"

Sofia's shout comes too late. The 1999 Côtes du Rhône falls from his hand and shatters.

"*Mamma mia.*" His head swings back and forth for the shopkeeper as he avoids Sofia's eyes. *La française* transforms into a poised blur at the end of the aisle amidst the fracas that ensues. *Fracas.* Interesting how that word comes to mind. He never uses it. It's never entered his frame of reference all these years. But here it is. *Fracas*, the perfume that would suit *la française* just now. A dangerous scent.

Sofia hands him the shopping basket and squats down to pick up the glass.

"No, no, madam. *S'il vous plait!*" The shopowner brings out a broom and dust pan and gestures for them to step aside. "You know this is one of our rarer wines," he says as he sweeps. A young boy from behind the bakery counter steps in with newspapers to wrap up the broken glass.

We will pay for it of course, Elio assures him. The man is grateful. I don't like to force a client to do that but you understand, it is so expensive and this month has been a difficult one. We understand. We are shopkeepers too. We run a perfumery in Florence. *Did you have to say that just now, Sofia?* There! You've done it. She's turned around and is now coming towards us, food basket on one arm, walking stick tucked under the other. She's an old woman now, she looks even older than her seventy-five years. She's hardly attractive. And so so frail. Careful she doesn't slip on the wet floor.

"Elio. Elio Barati," she says coquettishly. "*Finalement.*"

Elio's eyes snap to Sofia, whose face draws in before it shatters into a smile.

Later that night he will remember how he took apart the planes of the face of *la française*—sharp cheekbones scribbled over with tiny red veins, green eyes inside a crescent of fine lines, still as transparent as the emerald waters of Sardegna; a once lovely face marred by years, by a life that perhaps had not been good to her, the prideful set of her jaw, the disappointing smell of cigarette smoke on her breath. He will remember the press of her hand when she hugged him and Sofia ceremoniously and without emotion, as if they were all part of an inner circle. A circle of old people whose better days were far behind them. We are all growing old. She faster than me and certainly faster than Sofia. And, before he finally falls asleep, he will do what he's resisted until now. He will sniff the scent on his hand, and he will wonder where the years went because right now he feels just the way he did the night he grabbed his vials from her fireplace mantle, stashed them into his briefcase and walked out into the snow, away from his grand ambitions and freed of her demands forever.

She must have read his mind because her eyes suddenly light up with cynical satisfaction. They convey curiosity more than surprise or warmth. And perhaps a desire for vindication, to prove she was right about him. After all here he is, a common tourist in dusted-up clothes after a day in the fields, beside his equally disheveled spouse who holds a basket of food on her arm to take to their hotel and save money on dinner at a restaurant. He does not wear the mantle of prosperity. He has nothing to flaunt, to brag about. He has created *rien*.

Sofia knows exactly how to handle this. She steps forward into the space Elio should fill and slides effortlessly into the role she plays best, that of the purposeful life and business partner. She's thrilled to finally meet Palma, she says, after Elio's evasive and somewhat clumsy introduction. How marvelous that Elio should run into his former teacher. Does she still live in Grasse? *Mon dieu, non, Sofia.* I have had my fill of the country. I live in a condominium now, in Nice, right on the Promenade des Anglais where I can hear cars honk and revelers laugh and the waves slide in and out. I live alone with my small dog and a parakeet. I love the dog but detest the parakeet. He was a gift by a former lover whose name I don't even recall. There are some good things here of course. She nods at the storeowner. "The food in Grasse is superb, but after nine everyone is asleep. I understand. Fine. They have to wake up early to run their cafés and work in the fields. *Triste.*"

"*Una noia,*" agrees Sofia. Bucolic is nice in small doses, agree the women. How easily they seem to have connected. And yes, we must have the city fix, no matter what. I am definitely going to Paris before we leave France. Ah yes, it is still a magical city but difficult to live in, says Palma. I do so for thirty years. I still have a small studio there. She checks her watch.

"Thirty years?" He's kept quiet until now, on the sidelines where he feels safe.

"Oh yes. I sold out, Elio. You will be very disappointed in your old teacher." She winks playfully at Sofia. "I went to work for the commercial sector, a fragrance house, the *real* business of perfumery. *C'est la vie.* Too hard here, all the teaching and laboring over the creation of the *chef d'oeuvre* to rival those of Ernest Beaux, Roudniska, *alors*—" She twirls her hand in the air. A gesture that mocks. "After awhile, Sofia, you know what I'm talking about. What does it give you?" She rubs thumb and forefinger together. "*Rien.* No money, no real status. *Oof!* Maybe! A woman does all the work and the men get all the status. *Je m'en fiche*, I said one day. *Basta!*"

He must be frowning because she frowns back.

"Look, Elio. We all had high ideals then. We were going to create the next Shalimar, the next Diorama, the next No. 5. And we worked for free, or for so little we could barely pay the rent or afford a coffee at Nathalie's. Remember her?" Now she winks at Elio. "Ba! I went to Paris to work for Chanel, then for Guerlain, Dior, then for Chanel again, and I continued there until I retired just last year! It was a good and a lucrative life. And I got to live in Paris!"

She checks her watch triumphantly. She has a driver waiting for her, she confesses. Her eyesight is so bad she no longer drives at night. It's a shame we couldn't grab *un verre* and catch up. But who does she want to catch up with? She's barely looked at him. She hasn't even sized him up or commented on how good he looks for his age.

"Would you like to join us for dinner tomorrow evening then?" asks Sofia. She's ignoring him too. If she weren't she would have seen his jaw drop. "I want to go up to the fields to see the mimosa in the day, if you wish to join us."

"Absolutely not! Enjoy. I have seen and smelled enough mimosa for three lifetimes. When do you leave for Paris?"

"Monday morning on the Eurostar."

"Hmm. You will have to go through Nice. So why not come to my place for dinner the night before you leave? Let me host you. After all, you are in my country and I rarely venture across the border into yours. I don't much like Italy after Berlusconi. What were you Italians thinking? So! Sunday night at eight? No. At seven for cocktails, dinner at eight. And then maybe we can walk along the Promenade late at night. I suggest this—you check out of your hotel on Sunday morning. I'll book you into one of my favorites —you can stay just one night and take the train out the next morning."

"I would love an evening in Nice. What do you think, Elio?"

Does it matter? Palma cuts in, "Of course you do, and you should. And by Sunday you will have had enough of the damn hills. *Bon!* It's decided." She hands Elio her card but her interest is strictly with Sofia. He's relieved only to be released from the anxiety of returning to her stone house in Grasse with the jasmine tree in the backyard.

38

"I SHOULD INTRODUCE HER TO ENRICO."

"Seriously?"

"She's just like him. All about money and immediate gratification."

"You sound jealous."

"Me? Of her? Of what?"

"Then why are you so upset about this? She's a pragmatist. *Punto e basta.*"

"It's a good thing you're driving."

"I'm loving this drive actually." She rolls down the window. "You can smell the flowers going to sleep, that last jolt of scent. Do you smell it? Like small fireworks popping up here and there. Rose and lavender, jonquil. They float over the hills like a blanket of perfume."

"Now who is the poet and the romantic?"

"Me. You can share that role once in a while, can't you?"

What makes her so alluring this particular dusk? She wears the sheerest of makeup and her most delicate jewelry. Her hair is pinned up haphazardly but her face wears the burnished glow of a day in the sun, and everything about her, her movements, her loose linen dress and gem-embellished sandals, the day's revelations dancing inside her eyes, make him feel unusually happy.

She has a point, however. He is jealous. Palma's visible affluence is the result of her success, albeit a success he himself would never have pursued. Chanel. Guerlain. Dior. To have been chosen by these great dynasties of the fragrance world, to represent them in whatever capacity is an accomplishment. She had to have held a prestigious position to dress as she does and to live where she lives.

He had been chosen once. To be admitted as a student of perfumery at the then-most prestigious perfumery school in Grasse. After, no one has chosen him for anything. Well, in some respects his clients do when they buy from his shop. But that has been dropping off lately. And the reputation of Profumeria Barati within the commercial sector is the result of many factors outside his control. He has not, in effect, had any successes of his own. His old fragrance lies dormant in the pages of his perfumer's notebook and in dusty vials. He barely recollects its story, why he conceived it, why he chose the notes he did, what it was he was so proud of that evening at Palma's. Maybe she'd been right to discourage him.

"You're questioning your life choices now, aren't you?"

"How do you know?"

"Because you always do."

"She looked so old."

"Yes. What did you expect? You're going to be just the same in ten years."

"Not if I can help it."

"Correct."

"Don't turn to look at me like that when you need to keep your eyes on the road."

The car windshield is now dotted with raindrops. As the windshield wiper brushes them away, he sees the hills stenciled across the dark night sky and the Maritime Alps behind and he wonders if the ghosts of flowers past haunt the land. Do they sneak in and spread over the fields much as the full moon does now, reminiscent of an era that will never be erased from memory because, as Proust believed, every moment of life is stored in a taste and a smell? We carry those tastes and smells inside us, in our own human hard drive, and when they re-emerge, as they did a few days ago when Palma brushed past him in the market, there is no stopping the flood of real and complex emotions rendered no less powerful from the passage of time.

So, while the dominant scent in the air around them tonight is that of chemical and solvent residues from local factories, Sofia, a newcomer to Grasse is still able to detect and savor the subtlest nuances of what once was or what is struggling to re-emerge and re-invent itself. She, unlike Elio, is not restricted by the past.

"*ATTENTION!*" SHOUTS PALMA FROM THE BAR, where she pours champagne into three Lalique flutes. Behind her, *Casablanca* plays, muted, on a large TV screen.

They didn't know she lived in the penthouse until stepping out of the elevator and into a sunken living room wrapped in glass, the dark night sky speckled with glittering street lights below. They can still make out the Promenade des Anglais as it snakes along the coastline towards Monaco; quiet waves break in a spray of white along the shore.

She's wearing a silky black caftan that has grown too wide and too long for her shrinking frame. The champagne flutes, as long and as graceful as the fingers of a harpsichordist, sit on the art deco bar. That visual so enchants Elio, he's caught off guard. He almost misses seeing Palma stumble forward to greet them.

Sofia gives Elio that *do something and do it now!* look. Palma's walking stick leans inconveniently against a closet door. Her balance is off and she heads straight for a small foot stool. Elio grabs her elbow in the nick of time.

"A gentleman. That you always were," she says with a touch of nostalgia.

She takes his arm and they walk to where Sofia stands staring out at the sea.

"This is gorgeous, Palma. It's like a dream."

"It is. It was mine. I worked hard enough for it. Over thirty years."

She spins around, raises her arms up. "It always made me happy to come back here. I have a studio in Montmartre as well. But this is my haven, way up here above the noise and the craziness, but still a part of it. Make yourselves comfortable and I will bring your champagne."

"How about you sit down and I get it for you?" offers Elio.

"Absolutely not. You are my guests." She gestures towards a settee beside an end table and a vase of white gardenias. Elio and Sofia sit down reluctantly. Sofia tilts her head toward the walking stick. He shakes his head and whispers, "She's not going to let me—"

"I know," Sofia whispers back, "but if she falls..."

Palma descends the stairs with two filled champagne flutes but her hands shake. Elio stands, takes one flute, hands it to Sofia, takes the other one and places it on the end table beside the camellias. He offers his elbow. She takes it but this time it's apparent it bothers her to have to do so. She lets him guide her to the settee and points to the spot next to Sofia.

"Sofia, come sit closer to me. I always enjoy being served champagne by a handsome man, and you should too, even though he is your husband, and we take husbands for granted."

Elio looks at her quizzically.

"Oh don't give me that look. I never married anyone. Lots of lovers. No husbands. Good call if I say so myself."

She sits down gracefully, picks up the flute and holds it up to toast her guests. Now that she's seated, she's secure and in control. She frowns because Elio doesn't have a glass.

He swiftly remounts the steps to the bar and picks up the lone flute. How does she fare in here by herself? At seventy-five she should still be able to get around without falling. But she is terribly small and frail, and probably arthritic.

"The fragrance business on the corporate side can be pretty crazy from what I hear," says Sofia, eager to engage in conversation and keep her in her chair. "Did you have advertising input while you were at Chanel?"

"Oh yes, of course. That was my favorite part."

"Then you were involved in those fabulous *Égoïste* commercials."

"Oh my God yes! Égoïste, égoïste, égoïste! You know who my inspiration was for those, don't you, Elio?"

"Not me, I hope."

She gives him a sly look. "Not a chance. *You* know who. Jean Claude."

"Ah!" He decides it's best not to comment.

"Do you remember what a pompous idiot he was?"

"Well, yes. Problem was you didn't."

Sofia gives him *the* look.

"It was my absolute favorite launch of all! I had such fun with it. I oversaw all of the new fragrance launches. I even convinced them to bring some of the older fragrances back into the marketplace. There is always an interest in retro fragrance, retro fashion. And why not? Truth is, the most beautiful perfumes, like the world's greatest books, have already been created."

"You are most probably right," says Sofia, admiring the film-set living room worthy of Mademoiselle Chanel herself. Behind the grand piano is the Milton Greene photograph of Marlena Dietrich, seated with her gorgeous legs crossed. She leans over so her face is hidden by the fall of her blond hair as she touches the back of her knee. He's seen that pose re-created in perfume ads to great effect, but none approaches this original. The lighting is masterful, it falls across her golden hair and legs in such a way that it imparts a silvery sheen. It makes her all the more mysterious and desireable. You could imagine Marlena lifting her head. She might smile at you. She might not. But she holds you there just the same.

"I was Vice President of Fragrance Development for three companies: Chanel, Guerlain, Dior. I hated it and adored it all at once and every day. One has a lot of power. I wrote up the briefs, put the perfumers through their paces. They were all afraid of me, if you can imagine. As far as the companies were concerned they were thrilled to have someone on board who'd actually worked at a fragrance house."

"That's certainly an asset," says Elio. "Development teams comprised of marketing folks see only statistics and a marketing plan. You must have brought a lot to the table with all your experience as an actual perfumer."

He meant the compliment. She'd been brilliant. Funny how grudges soften over time.

"Well, thank you, dear Elio. But my talent as a perfumer was no match for yours."

He nearly spills his champagne.

"Oh, Palma, how gracious of you to say it. I know my husband regrets not continuing his studies in Grasse."

Is she drunk? Why is she offering this up? Because it's true. That's why. Sofia is nothing if not truthful.

What does he read in Palma's eyes? Tenderness? Regrets of her own? Such beautiful eyes they are. Even with all the lines around them. There is a part of him that will always love her.

"Life is too short. He chose a different future."

But I chose it for foolish reasons, he thinks. I was young, hot headed. Impulsive.

Palma continues, "So, Sofia darling, your husband is like Gaudi, Puccini, Schubert and all those other sad souls who almost finished masterpieces. We still enjoy *La Sagrada Famiglia*, *Turandot*, the *Unfinished Symphony*, do we not? Maybe we consider them masterpieces because these geniuses died or went crazy before they could finish them."

"I'm not about to die anytime soon," says Elio.

"Well! I never called you a genius either."

Elio grunts, swallowing a laugh. "My mother did."

"As a good mother should. She was not entirely wrong. You did show great promise and you used it in other ways. You built a family business. That is an act of creation too. Goodness knows it requires creative thinking to master the ins and outs of running a shop, to negotiate well with the fragrance and cosmetics houses, to know how to choose the collections you will carry year after year, to figure out how to offset expenses during a recession, such as the one we're experiencing now.

You have put your skills to good use." She clinks her glass against his and Sofia's. "I know all this because I Googled you earlier today."

"Ha! Hard to keep secrets with today's technology," he says, though secretly pleased.

"I Googled your mother too."

Now he spills champagne on his tie. She ignores him. And Sofia, as Sofia would, slides in closer. "Really?" But her face says, *Why would you do such a thing?*

Shrugging, Palma waves a hand. "I liked Elena very much when we met. If you remember, Elio, we had a connection, she and I. I was intrigued by her, and by your story years later of how she left your father."

"So," Elio pushes.

"So I asked myself even then, did you have the constitution to throw off the mantle of responsibility and take off for Grasse and Paris? I wasn't convinced you would do it."

She pauses for their comments. They say nothing so she goes on.

"But I was convinced that one day Elena would pursue some sort of path related to perfumery. She was your mentor. She was the one to lay the foundation for your interest and inspiration. When you came to Grasse you were already well schooled, tuned into the artistry of the *métier*, so to speak. She understood flowers, raw materials and fragrance oils. She had such an interest in the pulse and the rudiments of the perfume trade, in the actual composition of a scent from the initial inspiration or germ of the idea to the refining note. I had a sense way back then that she wanted to get to the heart of it all. That's why I'm not surprised that she's now owner of a citrus grove in Paros."

"Elio's mother is still alive and growing lemons?" Sofia gasps, setting down her flute and fixing her eyes quickly on Elio.

"Yes, for the fragrance trade. She's a small supplier but that life must suit her. I wasn't aware while I worked in the industry, but I'm sure we sourced from her from time to time."

Elio has nothing to say; the smell of bergamot against oysters and the sea too fully commands his attention.

A TOUR THROUGH PALMA'S APARTMENT reveals little else about her life other than her penchant for tiny *objets d'art*. A Baccarat bowl holds a collection of cocktail rings. Pearls of varying lengths are draped over a tall black-rimmed mirror. Drapes ressemble a box of No. 5, white linen trimmed in black grosgrain. There is not a single item out of place. It is as if no one really lives here, but she does, joyfully. Palma was never one for clutter or disorder in her life. There is little evidence of anything or anyone taking her off course, hence the marvelous photography collection but the complete absence of personal photos. There are portraits of Palma, artfully posed, throughout the decades of her life, all of them drawing forth her marvelous bone structure. But there are no photos of her with someone else, except for one where she receives an award from a well-dressed man half her age. One could chronicle her life experiences in the collection of perfume miniatures inside a mirrored vitrine, or the photos of cities and landscapes—various cities in France, the castle in Heidelberg, Germany, another of a cup of hot chocolate on the table of an outdoor café in Salzburg, yet another of Hagia Sofia and the Blue Mosque in Istanbul, and of the statue of an angel inside Central Park. Many are in black-and-white. A few in muted color. One is stretched on a canvas: a leopard climbing a tree at dusk. One whimsical shot captures a row of brightly colored motorcycles along a sepia-toned street in Rome. Excellent shots all of them, with no people in the frames.

So it's all the more touching that, after an abbreviated walk along the Promenade des Anglais and a late-night tea at her place, Palma sends them off with two things. A silk scarf for Sofia, in a white box and tied with a black grosgrain ribbon, and the key to her flat in Paris.

"We simply can't impose in this manner," objects Sofia. "And I'm not so sure we should go on to Paris."

"What are you saying? Of course we are going to Paris." Elio is beside himself. He could care less whether they stay at Palma's or not, but he's more intent than ever on going to Paris.

"I'm just worried about the shop, that's all."

"Please, when was the last time you were in Paris together?" Palma asks.

Elio hedges. "Sofia has gone alone, and with Romina or her friends. I've never been actually."

Elio accepts her glare with appropriate humility, because she is completely right.

"Seriously. You're worse than I thought." Dipping her hand into the small Chanel bag, she dangles her key. "My flat is teeny tiny. It's the baby version of this place, all black and white, but it's impeccably clean and stylish and on a step along a long flight of stairs in Montmartre. You will have to put up with people smoking pot outside, but other than that it's a short walk up to the Place du Tertre, which you must see in the morning light when all the bar patrons and tourists are gone and you see it then much as Toulous-Lautrec and Matisse did, with its painters, prostitutes, music. You'll feel in your bones the Montmartre of sin and ill-repute. An artistic and an erotic experience but the two must intermingle for either one to be exciting, no? Might be a romantic second honeymoon. I have a tiny red light above the bed. Up to you."

39

PALMA'S TINY RED LIGHT DID SERVE its romantic purpose for the two nights they passed there, as did the small flat with its own Twenties charm and the closeness of everything, which meant they behaved as young lovers with restricted means in a restricted space with restricted time. They made love in the mornings, ran up the stairs to the Place Du Tertre where they could wax philosophical about Paris in the Twenties and the artists who came from all over the world in search of a muse. Sofia enjoyed her long toasted baguettes slathered with melting butter and gobs of raspberry confiture. He loved the big bowls of *café au lait* that he could dip his croissants into, not minding when he dribbled on his shirt. And then they would return to the flat, make love again and later make the long hike down into the heart of the city and over the river to the Place Saint-Sulpice to shop, eat more good things and just meander. They moved about with the convenience of mobile phone maps and Elio's uncanny sense of direction. He'd never been to this city but it was logically divided by a river, much like Florence, with one side being more bohemian and the other more chic, although chic seemed to be bred in the bone of every Parisian whether it was in the way one rode one's bicycle in the street, tucked the mobile away courteously, or turned up the cuff of a soft leather jacket. The other word that sprung to mind over and over was *intellectual* perhaps because so many streets were named after poets, writers and essayists, and because the light had a silvery gray seriousness about it, like engraved words on stone or the dense pages of *Le Monde*. This is a city in which intellectuals reflected on the meanings of things and passed them on to descendants who acted out whatever was recommended with the ease of a Florentine selecting the most perfect leather accessory. He convinced Sofia to take one of the city bikes, assuring her that the drivers in Paris were no less crazy than in Florence. And she had ridden one in Rome, had she not? That was not only crazy, probably suicidal. Most fascinating, she admitted he was right. That, in and of itself, was a worth the entire exhorbitant cost of this totally unnecessary but blissful trip.

The moment that he will hold on to, however, is this one, right now, a mere accident. He and Sofia are simply ambling about in the late evening after a leisurely dinner and too much champagne at the Hôtel Costes on the Rue Saint-Honoré, and, coming to the Seine, find themselves here at just this time of day when the light softens and a misty blue haze starts to wrap itself around the bridges and streets. But he knows that, according to the Freudians, there are no real accidents. So perhaps he intended this. Maybe all along in his insistence that they come here to Paris has been his intention to stand, as he does now, on a bridge over the Seine at dusk, much as Jacques Guerlain, accompanied by his young son, had done in 1911.

"Still one of the loveliest of floral orientals," says Sofia without provocation.

He's recounted the story of L'Heure Bleue to her so many times, she hears him telling it inside his head. She looks down into the river at the watercolor reflection of the changing sky. "I love it here. Was it not amazing this afternoon at the Place Vendôme, the jewelers doing those settings? To create that very exact, uninterrupted flow of jewels with no visible metals. No wonder it takes six hundred hours to make a single brooch."

"Each piece was breathtaking." Elio nods as he leans into the bridge railing.

"And love. That's what I saw today. It was all about love. I see the same in our mosaicists at Lastrucci. You know it's been months since I've stopped in to watch Iacopo and Bruno work. I stop in whenever I'm in Santa Croce. I see the *pietre* in all their natural colors lined up along the walls and I think of all the times I went there as a child and I would ask how they made those thin perfectly shaped stones from those large rocks, how they cut them so fine to fit close. It seems the colors just flow into each other as if painted. But they're actually *stones*. I had the same feeling today when I saw those jewelers cut the tiniest wedges into those jewels to fit them together so as to have no metal in-between. I felt so fulfilled and so protective. You see, Elio, that's what I think Guerlain was feeling that night. An exuberant love for what Paris was at the time and the desire to hold on to it."

Elio stares at her, confused.

"I can imagine it, the afternoon fading into this mystical blue, all the stuff about the flowers. A bit sentimental if you ask me. But Guerlain was an astute and sensible man from what we've read, so what I get from the story is that he sensed a dramatic change was coming, an upheaval, and that it would be followed by great loss."

"The First World War," Elio replies.

"Exactly. Paris was such a different place then. It was the end of the Belle Époque when people, including Jacques Guerlain himself, would stroll through the Tuileries and take their children to sail model boats on the pond. And then it all changed, abruptly and violently."

He nods, but before he can speak, she continues. "Perfumers, like other artists, can sense change before it happens. They know intuitively that all of life's events are as vaporous as air." Sofia grabs the air before her. "You feel it now, Elio? The way the city grows quiet, and everything feels more immediate—especially here between the two banks of the river, choosing which side you're going to go to."

"It's that moment when the sky has lost its sun and has yet to find its stars," Elio whispers.

He wants to transport himself back to that dream-like evening in Palma's garden but Sofia won't let him. Neither will the setting. This is not the Belle Époque as Sofia pointed out. This is not 1960s Grasse. This is twenty-first-century Paris. The streets are busier, the lights brighter, and there is a splendid energy of people returning from work, greeting friends, checking mobile phones, moving precipitously into the anticipation and the rhythms of early evening.

"I know that quote, Elio. It's pretty. It positions a great fragrance. But, given the context within which it was conceived, there is a more profound message. When Guerlain made that statement, he knew that something dramatic was about to take place, that Paris would be forever changed, that *he* would be forever changed. He wrote that he experienced something so intense he had to express it in a perfume. Amazing how perfumes can be prophetic. But they are. They anticipate and define the times we live in. Like all the arts, perfumery records our history and tells our story to future generations. So I see his quote not as romantic reflection but as something far more urgent. I see it as a call to action."

40

BY THE TIME THE BARATI'S CAR pulls into their driveway, both Elio and Sofia have lived a few lifetimes. In the past three months they've escorted a friend to a life-saving clinic. They've toured the romantic city of Romeo and Juliet, the jasmine fields in Grasse, the casinos of Nice, and the cities of the Veneto and the streets of Paris. They have eaten well, listened to opera under the stars, laughed often, emptied many bottles of French wine and made love many times. They've visited Palladian villas and sprawling gardens and have had their share of late nights out and sleeping naked while reminiscing about passions and foibles, and all those dreams and plans that never came to pass, and those that still have a chance to sneak into their future.

But they're home now. He and Sofia sort their bills out together at the table in their kitchen. She takes one stack, he the other. Handle each piece of paper only once. Chop chop. And the sooner we finish this the quicker we go out to Michele's for an *aperitivo* before checking the shop to ensure all is in place.

And then they're going out to dinner, to Buca Lapi for a *bistecca fiorentina* and a bottle of Tignanello, because no one feels like cooking. Romina's placed a vase of irises and a bowl of white peaches in the center of the table. An easel leaning against the wall reveals an unfinished watercolor of the Arno. On the counter is a jar of her homemade "killer" granola, a box of fresh watercolors, and a basket with a bottle of Prosecco, a few wrapped up treasures, and a note.

Just wanted to welcome you back with morsels of home. I'm sure you've missed these. Let's meet at Michele's to celebrate. I have so much to tell you!

So Elio interrupts his bill sorting to ferret through the basket. Inside he finds: an engraved leather bookmark from La Scuola del Cuoio, a dupioni silk sachet from the Antico Setificio Fiorentino, a tiny bag of his favorite champagne truffles from Cioccolato Molto Bene, potpourri from Santa Maria Novella, and a delicious bottle of Aura Maris by Lorenzo Villoresi.

"Ah. Perfect. We need to re-order some of this for the shop." Sofia untwists the cap and sea, citrus, and floral scents fill the room. Villoresi intended that the first fragrance in his Mare Nostrum collection evoke impressions of sea breezes layered over nuances of citrus, flowers and shrubbery under a Mediterranean sun. He achieved it.

"Before you smell this and convince me to go on another holiday, let's see if there's anything here we can have for lunch."

As Elio fingers the last of the fresh bread found on the counter, Michele sends them a photo. Everything inside the shop looks simply gorgeous and very neat. Elio regrettably notes it actually looks better than it did when they left.

"Do you think it looks so good because there has been so little traffic in the shop?" asks Sofia.

"Ever the optimist." He turns up the background music on his computer, a CD mixed by Romina for last Christmas. Somewhere along these past week they decided they need more music in their lives. It even keeps his blood pressure down as he checks their charge card bills: Mara Broccardi, Faliero Sarti, more potpourri from Santa Maria Novella, jewelry from Angela Caputi.

"Oh don't complain about that, Elio," Sophia quickly rejoins. "Her pieces are gorgeous and affordable. I go into her studio in Santo Spirito and pull out those drawers and play— you feel like a young girl at dress-up. How can a woman resist?"

"She can't obviously."

Sofia points to one of the charges.

"Those where the huge Asian style earrings that look like jade. Oh, and the necklace, that thick red resin necklace that I wear with my eyelet sundress. You know the one."

"I do. I asked you about it. You said it was an old necklace, that it wasn't new."

"Well," she shrugs. "It's sort of old." She lays out four invoices for the shop: new flooring at the entryway to replace cracked marble tiles, a new front window, paint and plasterwork throughout, new recessed lighting. "It's all necessary, I'm afraid."

And all he can do is flip through invoice after invoice, calculate expenses in his head and question for the first time if this was how he and Sofia should spend the family finances. They have no debts. Their homes are paid for. And in spite of his complaints about Sofia's spending they are both quite prudent. They'd learned from their parents to *compra meglio, compra meno.* Buy better, buy less, whether it be a pair of shoes, a new piece of furniture, a kilo of peaches. Wherever possible buy from and support local artisans and local businesses. That's how you do your part to keep them alive. That way everything in your home has a heartbeat and a story of its own. When you return from a long trip and re-acquaint yourself with every room, you see inscribed in it a living family history. Elio still has his single row of perfectly polished shoes. Sofia drapes her jewelry pieces on silver hooks. Romina folds every article of clothing with care, as if it were the only one she'd ever own. Their paintings and sketches, whether by Florentine artists or artists Romina discovers during her travels, seem as new and fresh as the first moment they were hung. Their books have permanent homes on designated shelves so they can be re-visited from time to time. And their cherished foods—preserved in glass jars, tins or ceramics— acknowledge how truly fortunate they are to have such an abundance of good things to eat from their earth.

This delicious sense of permanence does not require they always be here, however. This is an easy home to live in and an easy home to leave for long periods of time. Of course there is Romina's graduate work at the Accademia to consider, if she doesn't go to New York. And he's not arguing that the shop needs refurbishing, although Sofia tends to make changes every two years. Successful changes, he can't argue. But right now as he watches Sofia tally up the costs, he considers what he will have to give up to keep it that way.

41

MICHELE HAS A *CLOSED* SIGN outside his door, but all the lights are on. He's seated at a table with Romina and Claudio. He points, enthusiastically, to wild graphics on his computer screen. They're drinking Negronis, and from the flushed looks on their faces, they're not on their first round.

"Shhh," says Sofia.

"What? You can't eavesdrop with the door shut."

"I'm just trying to guess what the fuss is about."

Romina has spread some of her New York photographs all over the tables and she's beaming. *I hope Claudio hasn't proposed*, Elio thinks before he can stop himself—then takes a deep breath. *It's her life to live.* So when Romina opens the door and hugs them both very hard and rushes them to the table to show her prints and talks so fast they can barely follow what she's saying—it's that single thought that makes him listen and congratulate. The Parsons School of Design in New York has accepted her. She's ecstatic. She's earned it, having sent in a portfolio of her best work and written an essay she translated herself in what Claudio describes as "perfect English."

"I can't believe it! I thought I had a chance but you never know. And then after awhile I realized that the *only* thing I wanted was to study art in New York. I wasn't going to settle. I'm determined to incorporate all the mediums I've worked in to become an installation artist. I *had* to get in. If they'd rejected me for the spring semester I would have re-applied for the fall."

"It also helped that they liked your work," adds Claudio. He looks pointedly at Elio. "Sometimes we're all so close to it we forget how truly brilliant she is. I want her to start preparing her first show, Mr. Barati." He slides a photograph across the table.

"Wait, Claudio," insists Michele. "They've just come home and you're throwing everything out at them at once." He brings out a platter of his best *stuzzichini*: chunks of parmiggiano, fettunta, crostini anointed with tomato and basil, some rolled up prosciutto. And it's fine that they drink their Negronis down so fast and ask for refills because they're intrigued by Romina's photographs of an elevated city park in New York built around an existing railroad track called the High Line. Michele has the same pictures in his computer so they watch Romina scroll excitedly through them on the wider screen.

"It's unbelievable. Here, look!" An unexpected streetscape. Railroad tracks underfoot, repurposed wood and steel benches, unruly vegetation sprouting on either side, graffiti on brick walls, metal bleachers piled high, unusual sculptures, and the occasional glimpse of the streets below. A jagged glass and steel office building resembles a cubist interpretation of the Swiss Alps. They all laugh at a billboard: *God is Too Busy to Find You a Parking Spot.*

"Even God doesn't want to argue with our young mayor," says Elio.

"Yes, but he's a forward thinker. He'll make a great prime minister," says Romina. "But don't you love this, Papa? I love when we bring art outdoors out of rarified spaces, out of museums and academies and into the streets where people can become a part of it." It *is* invigorating to see such stellar art stand unguarded on a scraggly, urban platform above the traffic lanes below. Romina looks happier than he's ever seen her.

And perhaps this is why Claudio decides now is the time to break the news. He looks at Michele, who nods then glides his fingers on the screen to show the High Line railing over a street facing west. Below, along a gray cobbled street leading to the docks, are rows of drab, square, metal and glass warehouse buildings.

"Mr. and Mrs. Barati, I want to show you the gallery where Romina will display her work. If all goes as planned we think she'll be ready by next summer."

Romina rests her elbows on the table, clasps her hands and closes her eyes.

"I am so so excited. I *have* to do this."

Claudio, ever the businessman, continues, "Here's what we're thinking. She would not be the only artist exhibiting inside the building of course, but since installation art is to be her *métier* this would be the place." He taps the screen definitively with the back of his hand.

"Perfect!" says Sofia, putting her hands on both sides of Romina's face before kissing her on the forehead. "I am so proud of you, s*tellina*."

Elio glances over quickly at her use of his name for Romina. Taking a deep breath: "I don't want to play devil's advocate—"

"But you will. You always do," sighs his daughter. Claudio shakes his head.

"Isn't it very difficult to show in those galleries unless you're already famous?"

"I'm part owner of that gallery, Mr. Barati."

"Ah!" A chorus of laughter follows.

"It doesn't hurt to have connections and to use them, especially when an artist is as talented as Romina. She's already a star and she *needs* to get noticed."

Michele slaps Elio on the back. "And I want to go to the opening. I just checked Airbnb and found a good two-week rental." He holds up his mobile phone mischievously. "You and Sofia had better book fast because this is happening."

"Yes! And please bring me another *Negroni*," smiles Sofia. He's not going to win.

But Romina is the most luminous of all tonight. Her dream is within reach. The chess pieces are lining up on the board. For the first time he sees in her the steely resolve of a confident young woman who will not stop until she gets what she wants.

"You have to hear what I am planning for my first exhibit." She looks at Michele, who gives her a determined thumbs up.

"Picture this, Papa. The sights, sounds, smells, textures and tastes of Florence and of Tuscany. My watercolors on huge canvases on all four walls."

"Like Monet's *Water Lilies*."

"Better, Mr. Barati."

"I want the watercolors to depict the four seasons in Florence or four different times of day. I want to show how our sky changes colors—morning, afternoon, dusk—that entire palette of light that is uniquely ours."

He knows his joy is apparent because she keeps talking.

"I'm not sure of what I'll have in the middle of the room. But I would do sculptures incorporating our Carrara marble, our pietra serena, alabaster from Volterra, silks from the Antico Setificio Fiorentino, leather swatches, handmade papers. I would have some of my more contemporary black-and-white photographs to portray the blend of old and new. For sound there will be music but I may even do voices, oral histories, like they did at Palazzo Strozzi for that exhibit on Italy in the '30s. I may incorporate video art and stage a small play. And for smell—you will love this, Papa—we could do a fragrance center with oils and raw ingredients. Picture giant cognac goblets, each one stuffed with a different colored fabric saturated with an oil typical of Tuscany: cypress, sunflower, poppy, lavender, chestnut—iris, of course. When people come into the room they will first take in the visual, the color, the changing light, the music, and voices. We will have things for them to touch and to taste. Wine and chocolate come to mind. And then they will sit down and take the fabric-filled goblets and put their noses inside the glass to breathe in the smells of our province. They will feel themselves infused with all the sensations that make us who we are. It's a true celebration of our heritage."

She stops and grins, impatient. "What do you think?"

What do I think, stellina? I think it's all marvelous.

42

"ELIO, I NEED YOU TO HAVE a little more patience," says Michele, exasperated. "I am technologically proficient but I am not Steve Jobs."

"You are far more charming than Jobs, but I want this website right by this afternoon. We have a deadline." Moving Romina's photographs across the screen with a few clicks on this chic stainless steel keyboard is far more fun than he thought.

"It's a self-imposed deadline, Elio."

"Exactly! That's why it's non-negotiable. Besides, you've all been nagging me to do this and now I'm making up for lost time."

He sits up in the tip-forward Plexiglas chair Sofia swears is better for his back. Michele leans forward in the chair next to him and makes Elio move pictures from left to right and to the center. Easy. He has an eye for layout, Michele tells him. *Che fortuna!* He also knows his merchandise, has a knack for how it needs to be presented on a screen. And Romina's photos capture the essence of every product. Okay. The text goes here. Bold the name of the fragrance. List the notes in a softer script but make them prominent. Maybe move the list of fragrance references—parfum, eau de parfum, eau de toilette—over to the left. Keep the fragrance stories. Every perfume has a story. But keep it brief, Michele warns him. Nice font. Clean. Sharp. A few more clicks and it may be right. Still.

"I still don't understand how you can order a perfume or an aftershave if you don't smell it, Michele. Part of the joy of buying a fragrance is holding the glass bottle in your palm, spraying it on your skin, listening to the words, the romance, seeing all those other beautiful things that tempt you—"

He points to the backlit glass shelves, the shimmering glass atomizers, fluffy body powder puffs, silver brushes, the prerequisite white scent strips twisted inside glass beakers. And, of course, in the back, standing proud, his beloved perfumer's organ.

"We'll put in a link so they can order samples. But what's most important is that you get them here. Someone in Shanghai deserves to know there is a real Florentine perfumery right here on Via della Vigna. So does someone in New York, in Capetown, in Auckland, or Mexico City."

"And we're in the middle of a new Renaissance in Florence," shouts Sofia from the aesthetician cabines upstairs.

"Correct!" Michele slaps his palm on the counter. "Look at our new opera house, an avant-garde music center for the rest of Europe. Paolo Desideri is a genius. But my point is we all have to take big steps now, into the future. Our fashion and design can rival Milan's. Look at your daughter, always cutting edge in everything she does."

"Ah yes. But it's her photography that amazes me. Where did she learn to do that?"

"She's like her father. She sees into the photograph and captures that insight, that intelligence. But, I agree. I wish I could invent a way to send perfume vapors up from the keyboard. Those Americans in Silicon Valley will come up with something. Like it or not, tourists today get their information off the Internet. They want to feel it's their own discovery. You have so much more competition now. In the old days you had just a few truly artisan *gelaterie*. Now all sorts of them are popping up all over the city selling those awful processed gelati. Look, just two blocks down, his pistachio is lime green! Looks like a Warhol silk screen."

"A what?"

"An artist you don't like, Elio. Although I do."

"He made silkscreens of canned soup," shouts Sofia.

"Ah! Who cares. I don't eat canned soup. But I agree about that pistachio down the street. Your father's gelato, Michele. I still remember how it tasted. *Una meraviglia!*" He clicks to a photo of Romina holding a chocolate and pistachio cone topped with panna at the door of Vestri near Santa Croce.

"But see, Michele, Vestri stands out because they are true to their craft."

"Now you get it. So my point is this, Elio. People have too much in their heads now. You need to stand out."

This is exactly the conversation Elio's been hoping for. "I'm listening, Michele."

"You need something new and fresh. Interactive."

"Like Diptyque on Via dè Tornabuoni, or that Jo Malone shop in New York Romina raves about?"

"Yes! Exactly! Do you see how much fun everyone has dipping scent strips into different oils, trying new scents, mixing their own fragrances, getting into it all like they're in a wine bar? You *definitely* should do something like that here!"

"And how do you see it?" Elio looks up at the mezzanine. Sofia looks down, winks.

Michele stands up, rubs his hands against the pockets of his jeans, points to the counter. "Get rid of that. No counters between you and the public."

"All right. Keep going."

"All this dark wood has to go. Keep the perfumer's organ. But if you lighten up everything around it, the organ will stand out. Paint everything white. More recessed lights. The ones that remind Sofia of the stars. Do a table in the center with oils and and scent strips and cool, maybe red, stools to sit on. Have irises in terracotta, and the artisan's star outside—"

Elio's about to shake his head and say *absolutely not,* but Michele beats him to it.

"You need to keep that. It defines the shop. It's your history. It's a mosaic, so it celebrates our mosaicists. I see the star the way I see a single Baroque piece in a very contemporary living room. It tells its own story. So, Elio, brighten and lighten everything else inside to make your star really shine."

43

IT IS AFTER THAT TIMELY MONOLOGUE that Elio and Sofia invite Michele into their back office to present Elio's plan. There's a reason they are renovating—to move forward into a future that's not just about them and the store. The store needs fresh hands, fresh vision. And they can think of no one they would rather sell the shop to than Michele. They will set a good price for him because Elio would like to retain fifteen percent, which he knows will grow under Michele's tutelage, but he will relinquish all control.

The one outstanding issue is the cost of refurbishing the perfumery the way Michele envisions. Elio has figured that out too. They need an investor. And it's with that purpose in mind that he calls Enrico and invites him to breakfast at the Four Seasons Firenze the next morning.

THERE IS NO DOUBT IN HIS MIND that the *Giardino della Gherardesca* is one of the most beautiful gardens in the city. He and Michele stand their battered bicycles outside the unassuming entrance off *Borgo Pinti*. The concierge leads them into an airy arcaded courtyard under a skylight, decorated with sixteenth-century Mannerist frescoes. Elio stops briefly to take in the soft gray-toned walls, the floral centerpieces, and the architectural history surrounding them. He wishes he could have been here in 1473 to thank Bartolomeo Scala for commissioning the Palazzo when he was chancellor to the Medici family. But just standing here where that history feels so present is what convinces him, yet again, that this plan is the right one.

They find Enrico seated at the garden café where Elio is temporarily distracted by the sculptures scattered about the grounds. This is like Romina's High Line. Art making itself accessible, in outdoor venues where people mill about doing what they do, not expecting they will come face to face with a sculptor's work.

But he has little time to investigate, although one sculpture in particular catches his eye, because Enrico has already unfolded his napkin and gestures for the waiter to bring *caffé* and *cornetti* for everyone. He doesn't have much time. Elio and Michele are well prepared. Over a generous buffet breakfast served by some of the most gracious waitstaff Elio has ever encountered, the deal is made. It was simple enough. Enrico is fine with being an investor. He has no desire to run things, create things, or devise marketing strategy.

"I trust those who know the business better than me to run it. End of story."

And so they shake hands. On the way out Elio hugs an ecstatic Michele.

"Thank you, Elio. I can't tell you how much this means to me."

"I *know* how much it means to you. That's why Sofia and I *chose* you."

He says goodbye and takes off on his bicycle, his mail-carrier bag that holds his perfumer's notebook positioned across his shoulder. He rides past Santa Croce, across the Ponte alle Grazie and pedals hard up hills until he arrives at Via de Bardi and the perfumery studio of Lorenzo Villoresi.

AS HE PARKS HIS BICYCLE, a scene plays out, like a film, inside his head. The revered perfumer won't be there. He and his staff are very preoccupied with a timely and exciting project—the design of Florence's first Museum and School of Perfumery. But what if

Villoresi *were* there and Elio handed him his old, beat-up perfumer's notebook and they actually had a conversation? What if it happened in just this way?

He would stand inside the lobby waiting for the small elevator to take him upstairs to the studio. And while he waited he would consider that soon this fifteenth-century family palazzo will be transformed into a museum and an academy to rival those in Grasse, but created with Italian heart, vision, and style. From what he's read, the intent is to host classes, lectures and workshops. There will also be an aromatic garden. Lorenzo Villoresi's passion for perfumery, which started with his love of gardens, spices and essences, peaked when he left his home province to explore the souks in the Middle East. He, more than anyone, truly understands how transformative gardens are. He would encourage Elio to take this next important step in his life.

A step involving irises.

He steps into the elevator. As it lurches up he feels his heart pound. The final moment for his perfume is arriving.

The elevator doors open and Elio starts. He steps directly into the humble studio. He looks at the fans of blotters on Villoresi's desk, at weighing scales, glass alembics, test tubes, tiny amber vials with their perfect printed labels and all around the room at walls lined with shelves upon shelves of natural essences, oils, absolutes, and more amber vials. He looks at the *Prix Coty* award affixed to the wall. He remembers the luscious scents along the stairwell on the way up. He stares at the perfumer's organ where Villoresi creates bespoke scents. If he says yes to Elio's request, this could be where he will craft Romina's fragrance. He stands, frozen in place, and has to be led past the organ, the sofa bed, the family portraits, and the piles of books to a place where he can sit down and where someone brings him a glass of water. His hand shakes as he removes his perfumer's notebook from his bag. He takes a deep breath and holds on to it. But once he regains his composure, he hands it over. Directly into the perfumer's hands.

44

THERE HAD BEEN NO RULES in Elena's garden, except that one had to treat the irises with respect because they were the symbol of *Firenze*, the city of flowers, and she liked that the three petals formed what she called the three essential parts of a human being: the mind, the heart, and the soul.

And years later he heard that same sentiment put another way. The heart, mind, and soul described as the structure of a fragrance—the top, middle and base. If one were to move three circles like chess pieces on a board, one could argue that the three were rarely on equal footing. The mind needed movement and range, the freedom to experiment without judgment. The heart, which he'd found the most complicated to construct, evolved through trial and error, illusory victories and inopportune setbacks. And it took an intense involvement of mind and heart to get to the soul, a worthwhile, albeit frustrating journey.

But all of that falls away as he talks with Giovanni, an iris farmer young enough to be his son. Giovanni's family owns one of the few remaining iris *fattorie* in Tuscany. They now stroll together under an ominous gray sky past rows of wilting irises. Mats of peeled iris roots dry in the sun, which is now dangerously behind the clouds.

Elio's heart aches. First, for the genuine and heartfelt effort Giovanni puts into his trade, and then for the ever-mounting odds. Elio remembers too well those shimmering summers under brilliant blue skies when his beloved violet-white *ghiacciolo* would carpet the hills outside San Polo, not unlike the jasmine of Grasse. He remembers the sunburned faces of the *contadini*, as they happily dug up the roots, peeled and tossed them into pails of water. He remembers the sound they made, a splash and a clang. He, Marina, and Elena would go into the iris fields to help, much as they did during the *vendemmia* and the olive oil harvest. They would join the *contadini* to sing the traditional Tuscan *stornelle*, their voices spreading over the fields the way the flowers did. And at dusk they would all gather around thick wooden tables and eat polenta and *fagioli all'uccelletto* with tomato sauce and *pinoli*. There would be a large, round basket with all the must- haves: tomatoes, bread, a twist full of salt, *salumi*, chunks of bread, cheeses, and they would drink it all down with a robust local wine that did not have a famous name and that probably cost the equivalent of one Euro. And as the Tuscan hills turned a misty blue they would banter about fictitious stories about trafficked wine and exclaim how fortunate they were to watch the sun set over their day's labor.

The curved knife with which Giovanni now trims a rhizome—a *roncollino*—is almost a relic because so few artisans make it.

"We cut off the top to re-plant. For me it's worth more than gold. Then we peel the roots until they're white like potatoes. See? We rinse them, soak them in water, put them in terra cotta to soften, then they have to dry. We spread them out on these cane mats for at least four days. We pray it doesn't rain because even a light rainfall will ruin the entire harvest. If there's even a slight chance of rain, we have to work fast and bring all of the roots inside."

He shows Elio the mats and the drying roots. An earthy, fennel-like vapor rises up like the air after a fresh summer rain. It's a warm, mossy scent tethered to the land. That a scent so seductive can emerge from a root is in and of itself a miracle.

Still, as Giovanni walks past the mats, checking the sky warily and looking out over the fields like a father observing a sleeping child, Elio wonders how long will this last? Giovanni is young, strong and smart. Which means he is free to be impulsive, to modify his dreams and to change his *métier* many times. He's free to leave Tuscany, leave the country, to strike out in a myriad of directions. How admirable that one so young is intent on preserving that which is truly Tuscan.

Because there is one thing that will be forever true. It's the single rhizome Giovannni's dug out of the earth with the precision of a surgeon, using an *ubbidiente* and his bare hands. Elio shakes off the dirt and smells it.

"This is it, Elio. And you saw how long it took me to hoe around it by hand and to pull it out so as not to damage. It's too precious to risk damaging even one. To extract just one liter of iris root butter you need forty tons of rhizomes." He wipes a blackened hand across his forehead. "This is more precious to me than a diamond, or a ruby. And it's becoming more precious because we're losing it. Even Lorenzo Villoresi has said that orris absolute is now worth three times its own weight in gold."

Elio brings the rhizome to his nose. The smell of the fertile Tuscan earth is unequaled. It's the smell of home. "I grow my own but my fields are small. It's always been a hobby, nothing more. And my life has been as a merchant."

Giovanni gives a wry smile "Well, Elio. I'm glad for merchants. They help keep the iris alive. So what if a perfume is commercial? Better for my business. Our *iris pallida* grows wild all over our hills, but you know what the problem is. The damn scent is in the roots, not in the petals. As you just saw back there on the mats, the harvested rhizomes have to dry in the sun for days. Then we have to load them all, thousands of them, into those huge sacks you saw piled up there behind the house. And the rhizomes have to stay in there to dehydrate for two years so the bulbs release chetone alpha irone, which is then distilled into an essential oil. Scientists have discovered a synthetic iris compound, but it can't replicate this specific oil. The truly authentic fragrances still use it. I'm glad for that, but the number is diminishing every year."

"From what I'm reading in various trade journals the rising trend is to have more authenticity, not less."

Giovanni guffaws. "But at what cost? Do you know that at one time we even had a special train that traveled between

Florence and Grasse? But now even the perfumers in Grasse are using the chemical synthetic iris."

A bit of sun filters through the clouds. Elio changes the subject. "So you sell the rhizomes to the manufacturing center, where they distill them over six months or so."

"Correct. Nothing much has changed over time. It just gets more and more expensive to produce. That's where the roots are first pulverized, then macerated in cold water. Then they distill them over and over again for six months. Then they warm them up moderately, not too much, until they produce orris butter they finally refine for the absolute."

They sit down on a stone bench just outside a cottage behind the fields. Giovanni's son, a small boy with wide, brown eyes and long lashes like his father, brings them two cups of espresso. Elio rubs the boy's head affectionately. Again he feels that pang in his stomach. With the number of iris farms declining, with the major French companies now sourcing from other countries or turning to synthetics, the future of Giovanni's farm and others like it is in jeopardy.

"I know you're considering becoming a grower for the industry, Elio. Why not? It would be a gift to the rest of us. It gives us more importance. With so many farms closing it says something when a professional of your caliber chooses to establish one. And you have credibility. You know the business from the retailer's side. You have insight into what the fragrance companies will seek out in the future. What I would like to do, Elio, is re-educate people. Revitalize and promote the idea that perfume must come from nature. But I'm not a marketer. I don't know how to get the word out. You, in your own way, have always done that in your shop. Why not take it to the next level?"

45

IN *THE CITY OF FLORENCE*, R.W.B. LEWIS writes that it is the *insieme* in Florence that beckons us back, whether we be natives, tourists or expatriates. *It is not any particular building or painting or statue or piazza or bridge; not even the whole unrivaled array of works of art. It is the city itself.*

Elio has his own interpretation. He sees the *insieme* in the tightly knit commercial and artisan community that, even in the midst of economic crisis, continues to bring beauty to its city and the world. Whether it be Taddei sculpting leather boxes in his tiny studio across from Dante's house, Chef Mario Stabile crafting art on a plate at Ora D'Aria, or Gianni Raffaelli fashioning etchings from copper plates using a five-hundred-year-old technique—whether it be Paola Quadretti fitting women with exquisite made-to-measure dresses or the ever-gracious Ferragamo family sponsoring an exhibit about the predominance of shoemaking in myths and fairy tales—there is a single unbreakable and unifying thread, the thread in a tapestry that weaves artisanship, history, science, and commerce together.

An American tourist once told him that he and his wife would spend their mornings at the Bargello and Palazzo Strozzi, and that in the afternoons his wife would continue to visit the other museums of Florentine art: Ferragamo, Gucci, Cavalli, Patrizia Pepe. The man had it right. Art is the thread. It's the center of that artisan's star at the entrance to his shop. Art informed Arnolfo di Cambio's design of its medieval heart, with Santa Maria del Fiore and Brunelleschi's Duomo at its center, roads branching out from it, like the rays of a star. Art is front and center in the heritage and daily life practices of every

Florentine, from the way he buttons his blazer to the way she parks her motorino.

"Even the way we set a table, Michele, is a work of art."

BUT FLORENCE IS NOT IMMUNE to reckless development. And on any other day, as they drive into the outskirts of town, Elio would rant about the ubiquitous industrial parks. On any other day he would not sit quietly in the back of Claudio's BMW while Romina drives and Michele and Sofia talk on and on about decorating the perfumery. She sees a bench at the entrance with a cashmere throw. Michele wants to revive Elio's shaving corner with both old-world travertine accessories and the latest high-tech shavers. Sofia insists there be a black-and-white photograph of a nude male model with dreamy dark eyes, towel around his waist, the featured razor in his hand.

Romina raises one hand off the steering wheel. "I get to photograph that one!"

"Not without your mother there to supervise." Sofia winks at Elio

"Elio. See the situation you have put me in!"

He smiles back at Michele, then turns to look out the window at a continuous reel of shopping malls and factories, assaults on the chiaroscuro landscape that once made artists and painters swoon. Imagine you have a terraced vineyard, a field of sunflowers, and silvery olive groves that stretch way up the hills, and there in the middle of a crown of cypresses you plop a gray block of steel that spews black smoke. And someone will come back and say, "But Elio, manufacturing and building are twenty-five percent of our economy and employ many workers. At a time of economic crisis, can we afford to turn that away?" We can't. And that is the honest and difficult truth.

But possibilities for re-invention still exist. And a Florentine knows how to do that better than anyone. That's why it's fitting that Marina invites them, and the entire city it seems, to a retirement dinner at the new Antinori winery in Bergino.

Who would argue that an evening tasting Chianti Classico and Tignanello while sampling local foods and perusing the family's eclectic art collection is anything but pure heaven? All of it from inside a structure architects and the international press have deemed an unprecedented architectural masterpiece.

"It blurs the boundary between landscape and architecture," says Romina, who has been here many times to photograph. "See. It's so integrated into the nature around it we barely see it. It doesn't occupy the landscape. It enhances it."

Elio listens but his mind is only on Marina.

Romina steers the car up the snaking driveway through the olive groves and down into an underground garage, dark except for the light from circular cutouts above. They walk up a twisting steel staircase into a soaring light-filled space. Unlike the others he is only mildly cognizant of the architectural details, the lighting, and the grace with which they are able to move up through one of the cuts in the ceiling onto an enormous sunlit terrazza whose curves, colors and contours mirror the equally magnificent landscape. This is where he does stop and gasp.

"*Incredibile.* It's as if the outside is coming in and the inside is going out."

"No boundaries, Elio. That's the idea."

And there is no mistaking that deep, smoky voice. There will never be a time it doesn't make his heart jump. Only this time when he turns to hug Marina, he sees lots of other people behind her. Amid the cheering, clapping, kisses and handshakes, he realizes that everyone he knows and has ever known is here to wish him and Sofia good fortune and happy travels. Marina, in a sapphire blue Indian tunic, and a cast of exquisitely attired waiters, hand out flutes of Prosecco. And in the sea of faces Elio sees every artisan, every merchant, members of illustrious Florentine families whose ancestors built palazzi and established the trades they still practice today, and the many young immigrant and emigrant entrepreneurs who take these trades around the world.

"Based on the number of people, I'm thinking Florence is a ghost town today."

Marina takes his hand and leads him away toward the restaurant that looks out over the vineyards and the distant hills. Her wrists smell of attar.

"Look out there, Elio." She lifts her arm, diva-style, toward the landscape. "They literally built this amazing place *into* the hill. Do you see how it's cantilevered? After they put it in, they replaced the hill on top. Who says it can't be done? It's a place one feels blissfully free in. Don't you think?"

He does. He feels very free and light, and about to float away on a cloud of sheer joy, as they find a quiet table, order a bottle of Tignanello and talk about where they are, where they've been and where they are going. He tells her about Grasse and about seeing Palma again. How strange it had felt at first, but how right in the end.

"That must have been difficult, but honestly, how exciting. She was your first real love, wasn't she?"

"No, you were."

"I was on the rebound."

"Not true. I was very much in love with you."

And in many ways I still am.

"Of course, how could you help it? But I was not right for you and I was not the first. Palma was the catalyst. She was at the beginning of that circle that brings you here today. She's like that pebble you throw in a pond making circles spread around it. She shook things up. I remember that story. Lucky you."

Yes he remembers that night with Marina, but he does so without the regret that it's gone and not to be repeated, but more with the satisfaction of knowing that it did happen.

"And perhaps the other very important catalyst is Romina. She shook things up too. If it weren't for her and her plans to go to New York, you'd be in your shop today, looking at twenty more years in captivity."

Even though it's a late summer day, he shudders at the prospect.

"Seriously, I like all the parts of your plan, Elio. It's ambitious. And you have it all laid out with precise dates and targets. Bravo." She touches her glass to his.

"And what about you, Marina? When do you leave for India?"

"We're planning the visit now. You know I will have to dig my hands into some fabrics. India is such a vibrant place, all those prickly smells and brilliant colors and that gold flailing about on veils and things. Pondicherry is where we want to spend a good amount of the time. I'm going to stay longer, for at least three months. Your daughter has always said that traveling to non-Western parts of the world made her feel the most alive. Of course New York City is her love, technically Western, but in its own category. I need that now. The business is fine. I've done all I can here."

He tells her he feels the same way. This formula feels right. Michele will manage the shop. Elio will devote his time to his iris fields, to mentoring and perhaps teaching. The only requirement is that he and Sofia reserve the time for travel. "I want to go to Romina's exhibit and visit her in New York whenever I want. I want to go back to Paris many times. And there is Morocco, and Istanbul, and other places."

Marina picks up her wine glass. "Yes, and one place in particular. Sofia tells me you are both going on a trip very soon—to the sea."

"I was hoping to tell you myself but that's correct."

"Well, when you *do* go I have a request. But let's have another toast first."

So they toast each with their glasses of Tignanello. The glints of garnet inside the glass flare like tiny fireworks. He glances quickly across the room to see if Romina is snapping their photograph. Of course she is.

Marina asks him to close his eyes. She opens her purse and places two sachets in his hand. The scent of gardenia wafts up. She closes his hand around it.

"When you arrive in Paros, Elio, please give her these, and my love."

The ferry to Paros cuts across the water faster than it did when he was a boy. Back then he didn't mind when it was late or slow because it meant he could talk his mother into one more donkey ride. But today, time is of the essence. It's the height of the lemon harvest. The light in Greece is as clear and transparent as glass, and the red-gold sun descends to bring them one of those glorious Cycladic sunsets etched in his memory. He and Sofia sit on the ferry's exterior so they can feel the salt spray and the sun on their faces. He checks the sky as it turns pink, looks down at his watch and smiles. Soon the lemon pickers will leave the fields and head right for the taverna, only steps from the rocks by the sea.

NINE MONTHS LATER

HE'S PULLING OFF HIS GARDENING GLOVES when Romina's package arrives from New York. He removes the cover of a long cardboard tube, unrolls a paper scroll, and gasps.

He sits down on the stone bench beside his irises. He holds a watercolor painting of the Arno at dusk. In her note, which he opens next, she explains how she wore the perfume he commissioned from Villoresi as she painted. The perfume made the colors alive for her, the brushstrokes fluid and quick enough to catch the light at just that moment, at just that time of day. So overjoyed, he feels as if he's stopped breathing. Romina has perfectly rendered the colors of the Tuscan sky above him.

It's that moment when the sky has lost its sun but has yet to find its stars.

Like his life, at this very moment. The music of a fragrance is like the arc of life itself. Its top note is youth, all sparkle and possibility. Its midnote, the emotional layers of middle age. And its base note, the seasoned transition into old age, the true sensual core of the scent, its very soul.

Sofia calls from inside. Elio's about to walk up the stairs when he stops and looks out across the garden, at the *chiaroscuro* light descending like a smoky blue dome over the jasmine, the oleander, the lilacs. Behind the flowers four tall cypresses rise up against the rose- and violet-brushed amber sky. In just a few lingering moments the sky has grown darker, the jasmine sweeter, the light more embracing, and he smells it all, as exuberantly as he had that night in Grasse.

Closing his eyes, the misty spires of his city rise up in his mind; the red, white, and green marbles of the Duomo. He sees himself again as a small boy wandering the Vasarian corridor with his father, pointing to the scary Medici portraits. He sees himself stealing flowers from the Boboli gardens with his mother. He sees the noble burnished arches of Santa Trinita, the shuttered goldsmith shops along the Ponte Vecchio, the street lamps, like sentries, sending sparkles of light along the riverbank.

He sees himself as a father with his daughter by the Arno the night he gave her her first bottle of perfume. He takes a deep breath and, all at once, the smells of his garden and of the city overwhelm him. He will never lose this. His sense of smell is not in his head but in his heart. And this city, this marvelous city he ran away from as a young man in pursuit of a dream, is the very city that brought the dream to him.

Dear Reader,

Thank you for embarking on this sensory journey with us. We've enjoyed being your storytellers, your tour guides, and your behind-the-scenes cognoscenti.

So we now invite you to travel deeper into our world, meet hoteliers who've mastered the art of 'receiving guests'; perfumers whose bespoke scents will transport you back to a cherished moment; and craftsmen, craftswomen, designers, restaurateurs, shopkeepers, winemakers, chefs and merchants whose passion for beauty and for the art of life itself keep our vibrant city in a constant state of rebirth.

Because whilst we, the characters in ARTISAN'S STAR are fictional, we inhabit real and unforgettable settings. We walk under the arches of the Uffizi every day, we cross the Ponte Santa Trinita at sunset just as the street lamps flicker on, and perhaps we will sit on the bridge with a gelato and watch the light change as if experiencing it for the first time.

So, if any of the places in this book set your heart racing there's a reason. Every encounter in Florence, even over decades, even when repeated, feels as fresh and illuminating as the first, but ever more deeply personal.

Most of all we hope our story has inspired you to either make your first visit to our beloved Florence, or to return to it again many times.

In the meantime please join us at WWW.GABRIELLACONTESTABILE.COM, where we will take you to our favorite cafes, galleries, restaurants, shops and local haunts—and into the stories, inspirations and practices of Florence's established and emerging artisans.

A Presto,

Elio, Michele, Romina, Sofia

ARTISANS ON FIRENZE ...

"When I was a young child, people called me Giuggiu'. It is an Italian term of endearment that means 'small agreeable thing.' It is used for something that is playful and cute, just like my jewelry."
-Angela Caputi, Angela Caputi Giuggiu'

"It seems to me that though my ideas are born out of the past, yet they reach me perfected. They come to me full-blown on the cosmic tide, all ancient errors smoothed away."
—Salvatore Ferragamo

"Tourism gives us the means to keep traditions alive. This is how Florence still works, producing high quality goods with artisans' spirit. This is what Florence is about, beyond its beauty and its museums; skills, talents, arts and crafts passed on from master to apprentice."
—Laura Gori, La Scuola del Cuoio

"Art is that untouchable string that chains man to history. When everything is turned off or becomes obsolete, or just lies in the general memory of a country, what is left is ART."
-Gianni Raffaelli, L'Ippogrifo

"Watching people work is like watching someone play the piano. Hands and feet alternate on the loom, a structure which has been working for two hundred years."
—Stefano Ricci, Antico Setificio Fiorentino

"My philosophy of being and feeling good is to surround ourselves with everything that gives pleasure to the mind and the senses and captures the emotions in precious fragrances encased in elegant glass bottles which compliment the virtual journey of continuous discovery."
—Paolo Vranjes

ACKNOWLEDGEMENTS

As with the ever-blossoming city of Firenze, the *insieme* brought Artisan's Star into the world.

Catherine Adams of Inkslinger Editing, peerless editor and artist. You are the Michelangelo. You knew where to chisel away, sculpt, and polish an unruly narrative that wanted to run in eight different directions like the rays in Elio's star. You plucked out the threads in the tapestry and directed my hand. Thank you for helping me find my voice.

Aviva Layton, years ago you pressed me to go deep into Elio's world. Your thoughtful analysis and first edits nurtured this book through its adolescence and early adulthood.

Wesley Gibson, you said this short story could be a novel. Don't know whether to thank you or curse you. But being that it's done, I will opt for the former. Your incisive reading and commentary in the initial stages gave shape and authenticity to Elio's story.

Angie Jernejcic. What a journey this has been! Working with a book cover designer of your skill makes me feel like a Medici commissioning a work of art. You read the entire novel, picked up the emotional threads, and re-imagined it as a painting on canvas. You are amazing.

Brilliant and tenacious teachers Carol Emschwiller, Wesley Gibson, and Adam Sexton—thank you for saying so often, *not good enough.*

My parents, Umberto and Clelia, who sailed with me on the Andrea Doria from Italy to North America and insisted we speak and "live in Italian" decades before it became fashionable to do so.

Umberto, thank you for finding joy in simple things: a new tomato in your garden, a perfect espresso from the *macchinetta* on our stove, a Puccini aria that evoked tears. You gave me a copy of *The Passionate Sightseer* by Bernard Berenson when I was but eleven years old. I re-opened it forty years later to research Artisan's Star. You were Elio in spirit and in gesture. You made him the easiest of all characters to write.

Clelia, at 90, thank you for forcing me to work on my terrible penmanship in grade school. I started writing stories because I got bored writing the same letters over and over again. You still create couture with your hands, making magic with every bolt of fabric you touch. When I can hand-embroider my daughter's name on her pillowcase, or roll out the *sfoglia* for lasagna as paper thin as yours, you will know your work is done.

My pesky younger brother Bert, who ripped up the stories emerging from penmanship lessons so I learned to re-write. Thank you for your dogged encouragement. I thank your co-conspirator, Maria, too. And my extended family on both sides of the ocean.

Friends and colleagues in the cosmetics and perfume industry, you made me aware that this delicious world existed. Karen Khoury, you describe perfume composition as the art form it truly is.

The talented and unforgettable people of Florence and Grasse, artisans of their *métier* and their lives. Their stories form the top, middle, and base notes of this composition.

My writing group mates: You guided the brushstrokes for my characters and their journeys.

My indomitable, irreplaceable friends, the rays of my star, you read, you critiqued, you would not let me put this manuscript aside.

Daniela, you brought into focus all those gorgeous facets of youth I had long forgotten, and foolishly underestimated.

And, Steve, you are the center of my star. Your *joie de vivre* and inimitable sense of humor showed me the joy and humor in Elio's world, and in my own.

BIBLIOGRAPHY

THE PASSIONATE SIGHTSEER BY BERNARD BERENSON launched me into a life of wanderlust and a fascination with art and all things Florentine. The literary world has been blessed with a wealth of illuminating writers whose work made my research both an educational journey and a sensorial joy.

BOOKS
Kinta Beevor, *A Tuscan Childhood* (London, 1993).

Bernard Berenson, *The Passionate Sightseer: From the Diaries of Bernard Berenson, 1947–56* (New York, 1960).

Robert R. Calkin and Jellinek, J.Stephan, *Perfumery, Practice and Principles* (New York 1994).

Michael Edwards, *Perfume Legends: French Feminine Fragrances* (Levallois, 1996).

Anton Gill, *Il Gigante, Michelangelo, Florence, and the David: 1492-1504* (New York, 2002).

R. W. B. Lewis, *The City of Florence: Historical Vistas and Present Sightings* (London, 1995).

Celia Lyttelton, *The Scent Trail: How One Woman's Quest for the Perfect Perfume Took Her Around the World* (New York 2007).

Frances Mayes, *Under the Tuscan Sun* (New York, 1996).

Mary McCarthy, *The Stones of Florence.* (New York, 1963).

Fabienne Pavia, *The World of Perfume* (New York, 1996).

Joe Wolf, *Café Life Florence: A Guidebook to the Cafés & Bars of the Renaissance Treasure* (Northampton, Massachusetts, 2005).

ARTICLES

Tina Gaudoin, "A Whiff of Something Real," *Departures Magazine*, Nov/Dec 2013.

Michael Kimmelman, "Vines and Vitner Beautify a Tuscan Hill," *New York Times*, August 26, 2013.

Edward Readicker-Henderson, "Heaven Scent, a Journey through the heart of France's Perfume Country," *AFAR Magazine*, July 05, 2013.

WEBSITES

Les Fleurs d'Exception du Pays de Grasse (http://www.fleurs-exception-grasse.com/?page_id=664)

ABOUT THE AUTHOR

GABRIELLA CONTESTABILE IS AN AUTHOR, educator, and owner of Su Misura Journeys, a boutique travel company connecting people to the artisans of Florence. She emigrated, with her parents, from Italy to New York City in 1959. In her pre-writer life, she worked as a foreign language teacher, management development specialist, and fragrance/cosmetics executive. She is a strong advocate of the arts, of multiculturalism, and of social justice—a passion inspired by reading Dickens and Dante at a very young age. She lives on the Upper West Side with her husband, her daughter, and a furry Shih–Tzu named Oreo.

This is her first novel.

Made in the USA
Middletown, DE
16 April 2017